DESIGN FOR A BRAIN

DESIGN FOR A BRAIN

W. ROSS ASHBY

M.A., M.D. (Cantab), D.P.M.

Director of Research
Barnwood House, Gloucester

□

REPRINTED
(WITH CORRECTIONS)

NEW YORK
JOHN WILEY & SONS INC.
440 FOURTH AVENUE
1954

First Published .   *1952*
Reprinted (with corrections)   *1954*

Printed in Great Britain by Butler & Tanner Ltd , Frome and London

Summary and Preface*

THE BOOK is not a treatise on all cerebral mechanisms but an attempt to solve a specific problem the origin of the nervous system's unique ability to produce adaptive behaviour. The work has as basis the fact that the nervous system behaves adaptively and the hypothesis that it is essentially mechanistic; it proceeds on the assumption that these two *data* are not irreconcilable. It attempts to deduce from the observed facts what sort of a mechanism it must be that behaves so differently from any machine made so far. Many other workers have proposed theories on the subject, but they have usually left open the question whether some different theory might not fit the facts equally well. I have attempted to deduce what is necessary, what properties the nervous system *must* have if it is to behave at once mechanistically and adaptively.

Proceeding in this way I have deduced that any system which shows adaptation must (1) contain many variables that behave as step-functions, (2) contain many that behave as part-functions, and (3) be assembled largely at random, so that its details are determined not individually but statistically. The last requirement may seem surprising· man-made machines are usually built to an exact specification, so we might expect a machine assembled at random to be wholly chaotic. But it appears that this is not so. Such a system has a fundamental tendency, shown most clearly when its variables are numerous, to so arrange its internal pattern of action that, in relation to its environment, it becomes stable. If the system were inert this would mean little; but in a system as active and complex as the brain, it implies that the system will be self-preserving through active and complex behaviour.

The work may also be regarded as amplifying the view that the nervous system is not only sensitive but ' delicate ' : that its encounters with the environment mark it readily, extensively, and permanently, with traces distributed according to the ' accidents ' of the encounter. Such a distribution might be expected to produce a merely chaotic alteration in the nervous system's behaviour, but this is not so as the encounters multiply there is a fundamental tendency for the system's adaptation to improve, for the traces tend to such a distribution as will make its behaviour adaptive in the subsequent encounters.

---

* The summary is too brief to be accurate ; the full text should be consulted for the necessary qualifications.

The work also in a sense develops a theory of the 'natural selection' of behaviour-patterns. Just as, in the species, the truism that the dead cannot breed implies that there is a fundamental tendency for the successful to replace the unsuccessful, so in the nervous system does the truism that the unstable tends to destroy itself imply that theie is a fundamental tendency for the stable to replace the unstable. Just as the gene-pattern, in its encounters with the environment, tends towards ever better adaptation of the inherited form and function, so does a system of step- and part-functions tend towards ever bettei adaptation of learned behaviour.

These remarks give an impressionist picture of the work's nature; but a description in these terms is not well suited to systematic exposition. The book therefore presents the evidence in rather different order. The first five chapters are concerned with foundations: with the accurate definition of concepts, with basic methods, and especially with the establishing of exact equivalences between the necessary physical, physiological, and psychological concepts. After the development of more advanced concepts in the next two chapters, the exposition arrives at its point: the principle of ultrastability, which in Chapter 8 is defined and described. The next two chapters apply it to the nervous system and show how it explains the organism's basic power of adaptation. The remainder of the book studies its developments. Chapters 11 to 13 show the inadequacy of the principle in systems that lack part-functions, Chapters 14 to 16 develop the properties of systems that contain them, and Chapters 17 and 18 offer evidence that the principle's power to develop adaptation is unlimited.

The thesis is stated twice. at first in plain words and then in mathematical form. Having experienced the confusion that tends to arise whenever we try to relate cerebral mechanisms to psychological phenomena, I made it my aim to accept nothing that could not be stated in mathematical form, for only in this language can one be sure, during one's progress, that one is not unconsciously changing the meaning of terms, or adding assumptions, or otherwise drifting towards confusion. The aim proved achievable. The concepts of organisation, behaviour, change of behaviour, part, whole, dynamic system, co-ordination, etc.— notoriously elusive but essential—were successfully given rigorous definition and welded into a coherent whole. But the rigour and coherence depended on the mathematical form, which is not read with ease by everybody. As the basic thesis, however, rested on essentially common-sense reasoning, I have been able to divide the account into two parts. The main account (Chapters 1–18) is non-mathematical and is complete in itself. The Appendix (Chapters 19–24) contains the definitive theory in mathematical form. So far as is possible, the main account and the Appendix have been written in parallel to facilitate cross-reference.

Since the reader will probably need cross-reference frequently, the chapters have been subdivided into sections. These are indicated thus S 4/5, which means Chapter 4's fifth section. Each figure and table is numbered within its own section: Fig. 4/5/2 is the second figure in S. 4/5. Section-numbers are given at the top of every page, so finding a section or a figure should be as simple and direct as finding a page.

Figs. 8/8/1 and 8/8/2 are reproduced by permission of the Editor of *Electronic Engineering*.

It is a pleasure to be able to express my indebtedness to the Governors of Barnwood House and to Dr. G. W. T. H. Fleming for their generous support during the prosecution of the work, and to Professor F. L. Golla and Dr. W. Grey Walter for much helpful criticism.

W. ROSS ASHBY

Contents

CHAPTER 1

The Problem

1/1. How does the brain produce adaptive behaviour? In attempting to answer the question, scientists have discovered two sets of facts and have had some difficulty in reconciling them. The physiologists have shown in a variety of ways how closely the brain resembles a machine· in its dependence on chemical reactions, in its dependence on the integrity of anatomical paths, and in many other ways. At the same time the psychologists have established beyond doubt that the living organism, whether human or lower, can produce behaviour of the type called ' purposeful ' or ' intelligent ' or ' adaptive ', for though these words are difficult to define with precision, no one doubts that they refer to a real characteristic of behaviour. These two characteristics of the brain's behaviour have proved difficult to reconcile, and some workers have gone so far as to declare them incompatible.

Such a point of view will not be taken here. I hope to show that a system can be both mechanistic in nature and yet produce behaviour that is adaptive. I hope to show that the essential difference between the brain and any machine yet made is that the brain makes extensive use of a principle hitherto little used in machines. I hope to show that by the use of this principle a machine's behaviour may be made as adaptive as we please, and that the principle may be capable of explaining even the adaptiveness of Man.

But first we must examine more closely the nature of the problem, and this will be commenced in this chapter. The succeeding chapters will develop more accurate concepts, and when we can state the problem with precision we shall be not far from its solution.

1

Behaviour, reflex and learned

1/2. The activities of the nervous system may be divided more or less distinctly into two types. The dichotomy is perhaps an over-simplification, but it will be sufficient for our purpose.

The first type is reflex behaviour. It is inborn, it is genetically determined in detail, it is a product, in the vertebrates, chiefly of centres in the spinal cord and in the base of the brain, and it is not appreciably modified by individual experience. The second type is learned behaviour. It is not inborn, it is not genetically determined in detail (more fully discussed in S. 1/9), it is a product chiefly of the cerebral cortex, and it is modified markedly by the organism's individual experiences

1/3. With the first or reflex type of behaviour we shall not be concerned. We assume that each reflex is produced by some neural mechanism whose physico-chemical nature results inevitably in the characteristic form of behaviour, that this mechanism is developed under the control of the gene-pattern and is inborn, and that the pattern of behaviour produced by the mechanism is usually adapted to the animal's environment because natural selection has long since eliminated all non-adapted variations. For example, the complex activity of ' coughing ' is assumed to be due to a special mechanism in the nervous system, inborn and developed by the action of the gene-pattern, and adapted and perfected by the fact that an animal who is less able to clear its trachea of obstruction has a smaller chance of survival.

Although the mechanisms underlying these reflex activities are often difficult to study physiologically and although few are known in all their details, yet it is widely held among physiologists that no difficulty of principle is involved. Such behaviour and such mechanisms will not therefore be considered further.

1/4. It is with the second type of behaviour that we are concerned . the behaviour that is not inborn but learned. Examples of such reactions exist in abundance, and any small selection must seem paltry. Yet I must say what I mean, if only to give the critic a definite target for attack. Several examples will therefore be given.

A dog selected at random for an experiment with a conditioned

reflex can be made at will to react to the sound of a bell either
with or without salivation. Further, once trained to react in
one way it may, with little difficulty, be trained to react later in
the opposite way. The salivary response to the sound of a bell
cannot, therefore, be due to a mechanism of fixed properties.

A rat selected at random for an experiment in maze-running
can be taught to run either to right or left by the use of an appropriately shaped maze. Further, once trained to turn to one side
it can be trained later to turn to the other.

A kitten approaching a fire for the first time is unpredictable
in its first reactions. The kitten may walk almost into it, or
may spit at it, or may dab at it with a paw, or may try to sniff
at it, or may crouch and ' stalk ' it. The initial way of behaving
is not, therefore, determined by the animal's species

Perhaps the most striking evidence that animals, after training,
can produce behaviour which cannot possibly have been inborn
is provided by the circus. A seal balances a ball on its nose for
minutes at a time , one bear rides a bicycle, and another walks
on roller skates. It would be ridiculous to suppose that these
reactions are due to mechanisms both inborn and specially perfected for these tricks.

Man himself provides, of course, the most abundant variety of
learned reactions · but only one example will be given here. If
one is looking down a compound microscope and finds that the
object is not central but to the right, one brings the object to
the centre by pushing the slide still farther to the right. The
relation between muscular action and consequent visual change
is the reverse of the usual. The student's initial bewilderment
and clumsiness demonstrate that there is no neural mechanism
inborn and ready for the reversed relation. But after a few days
co-ordination develops.

These examples, and all the facts of which they are representative. show that the nervous system is able to develop ways of
behaving which are not inborn and are not specified in detail
by the gene-pattern.

1/5. Learned behaviour has many characteristics, but we shall
be concerned chiefly with one . when animals and children learn,
not only does their behaviour change, but it changes usually for
the better. The full meaning of ' better ' will be discussed in

Chapter 5, but in the simpler cases the improvement is obvious enough. 'The burned child dreads the fire': after the experience the child's behaviour towards the fire is not only changed, but is changed to a behaviour which gives a *lessened* chance of its being burned again. We would at once recognise as abnormal any child who used its newly acquired knowledge so as to get to the flames more quickly.

To demonstrate that learning usually changes behaviour from a less to a more beneficial, i.e. survival-promoting, form would need a discussion far exceeding the space available. But in this introduction no exhaustive survey is needed. I require only sufficient illustration to make the meaning clear. For this purpose the previous examples will be examined seriatim.

When a conditioned reflex is established by the giving of food or acid, the amount of salivation changes from less to more. And the change benefits the animal either by providing normal lubrication for chewing or by providing water to dilute and flush away the irritant. When a rat in a maze has changed its behaviour so that it goes directly to the food at the other end, the new behaviour is better than the old because it leads more quickly to the animal's hunger being satisfied. The kitten's behaviour in the presence of a fire changes from being such as may cause injury by burning to an accurately adjusted placing of the body so that the cat's body is warmed by the fire neither too much nor too little. The circus animals' behaviour changes from some random form to one determined by the trainer, who applied punishments and rewards. The animals' later behaviour is such as has decreased the punishments or increased the rewards. In Man, the proposition that behaviour usually changes for the better with learning would need extensive discussion. But in the example of the finger movements and the compound microscope, the later movements, which bring the desired object directly to the centre of the field, are clearly better than the earlier movements, which were disorderly and ineffective.

Our problem may now be stated in preliminary form: what cerebral changes occur during the learning process, and why does the behaviour usually change for the better? What type of mechanistic process could show the same property?

But before the solution is attempted we must first glance at the peculiar difficulties which will be encountered.

4

1/6. The nervous system is well provided with means for action. Glucose, oxygen, and other metabolites are brought to it by the blood so that free energy is available abundantly. The nerve cells composing the system are not only themselves exquisitely sensitive, but are provided, at the sense organs, with devices of even higher sensitivity. Each nerve cell, by its ramifications, enables a single impulse to become many impulses, each of which is as active as the single impulse from which it originated. And by their control of the muscles, the nerve cells can rouse to activity engines of high mechanical power. The nervous system, then, possesses almost unlimited potentialities for action. But do these potentialities solve our problem? It seems not. We are concerned primarily with the question why, during learning, behaviour changes for the better: and this question is not answered by the fact that a given behaviour can change to one of lesser or greater activity. The examples given in S. 1/5, when examined for the energy changes before and after learning, show that the question of the quantity of activity is usually irrelevant.

But the evidence against regarding mere activity as sufficient for a solution is even stronger: often an increase in the amount of activity is not so much irrelevant as positively harmful.

If a dynamic system is allowed to proceed to vigorous action without special precautions, the activity will usually lead to the destruction of the system itself. A motor car with its tank full of petrol may be set into motion, but if it is released with no driver its activity, far from being beneficial, will probably cause the motor car to destroy itself more quickly than if it had remained inactive. The theme is discussed more thoroughly in S. 20/12; here it may be noted that activity, if inco-ordinated, tends merely to the system's destruction. How then is the brain to achieve success if its potentialities for action are partly potentialities for self-destruction?

The relation of part to part

1/7. It was decided in S. 1/5 that after the learning process the behaviour is usually better adapted than before. We ask, therefore, what property must be possessed by the neurons, or by the parts of a mechanical 'brain', so that the manifestation by the neuron of this property shall result in the whole animal's behaviour being improved.

Even if we allow the neuron all the properties of a living organism, it is still insufficiently provided. For the improvement in the animal's behaviour is often an improvement in relation to entities which have no counterpart in the life of a neuron. Thus when a dog, given food in an experiment on conditioned reflexes, learns to salivate, the behaviour improves because the saliva provides a lubricant for chewing. But in the neuron's existence, since all its food arrives in solution, neither ' chewing ' nor ' lubricant ' can have any direct relevance or meaning. Again, a rat learns to run through a maze without mistakes ; yet the learning has involved neurons which are firmly supported in a close mesh of glial fibres and never move in their lives.

Finally, consider an engine-driver who has just seen a signal and whose hand is on the throttle. If the light is red, the excitation from the retina must be transmitted through the nervous system so that the cells in the motor cortex send impulses down to those muscles whose activity makes the throttle *close*. If the light is green, the excitation from the retina must be transmitted through the nervous system so that the cells in the motor cortex make the throttle open. And the transmission is to be handled, and the safety of the train guaranteed, by neurons which can form no conception of 'red', 'green', 'train', 'signal', or ' accident ' ! Yet the system works.

1/8. In some cases there may be a simple mechanism which uses the method that a red light activates a chain of nerve-cells leading to the muscles which close the throttle while a green light activates another chain of nerve-cells leading to the muscles which make it open. In this way the effect of the colour of the signal might be transmitted through the nervous system in the appropriate way.

The simplicity of the arrangement is due to the fact that we are supposing that the two reactions are using two completely separate and independent mechanisms. This separation may well occur in the simpler reactions, but it is insufficient to explain the events of the more complex reactions. In most cases the ' correct ' and the ' incorrect ' neural activities are alike composed of excitations, of inhibitions, and of other changes that are all physiological,

6

so that the correctness is determined not by the process itself but by the relations which it bears to the other processes.

This dependence of the ' correctness ' of what is happening at one point in the nervous system on what is happening at other points would be shown if the engine-driver were to move over to the other side of the cab   For if previously a flexion of the elbow had closed the throttle, the same action will now open it ; and what was the correct pairing of red and green to push and pull must now be reversed   So the local action in the nervous system can no longer be regarded as ' correct ' or ' incorrect ', and the first simple solution breaks down.

Another example is given by the activity of chewing in so far as it involves the tongue and teeth in movements which must be related so that the teeth do not bite the tongue. No movement of the tongue can by itself be regarded as wholly wrong, for a movement which may be wrong when the teeth are just meeting may be right when they are parting and food is to be driven on to their line. Consequently the activities in the neurons which control the movement of the tongue cannot be described as either ' correct ' or ' incorrect ': only when these activities are related to those of the neurons which control the jaw movements can a correctness be determined ; and this property now belongs, not to either separately, but only to the activity of the two in combination.

These considerations reveal the main peculiarity of the problem. When the nervous system learns, it undergoes changes which result in its behaviour becoming better adapted to the environment. The behaviour depends on the activities of the various parts whose individual actions compound for better or worse into the whole action. Why, in the living brain, do they always compound for the better ?

If we wish to build an artificial brain the parts must be specified in their nature and properties. But how can we specify the ' correct ' properties for each part if the correctness depends not on the behaviour of each part but on its relations to the other parts ? Our problem is to get the parts properly co-ordinated. The brain does this automatically. What sort of a machine can be *self*-co-ordinating ?

This is our problem. It will be stated with more precision in S. 1/12. But before this statement is reached, some minor topics must be discussed.

7

The genetic control of cerebral function

1/9. The various species of the animal kingdom differ widely in their powers of learning . Man's intelligence, for instance, is clearly a species-characteristic, for the higher apes, however well trained, never show an intelligence equal to that of the average human being. Clearly the power of learning is determined to some extent by the inherited gene-pattern. In what way does the gene-pattern exert its effect on the learning process ? In particular, what part does it play in the adjustments of part to part which the previous section showed to be fundamental ? Does the gene-pattern determine these adjustments in detail ?

In Man, the genes number about 50,000 and the neurons number about 10,000,000,000. The genes are therefore far too few to specify every neuronic interconnection. (The possibility that a gene may control several phenotypic features is to some extent balanced by the fact that a single phenotypic feature may require several genes for its determination.)

But the strongest evidence against the suggestion that the genes exert, in the higher animals, a detailed control over the adjustments of part to part is provided by the evidence of S. 1/4. A dog, for instance, can be made to respond to the sound of a bell either with or without salivation, regardless of its particular gene-pattern. It is impossible, therefore, to relate the control of salivation to the particular genes possessed by the dog. This example, and all the other facts of which it is typical, show that the effect of the gene-pattern on the details of the learning process cannot be direct.

The effect, then, must be indirect : the genes fix permanently certain function-rules, but do not interfere with the function-rules in their detailed application to particular situations. Three examples of this type of control will be given in order to illustrate its nature.

In the game of chess, the laws (the function rules) are few and have been fixed for a century ; but their effects are as numerous as the number of positions to which they can be applied. The result is that games of chess can differ from one another though controlled by constant laws.

A second example is given by the process of evolution through natural selection. Here again the function-rule (the principle of

8

the survival of the fittest) is fixed, yet its influence has an infinite variety when applied to an infinite variety of particular organisms in particular environments.

A final example is given in the body by the process of inflammation. The function-rules which govern the process are genetically determined and are constant in one species. Yet these rules, when applied to an infinite variety of individual injuries, provide an infinite variety in the details of the process at particular points and times.

Our aim is now clear · we must find the function-rules. They must be few in number, much fewer than 50,000, and we must show that these few function-rules, when applied to an almost infinite number of circumstances and to 10,000,000,000 neurons, are capable of directing adequately the events in all these circumstances. The function-rules must be fixed, their applications flexible.

(The gene-pattern is discussed again in S. 9/9.)

Restrictions on the concepts to be used

1/10. Throughout the book I shall adhere to certain basic assumptions and to certain principles of method.

The nervous system, and living matter in general, will be assumed to be identical with all other matter. So no use of any ' vital ' property or tendency will be made, and no *deus ex machina* will be invoked. No psychological concept will be used unless it can be shown in objective form in non-living systems; and when used it will be considered to refer solely to its objective form. Related is the restriction that every concept used must be capable of objective demonstration. In the study of man this restriction raises formidable difficulties extending from the practical to the metaphysical. But as most of the discussion will be concerned with the observed behaviour of animals and machines, the peculiar difficulties will seldom arise.

No teleological explanation for behaviour will be used. It will be assumed throughout that a machine or an animal behaved in a certain way at a certain moment because its physical and chemical nature at that moment allowed it no other action. Never will we use the explanation that the action is performed because it will later be advantageous to the animal. Any such explanation would, of course, involve a circular argument; for our purpose is to explain the origin of behaviour which appears to be teleologically directed.

It will be further assumed that the nervous system, living matter, and the matter of the environment are all strictly determinate: that if on two occasions they are brought to the same state, the same behaviour will follow. Since at the atomic level of size the assumption is known to be false, the assumption implies that the functional units of the nervous system must be sufficiently large to be immune to this source of variation. For this there is some evidence, since recordings of nervous activity, even of single impulses, show no evidence of appreciable thermal noise. But we need not prejudge the question. The work to be described is an attempt to follow the assumption of determinacy wherever it leads. When it leads to obvious error will be time to question its validity.

Consciousness

1/11. The previous section has demanded that we shall make no use of the subjective elements of experience; and I can anticipate by saying that in fact the book makes no such use. At times its rigid adherence to the objective point of view may jar on the reader and may expose me to the accusation that I am ignoring an essential factor. A few words in explanation may save misunderstanding.

Throughout the book, consciousness and its related subjective elements are not used for the simple reason that at no point have I found their introduction necessary. This is not surprising, for the book deals with only one of the aspects of the mind-body relation, and with an aspect—learning—that has long been recognised to have no necessary dependence on consciousness. Here is an example to illustrate their independence. If a cyclist wishes to turn to the left, his first action must be to turn the front wheel to the *right* (otherwise he will fall outwards by centrifugal force). Every practised cyclist makes this movement every time he turns, yet many cyclists, even after they have made the movement hundreds of times, are quite unconscious of making it. The direct intervention of consciousness is evidently not necessary for adaptive learning.

10

Such an observation, showing that consciousness is sometimes not necessary, gives us no right to deduce that consciousness does not exist. The truth is quite otherwise, for the fact of the existence of consciousness is prior to all other facts. If I perceive —am aware of—a chair, I may later be persuaded, by other evidence, that the appearance was produced only by a trick of lighting; I may be persuaded that it occurred in a dream, or even that it was an hallucination; but there is no evidence in existence that could persuade me that my awareness itself was mistaken—that I had not really been aware at all. This knowledge of personal awareness, therefore, is prior to all other forms of knowledge.

If consciousness is the most fundamental fact of all, why is it not used in this book ? The answer, in my opinion, is that Science deals, and can deal, only with what one man can *demonstrate* to another. Vivid though consciousness may be to its possessor, there is as yet no method known by which he can demonstrate his experience to another. And until such a method, or its equivalent, is found, the facts of consciousness cannot be used in scientific method.

The problem

1/12. It is now time to state the problem. Later, when more exact concepts have been developed, it will be possible to state the problem more precisely (S. 8/1).

It will be convenient, throughout the discussion, to have some well-known, practical problem to act as type-problem, so that general statements can always be referred to it. I select the following. When a kitten first approaches a fire its reactions are unpredictable and usually inappropriate. Later, however, when adult, its reactions are different. It approaches the fire and seats itself at that place where the heat is moderate. If the fire burns low, it moves nearer. If a hot coal falls out, it jumps away. I might have taken as type-problem some experiment published by a psychological laboratory, but the present example has several advantages. It is well known; it is representative of a wide class of important phenomena; and it is not likely to be called in question by the discovery of some small technical flaw.

With this as specific example, we may state the problem

generally. We commence with the concepts that the organism is mechanistic in action, that it is composed of parts, and that the behaviour of the whole is the outcome of the compounded actions of the parts. Organisms change their behaviour by learning, and change it so that the later behaviour is better adapted to their environment than the earlier   Our problem is, first, **to identify the nature of the change which shows as learning, and secondly, to find why such changes should tend to cause better adaptation for the whole organism.**

CHAPTER 2

Dynamic Systems

2/1. In the previous chapter we have repeatedly used the concepts of a system, of parts in a whole, of the system's behaviour, and of its changes of behaviour. These concepts are fundamental and must be properly defined Accurate definition at this stage is of the highest importance, for any vagueness here will infect all the subsequent discussion ; and as we shall have to enter the realm where the physical and the psychological meet, a realm where the experience of centuries has found innumerable possibilities of confusion, we shall have to proceed with unusual caution.

We start by assuming that we have before us some dynamic system, i e. something that may change with time We wish to study it. It will be referred to as the ' machine ', but the word must be understood in the widest possible sense, for no restriction is implied other than that it should be objective.

2/2. As we shall be more concerned in this chapter with principles than with practice, we shall be concerned chiefly with constructing a method. When constructed, it must satisfy these axiomatic demands :—(1) Its procedure for obtaining information must be wholly objective (2) It must obtain its information solely from the 'machine', no other source being permitted. (3) It must be applicable, at least in principle, to all material ' machines ', whether animate or inanimate. (4) It must be precisely defined.

The actual form developed may appear to the practical worker to be clumsy and inferior to methods already in use , it probably is. But it is not intended to compete with the many specialised methods already in use. Such methods are usually adapted to a particular class of dynamic systems : electronic circuits, rats in mazes, solutions of reacting chemical substances, automatic pilots, or heart-lung preparations. The method proposed here

13

must have the peculiarity that it is applicable to all; it must, so to speak, specialise in generality.

Variable and system

2/3. The first step is to record the behaviours of the machine's individual parts To do this we identify any number of suitable variables. A **variable** is *a measurable quantity which at every instant has a definite numerical value.* A ' grandfather ' clock, for instance, might provide the following variables :—the angular deviation of the pendulum from the vertical ; the angular velocity with which the pendulum is moving ; the angular position of a particular cog-wheel ; the height of a driving weight ; the reading of the minute-hand on the scale ; and the length of the pendulum. If there is any doubt whether a particular quantity may be admitted as a ' variable ' I shall use the criterion whether it can be represented by a pointer on a dial. I shall, in fact, assume that such representation is always used : that the experimenter is observing not the parts of the real ' machine ' directly but the dials on which the variables are displayed, as an engineer watches a control panel

Only in this way can we be sure of what sources of information are used by the experimenter. Ordinarily, when an experimenter examines a machine he makes full use of knowledge ' borrowed ' from past experience. If he sees two cogs enmeshed he knows that their two rotations will not be independent, even though he does not actually see them rotate. This knowledge comes from previous experiences in which the mutual relations of similar pairs have been tested and observed directly. Such borrowed knowledge is, of course, extremely useful, and every skilled experimenter brings a great store of it to every experiment. Nevertheless, it must be excluded from any fundamental method, if only because it is not sufficiently reliable . the unexpected sometimes happens ; and the only way to be *certain* of the relation between two parts in a new ' machine ' is to test the relationship directly.

All the quantities used in physics, chemistry, biology, physiology, and objective psychology, are variables in the defined sense. Thus, the position of a limb can be specified numerically by co-ordinates of position, and movement of the limb can move a pointer

14

on a dial. Temperature at a point can be specified numerically and can be recorded on a dial. Pressure, angle, electric potential, volume, velocity, torque, power, mass, viscosity, humidity, surface tension, osmotic pressure, specific gravity, and time itself, to mention only a few, can all be specified numerically and recorded on dials. Eddington's statement on the subject is explicit: ' The whole subject matter of exact science consists of pointer readings and similar indications.' ' Whatever quantity we say we are " observing ", the actual procedure nearly always ends in reading the position of some kind of indicator on a graduated scale or its equivalent.'

Whether the restriction to dial-readings is justifiable with living subjects will be discussed in S. 3/4.

One minor point should be noticed as it will be needed later. The absence of an entity can always be converted to a reading on a scale simply by considering the entity to be present but in zero degree. Thus, ' still air ' can be treated as a wind blowing at 0 m.p.h.; ' darkness ' can be treated as an illumination of 0 footcandles ; and the giving of a drug can be represented by indicating that its concentration in the tissues has risen from its usual value of 0 per cent.

2/4. A **system** is *any arbitrarily selected set of variables.* It is a list nominated by the experimenter, and is quite different from the real ' machine '.

At this stage no naturalness of association is implied, and the selection is arbitrary. (' Naturalness ' is discussed in S. 2/14)

The variable ' time ' will always be used, so the dials will always include a clock. But the status of ' time ' in the method is unique, so it is better segregated. I therefore add the qualification that ' time ' is not to be included among the variables of a system.

The Method

2/5. It will be appreciated that every real ' machine ' embodies no less than an infinite number of variables, most of which must of necessity be ignored. Thus if we were studying the swing of a pendulum in relation to its length we would be interested in its angular deviation at various times, but we would often ignore the chemical composition of the bob, the reflecting power of its surface, the electric conductivity of the suspending string, the specific gravity of the bob, its shape, the age of the alloy, its degree of bacterial contamination, and so on. The list of what might be ignored could be extended indefinitely. Faced with this infinite number of variables, the experimenter must, and of course does, select a definite number for examination—in other words, he defines his system. Thus, an experimenter once drew up Table 2/5/1 He thereby defined a three-variable

Time (mins)	Distance of secondary coil (cm)	Part of skin stimulated	Secretion of saliva during 30 secs (drops)
. .	. .	. . .	. .

TABLE 2/5/1

system, ready for testing.   This experiment being finished, he later drew up other tables which included new variables or omitted old. By definition these new combinations were new systems.

2/6. The variables being decided on, the recording apparatus is now assumed to be attached to the ' machine ' and the experimenter ready to observe the dials. We must next specify what power the experimenter has over the experimental situation.

It is postulated that the experimenter can control any variable he pleases . that he can make any variable take any arbitrary value at any arbitrary time. The postulate specifies nothing about the methods   it demands only that certain end-results are to be available. In most cases the means to be used are obvious enough. Take the example of S. 2/3 : an arbitrary angular deviation of the pendulum can be enforced at any time by direct manipulation ; an arbitrary angular momentum can be enforced at any time by an appropriate impulse ; the cog can be disconnected and shifted, the driving-weight wound up, the hand moved, and the pendulum-bob lowered.

By repeating the control from instant to instant, the experimenter can force a variable to take any prescribed series of values. The postulate, therefore, implies that any variable can be forced to follow a prescribed course.

16

Some systems cannot be forced, for instance the astronomical, the meteorological, and those biological systems that are accessible to observation but not to experiment. Yet no change is necessary in principle : the experimenter simply waits until the desired set of values occurs during the natural changes of the system, and he counts that instant as if it were the instant at which the system were started. Thus, though we cannot create a thunderstorm, we can observe how swallows react to one simply by waiting till one occurs ' spontaneously '.

2/7. The ' machine ' will be studied by applying the **primary operation,** defined thus   The variables are brought to a selected state (S. 2/9) by the experimenter's power of control (S. 2/6) ; the experimenter decides which variables are to be released and which are to be controlled ; at a given moment the selected variables are released, so that their behaviour is controlled primarily by the ' machine ', while the others are forced by the experimenter to follow their prescribed courses (which often includes their being held constant) ; the behaviours of the variables are then recorded. This operation is always used in the practical investigation of dynamic systems. Here are some examples.

In chemical dynamics the variables are often the concentrations of substances. Selected concentrations are brought together, and from a definite moment are allowed to interact while the temperature is held constant. The experimenter records the changes which the concentrations undergo with time.

In a mechanical experiment the variables might be the positions and momenta of certain bodies. At a definite instant the bodies, started with selected velocities from selected positions, are allowed to interact. The experimenter records the changes which the velocities and positions undergo with time.

In studies of the conduction of heat, the variables are the temperatures at various places in the heated body. A prescribed distribution of temperatures is enforced, and, while the temperatures of some places are held constant, the variations of the other temperatures is observed after the initial moment.

In physiology, the variables might be the rate of a rabbit's heart-beat, the intensity of faradisation applied to the vagus nerve, and the concentration of adrenaline in the circulating blood. The intensity of faradisation will be continuously under the experimenter's control. Not improbably it will be kept first at zero and then increased   From a given instant the changes in the variables will be recorded.

In experimental psychology, the variables might be ‘the number of mistakes made by a rat on a trial in a maze’ and ‘the amount of cerebral cortex which has been removed surgically’. The second variable is permanently under the experimenter's control. The experimenter starts the experiment and observes how the first variable changes with time while the second variable is held constant, or caused to change in some prescribed manner.

While a single primary operation may seem to yield little information, the power of the method lies in the fact that the experimenter can repeat it with variations, and can relate the different responses to the different variations. Thus, after one primary operation the next may be varied in any of three ways : the system may be changed by the inclusion of new variables or by the omission of old ; the initial state may be changed ; or the prescribed courses may be changed. By applying these variations systematically, in different patterns and groupings, the different responses may be interrelated to yield relations.

By further orderly variations, these relations may be further interrelated to yield secondary, or hyper-, relations ; and so on. In this way the ‘machine’ may be made to yield more and more complex information about its inner organisation.

2/8. All our concepts will eventually be defined in terms of this method.   For example, ‘environment’ is so defined in S. 3/8, ‘adaptation’ in S. 5/8, and ‘stimulus’ in S. 6/6.   If any have been omitted it is by oversight ; for I hold that this procedure is sufficient for their objective definition.

The Field of a System

2/9. The state of a system at a given instant is *the set of numerical values which its variables have at that instant.*

Thus, the six-variable system of S. 2/3 might at some instant have the state : $-4°$, $0 \cdot 3$ radians/sec, $128°$, 52 cm., $42 \cdot 8$ minutes, $88 \cdot 4$ cm

Two states are equal if and only if the corresponding pairs of numerical values are all equal.

2/10.   A **line of behaviour** is specified by *a succession of states and the time-intervals between them*.   The first state in a line of behaviour will be called the *initial* state.   Two lines of behaviour are equal if all the corresponding pairs of states are equal, and if all the corresponding pairs of time-intervals are equal.   One primary operation yields one line of behaviour.

There are several ways in which a line of behaviour may be recorded.

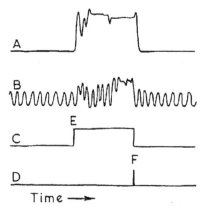

FIGURE 2/10/1 : Events during an experiment on a conditioned reflex in a sheep.   Attached to the left foreleg is an electrode by which a shock can be administered.   Line *A* records the position of the left forefoot. Line *B* records the sheep's respiratory movements.   Line *C* records by a rise (*E*) the application of the conditioned stimulus : the sound of a buzzer.   Line *D* records by a vertical stroke (*F*) the application of the electric shock.   (After Liddell *et al.*)

The graphical method is exemplified by Figure 2/10/1.   The four variables form, by definition, the system that is being examined.   The four simultaneous values at any instant define a state.   And the succession of states at their particular intervals constitute and specify the line of behaviour.   The four traces specify one line of behaviour.

Sometimes a line of behaviour can be specified in terms of elementary mathematical functions.   Such a simplicity is convenient when it occurs, but is rarer in practice than an

19

acquaintance with elementary mathematics would suggest. With biological material it is rare.

Another form is the tabular, of which an example is Table 2/10/1. Each column defines one state ; the whole table defines one line of behaviour (other tables may contain more than one line of behaviour). The state at 0 hours is the initial state.

		Time (hours)			
		0	1	3	6
Variable	w	7 35	7 26	7 28	7 29
	x	156 7	154 6	154 1	151 5
	y	110 3	116 7	118 3	118 5
	z	22 2	15 3	15 0	14 6

TABLE 2/10/1 : Blood changes after a dose of ammonium chloride. w = serum pH , x = serum total base ; y = serum chloride , z = serum bicarbonate ; (the last three in m. eq. per l.).

The tabular form has one outstanding advantage : it contains the facts and nothing more. Mathematical forms are apt to suggest too much : continuity that has not been demonstrated, fictitious values between the moments of observation, and an accuracy that may not be present. Unless specially mentioned, all lines of behaviour will be assumed to be recorded primarily in tabular form.

2/11. The behaviour of a system can also be represented in **phase-space**. By its use simple proofs may be given of many statements difficult to prove in the tabular form.

If a system is composed of two variables, a particular state will be specified by two numbers. By ordinary graphic methods, the two variables can be represented by axes ; the two values will then define a point in the plane. Thus the state in which variable x has the value 5 and variable y the value 10 will be represented by the point A in Figure 2/11/1. The **representative point** of a state is *the point whose co-ordinates are respectively equal to the values of the variables.* By S. 2/4 ' time ' is not to be one of the axes.

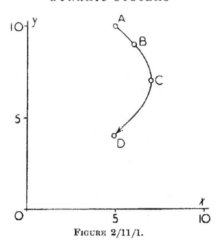

FIGURE 2/11/1.

2/12. Suppose next that a system of two variables gave the line of behaviour shown in Table 2/12/1. The successive states will be graphed, by the method, at positions *B*, *C*, and *D* (Figure 2/11/1). So the system's behaviour corresponds to a movement of the representative point along the line in the phase-space.

By comparing the Table and the Figure, certain exact correspondences can be found. Every state of the system corresponds

Time	x	y
0	5	10
1	6	9
2	7	7
3	5	4

TABLE 2/12/1.

uniquely to a point in the plane, and every point in the plane (or in some portion of it) to some possible state of the system. Further, every line of behaviour of the system corresponds uniquely to a line in the plane. If the system has three variables, the graph must be in three dimensions, but each state still corresponds to a point, and each line of behaviour to a line in the phase-space. If the number of variables exceeds three, this method of graphing is no longer physically possible, but the

21   c

correspondence is maintained exactly no matter how numerous the variables.

2/13. A system's **field** is *the phase-space containing all the lines of behaviour found by releasing the system from all possible initial states.*

In practice, of course, the experimenter would test only a representative sample of the initial states. Some of them will probably be tested repeatedly, for the experimenter will usually want to

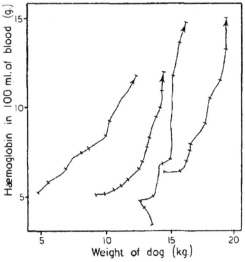

FIGURE 2/13/1 : Arrow-heads show the direction of movement of the representative point ; cross-lines show the positions of the representative point at weekly intervals.

make sure that the system is giving reproducible lines of behaviour. Thus in one experiment, in which dogs had been severely bled and then placed on a standard diet, their body-weight x and the concentration y of haemoglobin in their blood were recorded at weekly intervals. This two-variable system, tested from four initial states by four primary operations, gave the field shown in Figure 2/13/1. Other examples occur frequently later.

It will be noticed that a field is defined, in accordance with S. 2/8, by reference exclusively to the observed values of the variables and to the results of primary operations on them. It is therefore a wholly objective property of the system.

The concept of 'field' will be used extensively for two reasons. It defines the characteristic behaviour of the system, replacing the vague concept of what a system 'does' or how it 'behaves' (often describable only in words) by the precise construct of a 'field'. From this precision comes the possibility of comparing field with field, and therefore of comparing behaviour with behaviour. The reader may at first find the method unusual. Those who are familiar with the phase-space of mechanics will have no difficulty, but other readers may find it helpful if at first, whenever the word 'field' occurs, they substitute for it some phrase like 'typical way of behaving'.

The Natural System

2/14. In S 2/4 a system was defined as any arbitrarily selected set of variables. The right to arbitrary selection cannot be waived, but the time has now come to recognise that both science and common sense insist that if a system is to be studied with profit its variables must have some naturalness of association. But what is 'natural'? The problem has inevitably arisen after the restriction of S. 2/3, where we repudiated all borrowed knowledge. If we restrict our attention to the variables, we find that as every real 'machine' provides an infinity of variables, and as from them we can form another infinity of combinations, we need some test to distinguish the natural system from the arbitrary.

One criterion will occur to the practical experimenter at once. He knows that if an active and relevant variable is left unobserved or uncontrolled the system's behaviour will become capricious, not capable of being reproduced at will. This concept may readily be made more precise.

If, on repeatedly applying a primary operation to a system, it is found that all the lines of behaviour which follow an initial state S are equal, and if a similar equality occurs after every other initial state S', S'', . . . , then the system is **regular.**

Whether a system is regular or not may be decided by first constructing and then examining its field. For if the system is regular, from each initial state will go only one line of behaviour,

23

the subsequent trials merely confirming the first   The concept of 'regularity' thus conforms to the demand of S. 2/8; for it is definable in terms of the field and is therefore wholly objective.

The field of a regular system does not change with time.

If, on testing, a system is found to be not regular, the experimenter is faced with the common problem of what to do with a system that will not give reproducible results. Somehow he must get regularity. The practical details vary from case to case, but in principle the necessity is always the same: he must try a new system. This means that new variables must be added to the previous set, or, more rarely, some irrelevant variable omitted.

From now on we shall be concerned mostly with regular systems. We assume that preliminary investigations have been completed and that we have found a system, based on the real 'machine', that (1) includes the variables in which we are specially interested, and (2) includes sufficient other variables to render the whole system regular.

2/15. For some purposes regularity of the system may be sufficient, but more often a further demand is made before the system is acceptable to the experimenter: it must be 'absolute'.*
It will be convenient if I first define the concept, leaving the discussion of its importance to the next section.

If, on repeatedly applying primary operations to a system, it is found that all the lines of behaviour which follow a state S are equal, no matter how the system arrived at S, and if a similar equality occurs after every other state S', S", . . . , then the system is **absolute.**

Consider, for instance, the two-variable system that gave the two lines of behaviour shown in Table 2/15/1.

On the first line of behaviour the state $x = 0$, $y = 2 \cdot 0$ was followed after 0 1 seconds by the state $x = 0 \cdot 2$, $y = 2 \cdot 1$. On line 2 the state $x = 0$, $y = 2 \cdot 0$ occurred again; but after $0 \cdot 1$ seconds the state became $x = 0 \cdot 1$, $y = 1 \cdot 8$ and not $x = 0 \cdot 2$, $y = 2 \cdot 1$. As the two lines of behaviour that follow the state $x = 0$, $y = 2 \cdot 0$ are not equal, the system is not absolute.

A well-known example of an absolute system is given by the

* (O E D.) *Absolute* · existent without relation to any other thing; self-sufficing; disengaged from all interrupting causes.

simple pendulum swinging in a vertical plane. It is known that the two variables—(x) angle of deviation of the string from

		Time (seconds)			
Line	Variable	0	0·1	0·2	0·3
1	x	0	0·2	0·4	0·6
	y	2·0	2·1	2·3	2·6
2	x	− 0·2	− 0·1	0	0·1
	y	2·4	2·2	2·0	1·8

TABLE 2/15/1.

vertical, (y) angular velocity (or momentum) of the bob—are such that, all else being kept constant, their two values at a given instant are sufficient to determine the subsequent changes of the two variables (Figure 2/15/1.)

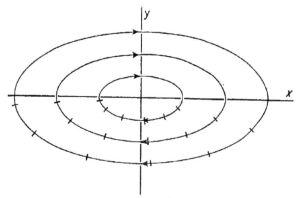

FIGURE 2/15/1 : Field of a simple pendulum 40 cm. long swinging in a vertical plane when g is 981 cm./sec.[2]. x is the angle of deviation from the vertical and y the angular velocity of movement. Cross-strokes mark the position of the representative point at each one-tenth second. The clockwise direction should be noticed.

An absolute system is thus ' state-determined ', and this is its most important property : the occurrence of a state is *sufficient* to determine the line of behaviour that ensues. The property is both necessary and sufficient ; so all state-determined systems are absolute. We shall use this fact repeatedly.

The field of an absolute system is characteristic · from every point there goes only one line of behaviour whether the point is initial on the line or not. The field of the two-variable system just mentioned is sketched in Figure 2/15/1 ; through every point passes only one line.

These relations may be made clearer if this field is contrasted with one that is regular but not absolute. Figure 2/15/2 shows

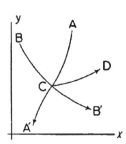

such a field (the system is described in S 19/15). The system's regularity would be established if we found that the system, started at A, always went to A', and, started at B, always went to B'. But such a system is not absolute ; for to say that the representative point is leaving C is insufficient to define its future line of behaviour, which may go to A' or B'.

FIGURE 2/15/2 · The field of the system shown in Figure 19/15/1

Even if the lines from A and B always ran to A' and B', the regularity in no way restricts what would happen if the system were started at C. it might go to D. If the system were absolute, the lines CA', CB', and CD would coincide.

A system's absoluteness is determined by its field ; the property is therefore wholly objective

An absolute system's field does not change with time.

2/16. We can now return to the question of what we mean when we say that a system's variables have a ' natural ' association. What we need is not a verbal explanation but a definition, which must have these properties

(1) it must be in the form of a test, separating all systems into two classes ,

(2) its application must be wholly objective ;

(3) its result must agree with common sense in typical and undisputed cases.

The third property makes clear that we cannot expect a proposed definition to be established by a few lines of verbal argument :

it must be treated as a working hypothesis and used ; only experience can show whether it is faulty or sound.

From here on I shall treat a ' natural ' system as equivalent to an ' absolute ' system. Various reasons might be given to make the equivalence plausible, but they would *prove* nothing and I shall omit them. Much stronger is the evidence in the Appendix. There it will be found that the equivalence brings clarity where there might be confusion ; and it enables proof to be given to propositions which, though clear to physical intuition, cannot be proved without it. The equivalence, in short, is indispensable.

Why the concept is so important can be indicated briefly. When working with determinate systems the experimenter always assumes that, if he is interested in certain variables, he can find a set of variables that (1) includes those variables, and (2) has the property that if all is known about the set at one instant the behaviour of all the variables will be predictable. The assumption is implicit in almost all science, but, being fundamental, it is seldom mentioned explicitly. Temple, though, refers to ' . . . the fundamental assumption of macrophysics that a complete knowledge of the present state of a system furnishes sufficient data to determine definitely its state at any future time or its response to any external influence '. Laplace made the same assumption about the whole universe when he stated that, given its state at one instant, its future progress should be calculable. The definition given above makes this assumption precise and gives it in a form ready for use in the later chapters.

2/17. To conclude, here is an example to illustrate this chapter's method.

Suppose someone constructed two simple pendulums, hung them so that they swung independently, and from this ' machine ' brought to an observation panel the following six variables ·

(v) the angular deviation of the first pendulum
(w) ,,   ,,   ,,   ,, ,, second   ,,
(x) the angular momentum of the first pendulum
(y) ,,   ,,   ,,   ,, ,, second   ,,
(z) the brightness of their illumination
(t) the time.

The experimenter, knowing nothing of the real ' machine ', or of the relations between the five variables, sits at the panel and applies the defined method.

He starts by selecting a system at random, constructs its field by S. 2/13, and deduces by S. 2/15 whether it is absolute. He then tries another system   It is clear that he will eventually be able to state, without using borrowed knowledge, that just three systems are absolute . (v, w, x, y), (v, x), and (w, y).   He will add that z is unpredictable. He has in fact identified the natural relations existing in the ' machine '.   He will also, at the end of his investigation, be able to write down the differential equations governing the systems (S. 19/20). Later, by using the method of S. 14/6, he will be able to deduce that the four-variable system really consists of two independent parts.

REFERENCES

EDDINGTON, A. S.   *The nature of the physical world.* Cambridge, 1929 ;
  The philosophy of physical science. Cambridge, 1939.
LIDDELL, H. S., ANDERSON, O D , KOTYUKA, E., and HARTMAN, F A.
  Effect of extract of adrenal cortex on experimental neurosis in sheep.
  Archives of Neurology and Psychiatry, **34,** 973 ; 1935.
TEMPLE, G.   *General principles of quantum theory.* London.   Second edition,
  1942.

CHAPTER 3

The Animal as Machine

3/1. WE shall assume at once that the living organism in its nature and processes is not essentially different from other matter. The truth of the assumption will not be discussed. The chapter will therefore deal only with the technique of applying this assumption to the complexities of biological systems.

The numerical specification of behaviour

3/2. If the method laid down in the previous chapter is to be followed, we must first determine to what extent the behaviour of an organism is capable of being specified by *variables*, remembering that our ultimate test is whether the representation can be by dial readings (S. 2/3).

There can be little doubt that any single quantity observable in the living organism can be treated at least in principle as a variable. All bodily movements can be specified by co-ordinates. All joint movements can be specified by angles. Muscle tensions can be specified by their pull in dynes. Muscle movements can be specified by co-ordinates based on the bony structure or on some fixed external point, and can therefore be recorded numerically. A gland can be specified in its activity by its rate of secretion. Pulse-rate, blood-pressure, temperature, rate of blood-flow, tension of smooth muscle, and a host of other variables can be similarly recorded.

In the nervous system our attempts to observe, measure, and record have met great technical difficulties. Nevertheless, much has been achieved. The action potential, the essential event in the activity of the nervous system, can now be measured and recorded. The excitatory and inhibitory states of the centres are at the moment not directly recordable, but there is no reason to suppose that they will never become so.

3/3. Few would deny that the elementary physico-chemical events in the living organism can be treated as variables. But some may hesitate before accepting that readings on dials are adequate for the description of *all* significant biological events. As the remainder of the book will assume that they are sufficient, I must show how the various complexities of biological experience can be reduced to this standard form.

A simple case which may be mentioned first occurs when an event is recorded in the form ' strychnine was injected at this moment ', or ' a light was switched on ', or ' an electric shock was administered '. Such a statement treats only the positive event as having existence and ignores the other state as a nullity. It can readily be converted to a numerical form suitable for our purpose by using the device mentioned in S. 2/3. Such events would then be recorded by assuming, in the first case, that the animal always had strychnine in its tissues but that at first the quantity present was 0 mg. per g. tissue ; in the second case, that the light was always on, but that at first it shone with a brightness of 0 candlepower ; and in the last case, that an electric potential was applied throughout but that at first it had a value of 0 volts. Such a method of description cannot be wrong in these cases for it defines exactly the same set of objective facts. Its advantage from our point of view is that it provides a method which can be used uniformly over a wide range of phenomena : the variable is always present, merely varying in value.

But this device does not remove all difficulties. It sometimes happens in physiology and psychology that a variable seems to have no numerical counter-part. Thus in one experiment two cards, one black and one brown, were shown alternately to an animal as stimuli. One variable would thus be ' colour ' and it would have two values The simplest way to specify colour numerically is to give the wave-length of its light ; but this method cannot be used here, for ' black ' means ' no light ', and ' brown ' does not occur in the spectrum. Another example would occur if an electric heater were regularly used and if its switch indicated only the degrees ' high ', ' medium ', and ' low '. Another example is given on many types of electric apparatus by a pilot light which, as a variable, takes only the two values ' lit ' and ' unlit '. More complex examples occur frequently in psychological experiments. Table 2/5/1, for instance, contains a variable ' part of skin stimu-

THE ANIMAL AS MACHINE

lated ' which, in Pavlov's table, takes only two values · ' usual place ' and ' new place '. Even more complicated variables are common in Pavlov's experiments. Many a table contains a variable ' stimulus ' which takes such values as ' bubbling water ', ' metronome ', ' flashing light '. A similar difficulty occurs when an experimenter tests an animal's response to injections of toxins, so that there will be a variable ' type of toxin ' which may take the two values ' Diphtheria type Gravis ' and ' Diphtheria type Medius '. And finally the change may involve an extensive re-organisation of the whole experimental situation. Such would occur if the experimenter, wanting to test the effect of the general surroundings, tried the effect of the variable ' situation of the experiment ' by giving it alternately the two values ' in the animal house ' and ' in the open air '. Can such variables be represented by number ?

In some of the examples, the variables might possibly be specified numerically by a more or less elaborate specification of their physical nature. Thus ' part of skin stimulated ' might be specified by reference to some system of co-ordinates marked on the skin , and the three intensities of the electric heater might be specified by the three values of the watts consumed   But this method is hardly possible in the remainder of the cases ; nor is it necessary. For numbers can be used cardinally as well as ordinally, that is, they may be used as mere labels without any reference to their natural order.   Such are the numberings of the divisions of an army, and of the subscribers on a telephone system ; for the subscriber whose number is, say, 4051 has no particular relation to the subscriber whose number is 4052 · the number identifies him but does not relate him.

It may be shown (S. 21/1) that if a variable takes a few values which stand in no simple relation to one another, then each value may be allotted an arbitrary number ; and provided that the numbers are used systematically throughout the experiment, and that their use is confined to the experiment, then no confusion can arise   Thus the variable ' situation of the experiment ' might be allotted the arbitrary value of ' 1 ' if the experiment occurs in the animal house, and ' 2 ' if it occurs in the open air

Although ' situation of the experiment ' involves a great number of physical variables, the aggregate may justifiably be treated as a single variable provided the arrangement of the experiment is

such that the many variables are used throughout as one aggregate which can take either of two forms. If, however, the
aggregate were split in the experiment, as would happen if we
recorded four classes of results ·

(1) in the animal house in summer
(2) in the animal house in winter
(3) in the open air in summer
(4) in the open air in winter

then we must either allow the variable ' condition of experiment '
to take four values, or we could consider the experiment as
subject to two variables : ' site of experiment ' and ' season of
year ', each of which takes two values. According to this method,
what is important is not the material structure of the technical
devices but the experiment's logical structure.

3/4. But is the method yet adequate ? Can all the living
organisms' more subtle qualities be numericised in this way ? On
this subject there has been much dispute, but we can avoid a part
of the controversy ; for here we are concerned only with certain
qualities defined.

First, we shall be dealing not so much with qualities as with
behaviour : we shall be dealing, not with what an organism feels
or thinks, but with what it does. The omission of all subjective
aspects (S. 1/11) removes from the discussion the most subtle of
the qualities, while the restriction to overt behaviour makes the
specification by variable usually easy. Secondly, when the non-
mathematical reader thinks that there are some complex quantities
that cannot be adequately represented by number, he is apt
to think of their representation by a single variable. The use of
many variables, however, enables systems of considerable complexity to be treated. Thus a complex system like ' the weather
over England ', which cannot be treated adequately by a single
variable, can, by the use of many variables, be treated as adequately as we please.

3/5. To illustrate the method for specifying the behaviour of a
system by variables, two examples will be given. They are of
little intrinsic interest ; more important is the fact that they
demonstrate that the method is exact and that it can be extended
to any extent without loss of precision.

The first example is from a physiological experiment. A dog was subjected to a steady loss of blood at the rate of one per cent of its body weight per minute. Recorded are the three variables :

(x) rate of blood-flow through the inferior vena cava,
(y) ,, ,, ,, ,, ,, muscles of a leg,
(z) ,, ,, ,, ,, ,, gut.

The changes of the variables with time are shown in Figure 3/5/1. It will be seen that the changes of the variables show a characteristic pattern, for the blood-flow through leg and gut falls more than that through the inferior vena cava, and this difference is characteristic of the body's reaction to haemorrhage. The use

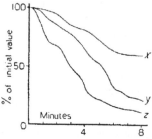

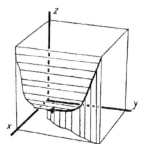

FIGURE 3/5/1 : Effect of haemorrhage on the rate of blood-flow through : x, the inferior vena cava ; y, the muscles of a leg ; and z, the gut. (From Rein.)

FIGURE 3/5/2 : Phase-space and line of behaviour of the data shown in Figure 3/5/1.

of more than one variable has enabled the *pattern* of the reaction to be displayed.

The changes specify a line of behaviour, shown in Figure 3/5/2. Had the line of behaviour pointed in a different direction, the change would have corresponded to a change in the pattern of the body's reaction to haemorrhage.

The second example uses certain angles measured from a cinematographic record of the activities of a man. His body moved forward but was vertical throughout. The four variables are :

(w) angle between the right thigh and the vertical
(x) ,, ,, ,, left ,, ,, ,, ,,
(y) ,, ,, ,, right ,, ., ,, right tibia
(z) ,, ,, ,, left ,, ,, ,, left ,,

In w and x the angle is counted positively when the knee comes forward . in y and z the angles are measured behind the knee. The line of behaviour is specified in Table 3/5/1. The reader can easily identify this well-known activity.

		Time (seconds)								
		0	0·1	0 2	0 3	0 4	0·5	0 6	0 7	0 8
Variable	w	45	10	−10	−20	−35	0	60	70	45
	x	−35	0	60	70	45	10	−10	−20	−35
	y	170	180	180	160	120	80	60	100	170
	z	120	80	60	100	170	180	180	160	120

TABLE 3/5/1.

The organism as system

3/6. In a physiological experiment the nervous system is usually considered to be absolute. That it can be made absolute is assumed by every physiologist before the work starts, for he assumes that it is subject to the fundamental assumption of S. 2/15 : that if every detail within it could be determined, its subsequent behaviour would also be determined. Many of the specialised techniques such as anaesthesia, spinal transection, root section, and the immobilisation of body and head in clamps are used to ensure proper isolation of the system—a necessary condition for its absoluteness (S. 2/15). So unless there are special reasons to the contrary, the nervous system in a physiological experiment has the properties of an absolute system.

3/7. Similarly it is usually agreed that an animal undergoing experiments on its conditioned reflexes is a physico-chemical system such that if we knew every detail we could predict its behaviour. Pavlov's insistence on complete isolation was intended to ensure that this was so. So unless there are special reasons to the contrary, the animal in an experiment with conditioned reflexes has the properties of an absolute system.

The environment

3/8. These two examples, however, are mentioned only as introduction ; rather we shall be concerned with the nature of the free-living organism within a natural environment.

Given an organism, its **environment** is defined as *those variables whose changes affect the organism, and those variables which are changed by the organism's behaviour*. It is thus defined in a purely functional, not a material, sense. It will be treated uniformly with our treatment of all variables : we assume it is representable by dials, is explorable (by the experimenter) by primary operations, and is intrinsically determinate.

Organism and environment

3/9. The theme of the chapter can now be stated . the free-living organism and its environment, taken together, form an absolute system.

The concepts developed in the previous sections now enable us to treat both organism and environment by identical methods, for the same primary assumptions are made about each. The two parts act and re-act on one another (S. 3/11), and are therefore properly regarded as two parts of one system. And since we have assumed that the conjoint system is state-determined, we may treat the whole as absolute.

3/10. As example, that the organism and its environment form a single absolute system, consider (in so far as the activities of balancing are concerned) a bicycle and its rider in normal progression.

First, the forward movement may be eliminated as irrelevant, for we could study the properties of this dynamic system equally well if the wheels were on some backward-moving band The variables can be identified by considering what happens. Suppose the rider pulls his right hand backwards : it will change the angular position of the front wheel (taking the line of the frame as reference). The changed angle of the front wheel will start the two points, at which the wheels make contact with the ground, moving to the right. (The physical reasons for this movement are irrelevant : the fact that the relation is determined is sufficient.)

The rider's centre of gravity being at first unmoved, the line vertically downwards from his centre of gravity will strike the ground more and more to the left of the line joining the two points   As a result he will start to fall to the left.   This fall will excite nerve-endings in the organs of balance in the ear, impulses will pass to the nervous system, and will be switched through it, if he is a trained rider, by such a route that they, or the effects set up by them, will excite to activity those muscles which push the *right* hand forwards.

We can now specify the variables which must compose the system if it is to be absolute.   We must include · the angular position of the handlebar, the velocity of lateral movement of the two points of contact between wheels and road, the distance laterally between the line joining these points and the point vertically below the rider's centre of gravity, and the angular deviation of the rider from the vertical.   These four variables are defined by S. 3/8 to be the ' environment ' of the rider.   (Whether the fourth variable is allotted to ' rider ' or to ' environment ' is optional (S. 3/12)).   To make the system absolute, there must be added the variables of the nervous system, of the relevant muscles, and of the bone and joint positions.

As a second example, consider a butterfly and a bird in the air, the bird chasing the butterfly, and the butterfly evading the bird. Both use the air around them.   Every movement of the bird stimulates the butterfly's eye and this stimulation, acting through the butterfly's nervous system, will cause changes in the butterfly's wing movements.   These movements act on the enveloping air and cause changes in the butterfly's position.   A change of position immediately changes the excitations in the bird's eye, and this leads through its nervous system to changed movements of the bird's wings.   These act on the air and change the bird's position.   So the processes go on.   The bird has as environment the air and the butterfly, while the butterfly has the bird and the air.   The whole may justifiably be assumed absolute.

3/11.   The organism affects the environment, and the environment affects the organism : such a system is said to have ' feedback ' (S. 4/12).

The examples of the previous section provide illustration. The rider's arm moves the handlebars, causing changes in the environment; and changes in these variables will, through the rider's sensory receptors, cause changes in his brain and muscles. When bird and butterfly manoeuvre in the air, each manoeuvre of one causes reactive changes to occur in the other.

The same feature is shown by the example of S. 1/12—the type problem of the kitten and the fire. The various stimuli from the fire, working through the nervous system, evoke some reaction from the kitten's muscles; equally the kitten's movements, by altering the position of its body in relation to the fire, will cause changes to occur in the pattern of stimuli which falls on the kitten's sense-organs. The receptors therefore affect the muscles (by effects transmitted through the nervous system), and the muscles affect the receptors (by effects transmitted through the environment). The action is two-way and the system possesses feedback.

The observation is not new :—

> ' In most cases the change which induces a reaction is brought about by the organism's own movements. These cause a change in the relation of the organism to the environment : to these changes the organism reacts. The whole behaviour of free-moving organisms is based on the principle that it is the movements of the organism that have brought about stimulation.'
>
> (Jennings.)

> ' The good player of a quick ball game, the surgeon conducting an operation. the physician arriving at a clinical decision—in each case there is the flow from signals interpreted to action carried out, back to further signals and on again to more action, up to the culminating point of the achievement of the task '.
>
> (Bartlett.)

> ' Organism and environment form a whole and must be viewed as such.'
>
> (Starling.)

It is necessary to point to the existence of feedback in the relation between the free-living organism and its environment because most physiological experiments are deliberately arranged to avoid feedback. Thus, in an experiment with spinal reflexes, a stimulus is applied and the resulting movement recorded ; but the movement is not allowed to influence the nature or duration of the stimulus. The action between stimulus and movement is therefore one-way. A similar absence of feedback is enforced in the Pavlovian experiments with conditioned reflexes : the stimulus may evoke salivation, but the salivation has no effect on the nature or duration of the stimulus.

Such an absence of feedback is, of course, useful or even essential in the analytic study of the behaviour of a mechanism, whether animate or inanimate. But its usefulness in the laboratory should not obscure the fact that the free-living animal is not subject to these constraints.

Sometimes systems which seem at first sight to be one-way prove on closer examination to have feedback. Walking on a smooth pavement, for instance, seems to involve so little reference to the structures outside the body that the nervous system might seem to be producing its actions without reference to their effects. *Tabes dorsalis*, however, prevents incoming sensory impulses from reaching the brain while leaving the outgoing motor impulses unaffected. If walking were due simply to the outgoing motor impulses, the disease would cause no disturbance to walking. In fact, it upsets the action severely, and demonstrates that the incoming sensory impulses are really playing an essential, though hidden, part in the normal action.

Sometimes the feedback can be demonstrated only with difficulty. Thus, Lloyd Morgan raised some ducklings in an incubator.

> ' The ducklings thoroughly enjoyed a dip   Each morning, at nine o'clock, a large black tray was placed in their pen, and on it a flat tin containing water. To this they eagerly ran, drinking and washing in it. On the sixth morning the tray and tin were given them in the usual way, but without any water. They ran to it, scooped at the bottom and made all the motions of the beak as if drinking. They squatted in it, dipping their heads, and waggling their tails as usual   For some ten minutes they continued to wash in non-existent water . . . '

Their behaviour might suggest that the stimuli of tray and tin were compelling the production of certain activities and that the results of these activities were having no back-effect. But further experiment showed that some effect was occurring :

> ' The next day the experiment was repeated with the dry tin. Again they ran to it, shovelling along the bottom with their beaks, and squatting down in it   But they soon gave up. On the third morning they waddled up to the dry tin, and departed.'

38

Their behaviour at first suggested that there was no feedback. But on the third day their change of behaviour showed that, in fact, the change in the bath had had some effect on them.

The importance of feedback lies in the fact that systems which possess it have certain properties (S 4/14) which cannot be shown by systems lacking it. Systems with feedback cannot adequately be treated as if they were of one-way action, for the feedback introduces properties which can be explained only by reference to the properties of the particular feedback used. (On the other hand a one-way system can, without error, be treated as if it contained feedback · we assume that one of the two actions is present but at zero degree (S. 2/3). In other words, systems without feedback are a sub-class of the class of systems with feedback.)

3/12. As the organism and its environment are to be treated as a single system, the dividing line between 'organism' and 'environment' becomes partly conceptual, and to that extent arbitrary. Anatomically and physically, of course, there is a unique and obvious distinction between the two parts of the system, but if we view the system functionally, ignoring purely anatomical facts as irrelevant, the division of the system into 'organism' and 'environment' becomes vague. Thus, if a mechanic with an artificial arm is trying to repair an engine, then the arm may be regarded either as part of the organism that is struggling with the engine, or as part of the machinery with which the man is struggling.

Once this flexibility of division is admitted, almost no bounds can be put to its application. The chisel in a sculptor's hand can be regarded either as a part of the complex biophysical mechanism that is shaping the marble, or it can be regarded as a part of the material which the nervous system is attempting to control. The bones in the sculptor's arm can be regarded either as part of the organism or as part of the 'environment' of the nervous system. Variables within the body may justifiably be regarded as the 'environment' of some other part. A child has to learn not only how to grasp a piece of bread, but how to chew without biting his own tongue; functionally both bread and tongue are part of the environment of the cerebral cortex But the environments with which the cortex has to deal are sometimes even deeper in the body than the tongue : the child has to learn how to play without exhausting itself utterly, and how to talk without getting out of breath.

These remarks are not intended to confuse, but to show that later arguments (S. 17/4 and Chapter 18) are not unreasonable. There it is intended to treat one group of neurons in the cerebral cortex as the environment of another group. These divisions, though arbitrary, are justifiable because we shall always treat the system as a whole, dividing it into parts in this unusual way merely for verbal convenience in description.

It should be noticed that from now on ' the system ' means not the nervous system but the whole complex of the organism and its environment. Thus, if it should be shown that ' the system ' has some property, it must not be assumed that this property is attributed to the nervous system   it belongs to the whole ; and detailed examination may be necessary to ascertain the contributions of the separate parts.

3/13. In some cases the dynamic nature of the interaction between organism and environment can be made intuitively more obvious by using the device, common in physics, of regarding the animal as the centre of reference. In locomotion the animal would then be thought of as pulling the world past itself. Provided we are concerned only with the relation between these two, and are not considering their relations to any third and independent body, the device will not lead to error. It was used in the ' rider and bicycle ' example.

By the use of animal-centred co-ordinates we can see that the animal has much more control over its environment than might at first seem possible. Thus when a dog puts its foot on a sharp and immovable stone, the latter does not seem particularly dynamic. Yet the dog can cause great changes in this environment—by moving its foot away. Again, while a frog cannot change air into water, a frog on the bank of a stream can, with one small jump, change its world from one ruled by the laws of mechanics to one ruled by the laws of hydrodynamics.

Static systems (like the sharp stone) can always be treated as if dynamic (though not conversely), for we have only to use the device of S. 2/3 and treat the static variable as one which is undergoing change of zero degree. *The dynamic view is therefore*

40

the more general. For this reason the environment will always be treated as wholly dynamic.

Essential variables

3/14. The biologist must view the brain, not as being the seat of the ' mind ', nor as something that ' thinks ', but, like every other organ in the body, as a specialised means to survival. We shall use the concept of ' survival ' repeatedly ; but before we can use it, we must, by S. 2/8, transform it to our standard form. What does it mean in terms of primary operations ?

Physico-chemical systems may undergo the most extensive transformations without showing any change obviously equivalent to death, for matter and energy are indestructible. Yet the distinction between a live horse and a dead one is obvious enough —they fetch quite different prices in the market. The distinction must be capable of objective definition.

It is suggested that the definition may be obtained in the following way. That an animal should remain ' alive ' certain variables must remain within certain ' physiological ' limits. What these variables are, and what the limits, are fixed when we have named the species we are working with. In practice one does not experiment on animals in general, one experiments on one of a particular species. In each species the many physiological variables differ widely in their relevance to survival. Thus, if a man's hair is shortened from 4 inches to 1 inch, the change is trivial ; if his systolic blood-pressure drops from 120 mm. of mercury to 30, the change will quickly be fatal.

Every species has a number of variables which are closely related to survival and which are closely linked dynamically so that marked changes in any one leads sooner or later to marked changes in the others. Thus, if we find in a rat that the pulse-rate has dropped to zero, we can predict that the respiration rate will soon become zero, that the body temperature will soon fall to room temperature, and that the number of bacteria in the tissues will soon rise from almost zero to a very high number. These important and closely linked variables will be referred to as the **essential** variables of the animal.

How are we to discover them, considering that we may not use borrowed knowledge but must find them by the method of

41

S. 2/8 ? There is no difficulty. Given a species, we observe what follows when members of the species are started from a variety of initial states. We shall find that large initial changes in some variables are followed in the system by merely transient deviations, while large initial changes in others are followed by deviations that become ever greater till the ' machine ' changes to something very different from what it was originally. The results of these primary operations will thus distinguish, quite objectively, the essential variables from the others. This distinction may not be quite clear, for an animal's variables cannot be divided sharply into ' essential ' and ' not essential '; but exactness is not necessary here. All that is required is the ability to arrange the animal's variables in an approximate order of importance. Inexactness of the order is not serious, for nowhere will we use a particular order as a basis for particular deductions.

We can now define ' survival ' objectively and in terms of a field it occurs when a line of behaviour takes no essential variable outside given limits.

References

BARTLETT, F. C   The measurement of human skill   *British Medical Journal,* **1**, 835 ; 14 June 1947

JENNINGS, H S   *Behavior of the lower organisms*   New York, 1906

MORGAN, C. LLOYD   *Habit and instinct.* London, 1896

REIN, H   Die physiologischen Grundlagen des Kreislaufkollapses. *Archiv fur klinische Chirurgie,* **189**, 302 ; 1937.

STARLING, E. H.   *Principles of human physiology.*   London, 6th edition, 1933

CHAPTER 4

Stability

4/1. THE words ' stability ', ' steady state ', and ' equilibrium ' are used by a variety of authors with a variety of meanings, though there is always the same underlying theme. As we shall be much concerned with stability and its properties, an exact definition must be provided.

The subject may be opened by a presentation of the three standard elementary examples. A cube resting with one face on a horizontal surface typifies ' stable ' equilibrium ; a sphere resting on a horizontal surface typifies ' neutral ' equilibrium ; and a cone balanced on its point typifies ' unstable ' equilibrium. With neutral and unstable equilibria we shall have little concern, but the concept of ' stable equilibrium ' will be used repeatedly.

These three dynamic systems are restricted in their behaviour by the fact that each system contains a fixed quantity of energy, so that any subsequent movement must conform to this invariance. We, however, shall be considering systems which are abundantly supplied with free energy so that no such limitation is imposed. Here are two examples.

The first is the Watt's governor. A steam-engine rotates a pair of weights which, as they are rotated faster, separate more widely by centrifugal action ; their separation controls mechanically the position of the throttle ; and the position of the throttle controls the flow of steam to the engine. The connections are arranged so that an increase in the speed of the engine causes a decrease in the flow of steam. The result is that if any transient disturbance slows or accelerates the engine, the governor brings the speed back to the usual value. By this return the system demonstrates its stability.

The second example is the thermostat, of which many types exist. All, however, work on the same principle · a chilling of the bath causes a change which in its turn causes the heating to become more intense or more effective ; and vice versa. The

43

result is that if any transient disturbance cools or overheats the bath, the thermostat brings the temperature back to the usual value. By this return the system demonstrates its stability.

4/2. An important feature of stability is that it does not refer to a material body or ' machine ' but only to some aspect of it. This statement may be proved most simply by an example showing that a single material body can be in two different equilibrial states at the same time. Consider a square card balanced exactly on one edge : to displacements at right angles to this edge the card is unstable ; to displacements exactly parallel to this edge it is, theoretically at least, stable.

The example supports the thesis that we do not, in general, study physical bodies but only entities carefully abstracted from them. The concept of stability must therefore be defined in terms of the basic primary operations (S. 2/3).

4/3. Consider next a corrugated surface, laid horizontally, with a ball rolling from a ridge down towards a trough. A photograph taken in the middle of its roll would look like Figure 4/3/1. We might think of the ball as being unstable because it has rolled away from the ridge, until we realise that we can also think of it as stable because it is rolling towards the trough. The duality shows we are approaching the concept in the wrong way. The situation can be made clearer if we remove the ball and consider only the surface. The top of the ridge, as it would affect the roll of a ball, is now recognised as a position of unstable equilibrium, and the bottom of the trough as a position of stability. We now see that, if friction is sufficiently marked for us to be able to neglect momentum, the system composed of the single variable ' distance of the ball laterally ' is absolute and has a definite, permanent field, which is sketched in the Figure.

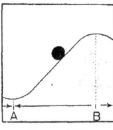

FIGURE 4/3/1.

From B the lines of behaviour diverge, but to A they converge. We conclude tentatively that the concept of ' stability ' belongs not to a material body but to a field. It is shown by a field if the lines of behaviour converge. (An exact definition is given in S. 4/8.)

4/4. This preliminary remark begins to justify the emphasis placed on absoluteness. Since stability is a feature of a field, and since only regular systems have unchanging fields (S. 19/16) it follows that to discuss stability in a system we must suppose that the system is regular: we cannot test the stability of a thermostat if some arbitrary interference continually upsets it.

But regularity in the system is not sufficient. If a field had lines criss-crossing like those of Figure 2/15/2 we could not make any simple statement about them. Only when the lines have a smooth flow like those of Figures 4/5/1, 4/5/2 or 4/10/1 can a simple statement be made about them. And this property implies (S. 19/12) that the system must be absolute.

4/5. To illustrate that the concept of stability belongs to a field, let us examine the fields of the previous examples.

The cube resting on one face yields an absolute system which has two variables:

(x) the angle which the face makes with the horizontal, and
(y) the rate at which this angle changes.

(This system allows for the momentum of the cube.) If the cube does not bounce when the face meets the table, the field is similar

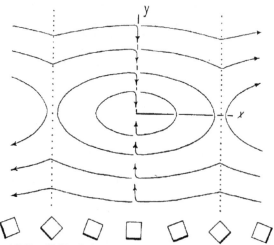

FIGURE 4/5/1: Field of the two-variable system described in the text. Below is shown the cube as it would appear in elevation when its main face, shown by a heavier line, is tilted through the angle x.

to that sketched in Figure 4/5/1. The stability of the cube when resting on a face corresponds in the field to the convergence of the lines of behaviour to the centre.

The square card balanced on its edge can be represented approximately by two variables which measure displacements at right

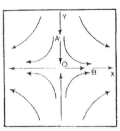

FIGURE 4/5/2.

angles (x) and parallel (y) to the lower edge. The field will resemble that sketched in Figure 4/5/2. Displacement from the origin O to A is followed by a return of the representative point to O, and this return corresponds to the stability. Displacement from O to B is followed by a departure from the region under consideration, and this departure corresponds to the instability. The uncertainty of the movements near O corresponds to the uncertainty in the behaviour of the card when released from the vertical position.

The Watt's governor has a more complicated field, but an approximation may be obtained without difficulty. The system may be specified to an approximation sufficient for our purpose by three variables :

(x) the speed of the engine and governor (r.p.m.),

(y) the distance between the weights, or the position of the throttle, and

(z) the velocity of flow of the steam.

(y represents either of two quantities because they are rigidly connected). If, now, a disturbance suddenly accelerates the engine, increasing x, the increase in x will increase y ; this increase in y will be followed by a decrease of z, and then by a decrease of x. As the changes occur not in jumps but continuously, the line of behaviour must resemble that

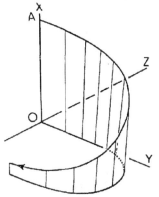

FIGURE 4/5/3 : One line of behaviour in the field of the Watt's governor. For clarity, the resting state of the system has been used as origin. The system has been displaced to A and then released.

46

sketched in Figure 4/5/3. The other lines of the field could be added by considering what would happen after other disturbances (lines starting from points other than A). Although having different initial states, all the lines would converge towards O.

4/6. In some of our examples, for instance that of the cube, the lines of behaviour terminate in a point at which all movement ceases. In other examples the movement does not wholly cease; many a thermostat settles down, when close to its resting state, to a regular small oscillation. We shall be little interested in the details of what happens at the exact centre.

4/7. More important is the underlying theme that in all cases the stable system is characterised by the fact that after a displacement we can assign some *limit* to the subsequent movement of the representative point, whereas in the unstable system such limitation is either impossible or depends on facts outside the subject of discussion Thus, if a thermostat is set at 37° C. and displaced to 40°, we can predict that in the future it will not go outside specified limits, which might be in one apparatus 36° and 40°. On the other hand, if the thermostat has been assembled with a component reversed so that it is unstable (S. 4/12) and if it is displaced to 40°, then we can give no limits to its subsequent temperatures ; unless we introduce such new topics as the melting-point of its solder.

4/8. These considerations bring us to the definition which will be used. Given an absolute system and a region within its field, *a line of behaviour from a point within the region is* **stable** *if it never leaves the region.* Within one absolute system a change of the region or of the line of behaviour may change the result of the criterion.

Thus, in Figure 4/3/1 the stability around A can be decided thus : make a mark on each side of A so as to define the region ; then as the line of behaviour from any point within this region never leaves it, the line of behaviour is stable. On the other hand, no region can be found around B which gives a stable line of behaviour. Again, consider Figure 4/5/2 : a boundary line is first drawn to enclose A, O and B, in order to define which part of the field is being discussed. The line of behaviour from

47

A is then found to be stable, and the line from *B* unstable. This example makes it obvious that the concept of ' stability ' belongs primarily to a line of behaviour, not to a whole field. In particular it should be noted that in all cases the definition gives a unique answer once the line, the region, and the initial state are given.

The examples above have been selected to test the definition severely. Sometimes the fields are simpler. In the field of the cube, for instance, it is possible to draw many boundaries, each oval in shape, such that all lines within the boundary are stable. The field of the Watt's governor is also of this type. It will be noticed that before we can discuss stability in a particular case we must always define which region of the phase-space we are referring to.

A field within a given region is ' stable ' if every line of behaviour in the region is stable. A system is ' stable ' if its field is stable.

4/9. **A resting state** *is one from which an absolute system does not move when released.* Such states occur in Figure 4/3/1 at *A* and *B*, and in Figure 4/5/1 at the origin.

Although the variables do not change value when at a resting state this invariance does not imply that the ' machine ' itself is inactive. Thus, a steady Watt's governor implies that the engine is working at a non-zero rate. And a living muscle, even if unchanging in tension, is continually active in metabolism. ' Resting ' applies to the variables, not necessarily to the ' machine ' that yields the variables.

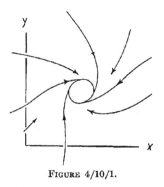

FIGURE 4/10/1.

4/10. If a line of behaviour is re-entrant to itself, the system undergoes a recurrent cycle. If the cycle is wholly contained in a given region, and the lines of behaviour lead *into* the cycle, the cycle is stable.

Such a cycle is commonly shown by thermostats which, after correcting any gross displacement, settle down to a steady oscillation. In such a case the field will show, not convergence to a point but convergence to a cycle, such as is shown exaggerated in Figure 4/10/1.

4/11. This definition of stability conforms to the requirement of S. 2/8; for the observed behaviour of the system determines the field, and the field determines the stability.

Feedback

4/12. The description given in S. 4/1 of the working of the Watt's governor showed that it is arranged in a functional circuit: the chain of cause and effect is re-entrant. Thus if we represent ' A has a direct effect on B ' or ' A directly disturbs B ' by the symbol $A \rightarrow B$, then the construction of the Watt's governor may be represented by the diagram:

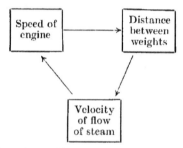

(The number of variables named here is partly optional.)

Lest the diagram should seem based on some metaphysical knowledge of causes and effects, its derivation from the actual machine, using only primary operations, will be described.

Suppose the relation between ' speed of engine ' and ' distance between weights ' is first investigated. The experimenter would fix the variable ' velocity of flow of steam '. Then he would try various speeds of the engine, and would observe how these changes affected the behaviour of ' distance between the weights '. He would find that changes in the speed of the engine were regularly followed by changes in the distance between the weights. He need know nothing of the nature of the ultimate physical linkages, but he would observe the fact. Then, still keeping ' velocity of flow of steam ' constant, he would try various distances between the weights, and would observe the effect of such changes on the speed of the engine; he would find them to be without effect.

49

He would thus have established that there is an arrow from left to right but not from right to left in

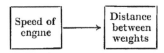

This procedure could then be applied to the two variables 'distance between weights' and 'velocity of flow of steam', while the other variable 'speed of engine' was kept constant. And finally the relations between the third pair could be established.

The method is clearly general. To find the immediate effects in a system with variables A, B, C, D . . . take one pair, A and B say; hold all other variables C, D . . . constant; note B's behaviour when A starts, or is held, at A_1; and also its behaviour when A starts, or is held, at A_2. If these behaviours of B are the same, then there is no immediate effect from A to B. But if the B's behaviours are unequal, and regularly depend on what value A starts from, or is held at, then there is an immediate effect, which we symbolise by $A \rightarrow B$.

By interchanging A and B in the process we can test for $B \rightarrow A$. And by using other pairs in turn we can determine all the immediate effects. The process is clearly defined, and consists purely of primary operations. It therefore uses no borrowed knowledge. We shall frequently use this **diagram of immediate effects.**

If A has an immediate effect on B, and B has an immediate effect on A, the relation will be represented by $A \rightleftarrows B$. If A affects B, and B also affects C, but A does not affect C directly, the relation will be shown by $A \rightarrow B \rightarrow C$. If there is a sequence of arrows joined head to tail and we are not interested in the intermediate steps, the sequence may often be contracted without ambiguity to $A \rightarrow C$. The diagram will be used only for illustration and not for rigorous proofs, so further precision is not required. (It should be carefully distinguished from the diagram of 'ultimate' effects, but this is not required yet and will be described in S. 14/6. At the moment we regard the concept of one variable 'having an effect' on another as well understood. But the concept will be examined more closely, and given more precision, in S. 14/3.)

A gas thermostat also shows a functional circuit or feedback;

for if it is controlled by a capsule which by its swelling moves a lever which controls the flow of gas to the heating flame, the diagram of immediate effects would be :

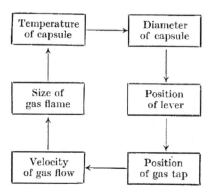

The reader should verify that each arrow represents a physical action which can be demonstrated if all variables other than the pair are kept constant.

Another example is provided by ' reaction ' in a radio receiver. We can represent the action by two variables linked in two ways :

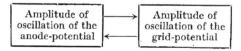

The lower arrow represents the grid-potential's effect within the valve on the anode-current. The upper arrow represents some arrangement of the circuit by which fluctuation in the anode-potential affects the grid-potential. The effect represented by the lower arrow is determined by the valve-designer, that of the upper by the circuit-designer.

Such systems whose variables affect one another in a circuit possess what the radio-engineer calls ' feedback ' ; they are also sometimes described as ' servo-mechanisms '. They are at least as old as the Watt's governor and may be older. But only during the last decade has it been realised that the possession of feedback gives a machine potentialities that are not available to a machine lacking it. The development occurred mainly during the last war, stimulated by the demand for automatic methods of control of searchlight, anti-aircraft guns, rockets, and torpedoes, and facilitated by the great advances that had occurred in electronics. As a result, a host of new machines appeared which acted with powers of self-adjustment and correction never before achieved. Some of their main properties will be described in S. 4/14.

The nature, degree, and polarity of the feedback has a decisive effect on the stability or instability of the system. In the Watt's governor or in the thermostat, for instance, the connection of a part in reversed position, reversing the polarity of action of one component on the next, may, and probably will, turn the system from stable to unstable. In the reaction circuit of the radio set, the stability or instability is determined by the quantitative relation between the two effects.

Instability in such systems is shown by the development of a ' runaway '. The least disturbance is magnified by its passage round the circuit so that it is incessantly built up into a larger

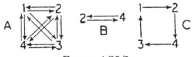

FIGURE 4/12/1.

and larger deviation from the resting state. The phenomenon is identical with that referred to as a ' vicious circle '.

The examples shown have only a simple circuit. But more complex systems may have many interlacing circuits. If, for instance, as in S. 8/8, four variables all act on each other, the diagram of immediate effects would be that shown in Figure 4/12/1 (A). It is easy to verify that such a system contains twenty interlaced circuits, two of which are shown at B and C.

The further development of the theory of systems with feed-back cannot be made without mathematics. But here it is sufficient to note two facts : a system which possesses feedback is usually actively stable or actively unstable ; and whether it is stable or unstable depends on the quantitative details of the particular arrangement.

4/13. It will be noticed that stability, as defined, in no way implies fixity or rigidity. It is true that stable systems may have a resting state at which they will show no change , but the lack

of change is deceptive if it suggests rigidity : they have only to be
disturbed to show that they are capable of extensive and active
movements.   They are restricted only in that they do not show
the unlimited divergencies of instability.

Goal-seeking

4/14. Every stable system has the property that if displaced
from a resting state and released, the subsequent movement is
so matched to the initial displacement that the system is brought
back to the resting state.   A variety of disturbances will therefore
evoke a variety of matched reactions.   Reference to a simple field
such as that of Figure 4/5/1 will establish the point.

This pairing of the line of return to the initial displacement
has sometimes been regarded as 'intelligent' and peculiar to living
things.   But a simple refutation is given by the ordinary pendulum : if we displace it to the right, it develops a force which
tends to move it to the left ; and if we displace it to the left, it
develops a force which tends to move it to the right.   Noticing

FIGURE 4/14/1   Tracing of the temperature (solid line), of a thermostatically
controlled bath, and of the control setting (broken line).

that the pendulum reacted with forces which though varied in
direction always pointed towards the centre, the mediaeval scien-
tist would have said 'the pendulum seeks the centre'.   By this
phrase he would have recognised that the behaviour of a stable
system may be described as 'goal-seeking'.   Without introducing
any metaphysical implications we may recognise that this type of
behaviour does occur in the stable dynamic systems.   Thus
Figure 4/14/1 shows how, as the control setting of a thermostat
was altered, the temperature of the apparatus always followed it,
the set temperature being treated as if it were a goal.

Such a movement occurs here in only one dimension (temperature), but other goal-seeking devices may use more. The radar-controlled searchlight, for example, uses the reflected impulses to alter its direction of aim so as to minimise the angle between its direction of aim and the bearing of the source of the reflected impulses. So if the aircraft swerves, the searchlight will follow it actively, just as the temperature followed the setting.

The examples show the common feature that each is 'error-controlled'. each is partly controlled by the deviation of the system's state from the resting state (which, in these examples, can be moved by an outside operation). The thermostat is affected by the difference between the actual and the set temperatures. The searchlight is affected by the difference between the two directions. So it will be seen that machines with feedback are not subject to the oft-repeated dictum that machines must act blindly and cannot correct their errors. Such a statement is true of machines without feedback, but not of machines in general.

Once it is appreciated that feedback can be used to correct any deviation we like, it is easy to understand that there is no limit to the complexity of goal-seeking behaviour which may occur in machines quite devoid of any 'vital' or 'intelligent' factor. Thus, an automatic anti-aircraft gun may be controlled by the radar-pulses reflected back both from the target aeroplane and from its own bursting shells, in such a way that it tends to minimise the distance between shell-burst and plane Such a system, wholly automatic, cannot be distinguished by its behaviour from a humanly operated gun . both will fire at the target, following it through all manoeuvres, continually using the errors to improve the next shot. It will be seen, therefore, that a system with feedback may be both wholly automatic and yet actively and complexly goal-seeking. There is no incompatibility.

4/15. An important feature of a system's stability (or instability) is that it is a property of the whole system and can be assigned to no part of it. The statement may be illustrated by a consideration of the third diagram of S. 4/12 as it is related to the practical construction of the thermostat. In order to ensure the stability of the final assembly, the designer must consider :

(1) The effect of the temperature on the diameter of the capsule, i.e. whether a rise in temperature makes the capsule expand or shrink.

(2) Which way an expansion of the capsule moves the lever.

(3) Which way a movement of the lever moves the gas-tap.

(4) Whether a given movement of the gas-tap makes the velocity of gas-flow increase or decrease.

(5) Whether an increase of gas-flow makes the size of the gas-flame increase or decrease.

(6) How an increase in size of the gas-flame will affect the temperature of the capsule.

Some of the answers are obvious, but they must none the less be included. When the six answers are known, the designer can ensure stability only by arranging the components (chiefly by manipulating (2), (3) and (5)) so that as a whole they form an appropriate combination. Thus five of the effects may be decided, yet the stability will still depend on how the sixth is related to them. The stability belongs only to the combination; it cannot be related to the parts considered separately.

In order to emphasise that the stability of a system is independent of any conditions which may hold over the parts which compose the whole, some further examples will be given. (Proofs of the statements will be found in S. 21/5–7.)

(a) Two systems may be joined so that they act and interact on one another to form a single system : to know that the two systems when separate were both stable is to know nothing about the stability of the system formed by their junction : it may be stable or unstable.

(b) Two systems, both unstable, may join to form a whole which is stable.

(c) Two systems may form a stable whole if joined in one way, and may form an unstable whole if joined in another way

(d) In a stable system the effect of fixing a variable may be to render the remainder unstable.

Such examples could be multiplied almost indefinitely. They illustrate the rule that the stability (or instability) of a dynamic system depends on the parts and their interrelations as a whole.

4/16. The fact that the stability of a system is a property of the system as a whole is related to the fact that the presence of stability (as contrasted with instability) always implies some co-ordination of the actions between the parts. In the thermostat the necessity for co-ordination is clear, for if the components were assembled at random there would be only an even chance that the assembly would be stable. But as the system and the feedbacks become more complex, so does the achievement of stability become more difficult and the likelihood of instability greater. Radio engineers know only too well how readily complex systems with feedback become unstable, and how difficult is the discovery of just that combination of parts and linkages which will give stability.

The subject is discussed more fully in S. 20/12 : here it is sufficient to note that as the number of variables increases so usually do the effects of variable on variable have to be co-ordinated with more and more care if stability is to be achieved.

REFERENCE

WIENER, NORBERT. *Cybernetics.* New York, 1948

CHAPTER 5

Adaptation as Stability

5/1. THE concept of 'adaptation' has so far been used without definition; this vagueness must be corrected. Not only must the definition be precise, but it must be given in terms that conform to the demand of S. 2/8.

5/2. The suggestion that an animal's behaviour is 'adaptive' if the animal 'responds correctly to a stimulus' may be rejected at once. First, it presupposes an action by an experimenter and therefore cannot be applied when the free-living organism and its environment affect each other reciprocally. Secondly, the definition provides no meaning for 'correctly' unless it means 'conforming to what the experimenter thinks the animal ought to do'. Such a definition is useless.

Homeostasis

5/3. I propose the definition that *a form of behaviour is adaptive if it maintains the essential variables* (S. 3/14) *within physiological limits*. The full justification of such a definition would involve its comparison with all the known facts—an impossibly large task. Nevertheless it is fundamental in this subject and I must discuss it sufficiently to show how fundamental it is and how wide is its applicability.

First I shall outline the facts underlying Cannon's concept of 'homeostasis'. They are not directly relevant to the problem of learning, for the mechanisms are inborn; but the mechanisms are so clear and well known that they provide an ideal basic illustration. They show that:

    (1) Each mechanism is 'adapted' to its end.
    (2) Its end is the maintenance of the values of some essential variables within physiological limits.

(3) Almost all the behaviour of an animal's vegetative system is due to such mechanisms.

5/4. As first example may be quoted the mechanisms which tend to maintain within limits the concentration of glucose in the blood. The concentration should not fall below about 0·06 per cent or the tissues will be starved of their chief source of energy; and the concentration should not rise above about 0·18 per cent or other undesirable effects will occur. If the blood-glucose falls below about 0·07 per cent the adrenal glands secrete adrenaline, which makes the liver turn its stores of glycogen into glucose , this passes into the blood and the fall is opposed. In addition, a falling blood-glucose stimulates the appetite so that food is taken, and this, after digestion, provides glucose. On the other hand, if it rises excessively, the secretion of insulin by the pancreas is increased, causing the liver to remove glucose from the blood. The muscles and skin also remove it ; and the kidneys help by excreting glucose into the urine if the concentration in the blood exceeds 0·18 per cent   Here then are five activities all of which have the same final effect. Each one acts so as to *restrict* the fluctuations which might otherwise occur. Each may justly be described as ' adaptive ', for it acts to preserve the animal's life.

The temperature of the interior of the warm-blooded animal's body may be disturbed by exertion, or illness, or by exposure to the weather. If the body temperature becomes raised, the skin flushes and more heat passes from the body to the surrounding air ; sweating commences, and the evaporation of the water removes heat from the body : and the metabolism of the body is slowed, so that less heat is generated within it.   If the body is chilled, these changes are reversed.   Shivering may start, and the extra muscular activity provides heat which warms the body.   Adrenaline is secreted, raising the muscular tone and the metabolic rate, which again supplies increased heat to the body. The hairs or feathers are moved by small muscles in the skin so that they stand more erect, enclosing more air in the interstices and thus conserving the body's heat.   In extreme cold the human being, when almost unconscious, reflexly takes a posture of extreme flexion with the arms pressed firmly against the chest and the legs fully drawn up against the abdomen.   The posture is clearly one which exposes to the air a minimum of surface. In all these ways, the body acts so as to maintain its temperature within limits.

The water content of the blood is disturbed by the intake of water at drinking and eating, by the output during excretion and secretion, and by sweating. When the water content is lowered, sweating, salivation, and the excretion of urine are all diminished; thirst is increased, leading to an increased intake, and the tissues of the body pass some of their water into the blood-stream. When the water content is excessive, all these activities are reversed. By these means the body tends to maintain the water-content of the blood within limits.

The pressure of the blood in the aorta may be disturbed by haemorrhage or by exertion. When the pressure falls, centres in the brain and spinal cord make the heart beat faster, increasing the quantity of blood forced into the aorta; they make the small arteries contract, impeding the flow of blood out of it. If the pressure is too high, these actions are reversed. By these and other mechanisms the blood pressure in the aorta is maintained within limits.

The amount of carbon dioxide in the blood is important in its effect on the blood's alkalinity. If the amount rises, the rate and depth of respiration are increased, and carbon dioxide is exhaled at an increased rate. If the amount falls, the reaction is reversed   By this means the alkalinity of the blood is kept within limits.

The retina works best at a certain intensity of illumination. In bright light the nervous system contracts the pupil, and in dim relaxes it. Thus the amount of light entering the eye is maintained within limits.

If the eye is persistently exposed to bright light, as happens when one goes to the tropics, the pigment-cells in the retina grow forward day by day until they absorb a large portion of the incident light before it reaches the sensitive cells. In this way the illumination on the sensitive cells is kept within limits.

If exposed to sunshine, the pigment-bearing cells in the skin increase in number, extent, and pigment-content. By this change the degree of illumination of the deeper layers of the skin is kept within limits.

When dry food is chewed, a copious supply of saliva is poured into the mouth. Saliva lubricates the food and converts it from a harsh and abrasive texture to one which can be chewed without injury. The secretion therefore keeps the frictional stresses below the destructive level

The volume of the circulating blood may be disturbed by haemorrhage. Immediately after a severe haemorrhage a number of changes occur : the capillaries in limbs and muscles undergo constriction, driving the blood from these vessels to the more essential internal organs ; thirst becomes extreme, impelling the subject to obtain extra supplies of fluid ; fluid from the tissues passes into the blood-stream and augments its volume ; and clotting at the wound helps to stem the haemorrhage. A haemorrhage has a second effect in that, by reducing the number of red corpuscles, it reduces the amount of oxygen which can be carried to the tissues; the reduction, however, itself stimulates the bone-marrow to an increased production of red corpuscles. All these actions tend to keep the variables ' volume of circulating blood ' and ' oxygen supplied to the tissues ' within normal limits.

Every fast-moving animal is liable to injury by collision with hard objects. Animals, however, are provided with reflexes that tend to minimise the chance of collision and of mechanical injury. A mechanical stress causes injury—laceration, dislocation, or fracture—only if the stress exceeds some definite value, depending on the stressed tissue—skin, ligament, or bone. So these reflexes act to keep the mechanical stresses within physiological limits.

Many more examples could be given, but all can be included within the same formula. Some external disturbance tends to drive an essential variable outside its normal limits ; but the commencing change itself activates a mechanism that *opposes* the external disturbance. By this mechanism the essential variable is maintained within limits much narrower than would occur if the external disturbance were unopposed. The narrowing is the objective form of the mechanism's adaptation.

5/5. The mechanisms of the previous section act mostly within the body, but it should be noted that some of them have acted partly through the environment. Thus, if the body-temperature is raised, the nervous system lessens the generation of heat within the body and the body-temperature falls, but only because the body is continuously losing heat to its surroundings. Flushing of the skin cools the body only if the surrounding air is cool; and sweating lowers the body-temperature only if the surrounding air is unsaturated. Increasing respiration lowers the carbon dioxide content of the blood, but only if the atmosphere contains less than 5 per cent. In each case the chain of cause and effect passes partly through the environment. The mechanisms that work wholly within the body and those that make extensive use of the environment are thus only the extremes of a continuous series. Thus, a thirsty animal seeks water: if it is a fish it does no more than swallow, while if it is an antelope in the veldt it has to go through an elaborate process of search, of travel, and of finding a suitable way down to the river or pond. The homeostatic mechanisms thus extend from those that work wholly within the animal to those that involve its widest-ranging activities; the principles are uniform throughout.

5/6. Just the same criteria for 'adaptation' may be used in judging the behaviour of the free-living animal in its learned reactions. Take the type-problem of the kitten and the fire. When the kitten first approaches an open fire, it may paw at the fire as if at a mouse, or it may crouch down and start to 'stalk' the fire, or it may attempt to sniff at the fire, or it may walk unconcernedly on to it. Every one of these actions is liable to lead to the animal's being burned. Equally the kitten, if it is cold, may sit far from the fire and thus stay cold. The kitten's behaviour cannot be called adapted, for the temperature of its skin is not kept within normal limits. The animal, in other words, is not acting homeostatically for skin temperature. Contrast this behaviour with that of the experienced cat · on a cold day it approaches the fire to a distance adjusted so that the skin temperature is neither too hot nor too cold. If the fire burns fiercer, the cat will move away until the skin is again warmed to a moderate degree. If the fire burns low the cat will move nearer If a red-hot coal drops from the fire the cat takes such action as will keep the skin temperature within normal limits. Without making any enquiry at this stage into what has happened to the kitten's brain, we can at least say that whereas

61

at first the kitten's behaviour was not homeostatic for skin temperature, it has now become so. Such behaviour is ' adapted ' : it preserves the life of the animal by keeping the essential variables within limits.

The same thesis can be applied to a great deal, if not all, of the normal human adult's behaviour. In order to demonstrate the wide application of this thesis, and in order to show that even Man's civilised life is not exceptional, some of the surroundings which he has provided for himself will be examined for their known physical and physiological effects. It will be shown that each item acts so as to narrow the range of variation of his essential variables

The first requirement of a civilised man is a house, and its first effect is to keep the air in which he lives at a more equable temperature. The roof keeps his skin at a more constant dryness. The windows, if open in summer and closed in winter, assist in the maintenance of an even temperature, and so do fires and stoves. The glass in the windows keeps the illumination of the rooms nearer the optimum, and artificial lighting has the same effect. The chimneys keep the amount of irritating smoke in the rooms near the optimum, which is zero.

Many of the other conveniences of civilisation could, with little difficulty, be shown to be similarly variation-limiting. An attempt to demonstrate them all would be interminable. But to confirm the argument we will examine a motor-car, part by part, in order to show its homeostatic relation to man.

Travel in a vehicle, as contrasted with travel on foot, keeps several essential variables within narrower limits. The fatigue induced by walking for a long distance implies that some variables, as yet not clearly known, have exceeded limits not transgressed when the subject is carried in a vehicle. The reserves of food in the body will be less depleted, the skin on the soles of the feet will be less chafed, the muscles will have endured less strain, in winter the body will have been less chilled, and in summer it will have been less heated, than would have happened had the subject travelled on foot.

When examined in more detail, many ways are found in which it serves us by maintaining our essential variables within narrower limits. The roof maintains our skin at a constant dryness. The windows protect us from a cold wind, and if open in summer, help to cool us. The carpet on the floor acts similarly in winter, helping to prevent the temperature of the feet from falling below its optimal value. The jolts of the road cause, on the skin and bone of the human frame, stresses which are much lessened by the presence of springs. Similar in action are the shock-absorbers and tyres. A collision would cause an extreme deceleration which leads to very high values for the stress on the skin and bone of the passengers. By the brakes these very high values may be avoided, and in this way the brakes keep the variables ' stress on bone ' within narrower limits. Good headlights keep the luminosity of the road within limits narrower than would occur in their absence.

The thesis that ' adaptation ' means the maintenance of essential variables within physiological limits is thus seen to hold not only over the simpler activities of primitive animals but over the more complex activities of the ' higher ' organisms.

5/7. Before proceeding further, it must be noted that the word ' adaptation ' is commonly used in two senses which refer to different processes.

The distinction may best be illustrated by the inborn homeo-static mechanisms : the reaction to cold by shivering, for instance. Such a mechanism may undergo two types of ' adaptation '. The first occurred long ago and was the change from a species too primitive to show such a reaction to a species which, by natural selection, had developed the reaction as a characteristic inborn feature. The second type of ' adaptation ' occurs when a member of the species, born with the mechanism, is subjected to cold and changes from not-shivering to shivering. The first change involved the development of the mechanism itself ; the second change occurs when the mechanism is stimulated into showing its properties

In the learning process, the first stage occurs when the animal ' learns ' : when it changes from an animal not having an adapted mechanism to one which has such a mechanism. The second stage occurs when the developed mechanism changes from in-activity to activity. In this chapter we are concerned with the characteristics of the developed mechanism. The processes which led to its development are discussed in Chapter 8.

5/8. We can now recognise that '*adaptive*' *behaviour is equivalent to the behaviour of a stable system, the region of the stability being the region of the phase-space in which all the essential variables lie within their normal limits.*

The view is not new (though it can now be stated with more precision):

'Every phase of activity in a living being must be not only a necessary sequence of some antecedent change in its environment, but must be so adapted to this change as to tend to its neutralisation, and so to the survival of the organism. . . . It must also apply to *all* the relations of living beings It must therefore be the guiding principle, not only in physiology . . . but also in the other branches of biology which treat of the relations of the living animal to its environment and of the factors determining its survival in the struggle for existence.'

(Starling.)

'In an open system, such as our bodies represent, compounded of unstable material and subjected continuously to disturbing conditions, constancy is in itself evidence that agencies are acting or ready to act, to maintain this constancy.'

(Cannon.)

'Every material system can exist as an entity only so long as its internal forces, attraction, cohesion, etc., balance the external forces acting upon it. This is true for an ordinary stone just as much as for the most complex substances ; and its truth should be recognised also for the animal organism. Being a definite circumscribed material system, it can only continue to exist so long as it is in continuous equilibrium with the forces external to it : so soon as this equilibrium is seriously disturbed the organism will cease to exist as the entity it was.'

(Pavlov.)

McDougall never used the concept of 'stability' explicitly, but when describing the type of behaviour which he considered to be most characteristic of the living organism, he wrote :

'Take a billiard ball from the pocket and place it upon the table. It remains at rest, and would continue to remain so for an indefinitely long time, if no forces were applied to it. Push it in any direction, and its movement in that direction persists until its momentum is exhausted, or until it is deflected by the resistance of the cushion and follows a new

64

path mechanically determined. . . . Now contrast with this an instance of behaviour. Take a timid animal such as a guinea-pig from its hole or nest, and put it upon the grass plot. Instead of remaining at rest, it runs back to its hole ; push it in any other direction, and, as soon as you withdraw your hand, it turns back towards its hole ; place any obstacle in its way, and it seeks to circumvent or surmount it, restlessly persisting until it achieves its end or until its energy is exhausted.'

He could hardly have chosen an example showing more clearly the features of stability.

Survival

5/9. The forces of the environment, and even the drift of time, tend to displace the essential variables by amounts to which we can assign no limit. For survival, the essential variables *must* be kept within their physiological limits. In other words, the values of the essential variables must stay within some definite region in the system's phase-space. It follows therefore that unless the environment is wholly inactive, stability is *necessary* for survival.

5/10. If an animal's behaviour always maintains its essential variables within their physiological limits, then the animal can die only of old age. Disease might disturb the essential variables, but the processes of repair and immunity would tend to restore them. But it is equally clear that the environment sometimes causes disturbances for which the body's stabilising powers are inadequate ; infections may prove too virulent, cold too extreme, a famine too severe, or the attack of an enemy too swift.

The possession of a mechanism which stabilises the essential variables is therefore of advantage : against moderate disturbances it may be life-saving even if it eventually fails at some severe disturbance. It promotes, but does not guarantee, survival.

5/11. Are there aspects of ' adaptation ' not included within the definition of ' stability ' ? Is ' survival ' to be the sole criterion of adaptation ? Is it to be maintained that the Roman soldier who killed Archimedes in Syracuse was better ' adapted ' in his behaviour than Archimedes ?

The question is not easily answered. It is similar to that of S. 3/4 where it was asked whether all the qualities of the living organism could be represented by number ; and the answer must be similar. It is assumed that we are dealing primarily with the simpler rather than with the more complex creatures, though the examples of S. 5/6 have shown that some at least of man's activities may be judged properly by this criterion

In order to survey rapidly the types of behaviour of the more primitive animals, we may examine the classification of Holmes, who intended his list to be exhaustive but constructed it with no reference to the concept of stability. The reader will be able to judge how far our formulation (S. 5/8) is consistent with his scheme, which is given in Table 5/11/1.

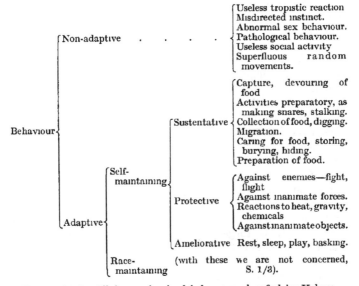

TABLE 5/11/1 : All forms of animal behaviour, classified by Holmes

For the primitive organism, and excluding behaviour related to racial survival, there seems to be little doubt that the ' adaptiveness ' of behaviour is properly measured by its tendency to promote the organism's survival.

The stable organism

5/12. A most impressive characteristic of living organisms is their mobility, their tendency to change. McDougall expressed this characteristic well in the example of S. 5/8. Yet our formulation transfers the centre of interest to the resting state, to the fact that the essential variables of the adapted organism change *less* than they would if they were unadapted. Which is important : constancy or change ?

The two aspects are not incompatible, for *the constancy of some variables may involve the vigorous activity of others.* A good thermostat reacts vigorously to a small change of temperature, and the vigorous activity of some of its variables keeps the others within narrow limits. The point of view taken here is that the constancy of the essential variables is fundamentally important, and that the activity of the other variables is important only in so far as it contributes to this end.

5/13. So far the discussion has traced the relation between the concepts of 'adaptation' and of 'stability'. It will now be proposed that 'motor co-ordination' also has an essential connection with stability.

'Motor co-ordination' is a concept well understood in physiology, where it refers to the ability of the organism to combine the activities of several muscles so that the resulting movement follows accurately its appropriate path. Contrasted to it are the concepts of clumsiness, tremor, ataxia, athetosis. It is suggested that the presence or absence of co-ordination may be decided, in accordance with our methods, by observing whether the movement does, or does not, deviate outside given limits.

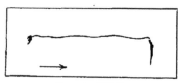

FIGURE 5/13/1.

The formulation seems to be adequate provided that we measure the limb's deviations from some line which is given arbitrarily, usually by a knowledge of the line followed by the normal limb. A first example is given by Figure 5/13/1, which shows the line traced by the point of an expert fencer's foil during a lunge.

Any inco-ordination would be shown by a divergence from the intended line.

A second example is given by the record of Figure 5/13/2.

The subject, a patient with a tumour in the left cerebellum, was asked to follow the dotted lines with a pen. The left- and right-hand curves were drawn with the respective hands. The tracing shows clearly that the co-ordination is poorer in the left hand. What criterion reveals the fact? The essential distinction is that the deviations of the lines from the dots are larger on the left than on the right.

FIGURE 5/13/2: Record of the attempts of a patient to follow the dotted lines with the left and right hands. (By the courtesy of Dr. W. T. Grant of Los Angeles.)

The degree of motor co-ordination achieved may therefore be measured by the smallness of the deviations from some standard line. Later it will be suggested that there are mechanisms which act to maintain variables within narrow limits. If the identification of this section is accepted, such mechanisms could be regarded as appropriate for the co-ordination of motor activity.

5/14. So far we have noticed in stable systems only their property of keeping variables within limits. But such systems have other properties of which we shall notice two. They are also shown by animals, and are then sometimes considered to provide evidence that the organism has some power of 'intelligence' not shared by non-living systems. In these two instances the assumption is unnecessary.

The first property is shown by a stable system when the lines of behaviour do not return directly, by a straight line, to the resting state (e.g. Figure 4/5/3). When this occurs, variables may be observed to move away from their values in the resting state, only to return to them later. Thus, suppose in Figure 5/14/1 that the field is stable and that at the resting state R x and y have the values X and Y. For clarity, only one line of behaviour is drawn. Let the system be displaced to A and its subsequent behaviour observed. At first, while the representative point moves towards B, y hardly alters; but x, which started at X', moves to X and goes past it to X''. Then x remains almost constant and y changes until the representative point

reaches C. Then y stops changing, and x changes towards, and reaches, its resting value X. The system has now reached its resting state and no further changes occur. This account is just a transcription into words of what the field defines graphically

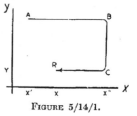

FIGURE 5/14/1.

Now the shape and features of any field depend ultimately on the real physical and chemical construction of the 'machine' from which the variables are abstracted. The fact that the line of behaviour does not run straight from A to R must be due to some feature in the 'machine' such that if the machine is to get from state A to state R, states B and C must be passed through of necessity. Thus, if the machine contained moving parts, their shapes might prohibit the direct route from A to R; or if the system were chemical the prohibition might be thermodynamic. But in either case, if the observer watched the machine work, and thought it alive, he might say: 'How clever! x couldn't get from A to R directly because this bar was in the way; so x went to B, which made y carry x from B to C; and once at C, x could get straight back to R. I believe x shows foresight.'

Both points of view are reasonable. A stable system may be regarded both as blindly obeying the laws of its nature, and also as showing a rudimentary skill in getting back to its resting state in spite of obstacles.

5/15. The second property is shown when an organism reacts to a variable with which it is not directly in contact. Suppose, for instance, that the diagram of immediate effects (S. 4/12) is that of Figure 5/15/1, the variables have been divided by the dotted line into 'animal' on the right and 'environment' on the left, and the animal is not in direct contact with the variable marked X. The system is assumed to be stable, i e. to have arrived at the 'adapted' condition (S. 5/7). If disturbed, its changes will show co-ordination of part with part (S. 5/14), and this co-ordination will hold over the whole system (S. 4/15).   It follows that the behaviour of the ' animal '-part will be co-ordinated with the behaviour of X although the ' animal ' has no immediate contact with it.

In the higher organisms, and especially in man, the power to react correctly to something not immediately visible or tangible

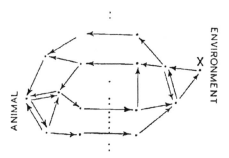

FIGURE 5/15/1.

has been called ' imagination ', or ' abstract thinking ', or several other names whose precise meaning need not be discussed at the moment.   Here we should notice that the co-ordination of the behaviour of one part with that of another part not in direct contact with it is simply an elementary property of the stable system.

5/16.   At this stage it is convenient to re-state our problem in the new vocabulary.   If, for brevity, we omit minor qualifications, we can state it thus : A determinate ' machine ' changes from a form that produces chaotic, unadapted behaviour to a form in which the parts are so co-ordinated that the whole is stable, acting to maintain certain variables within certain limits—how can this happen ?   For example, what sort of a thermostat could, if assembled at random, rearrange its own parts to get itself stable for temperature ?

It will be noticed that the new statement involves the concept of a machine changing its internal organisation.   So far, nothing has been said of this important concept ; so it will be treated in the next two chapters.

REFERENCES

ASHBY, W. ROSS. Adaptiveness and equilibrium. *Journal of Mental Science,*
    86, 478 , 1940.
Idem. The behavioral properties of systems in equilibrium. *American
    Journal of Psychology,* **59**, 682 , 1946.
CANNON, W. B. *The wisdom of the body* London, 1932.
CONFERENCE ON TELEOLOGICAL MECHANISMS. *Annals of the New York
    Academy of Science,* **50**, 187 ; 1948.
GRANT, W T. Graphic methods in the neurological examination : wavy
    tracings to record motor control   *Bulletin of the Los Angeles Neurological
    Society,* **12**, 104 ; 1947
HOLMES, S J   A tentative classification of the forms of animal behavior.
    Journal of Comparative Psychology, **2**, 173 ; 1922
McDOUGALL, W. *Psychology* New York, 1912
PAVLOV, I P. *Conditioned reflexes.* Oxford, 1927
ROSENBLUETH, A., WIENER, N , and BIGELOW, J Behavior, purpose and
    teleology *Philosophy of Science,* **10**, 18 ; 1943.
SOMMERHOFF, G. *Analytical biology.* Oxford, 1950.

CHAPTER 6

Parameters

6/1. So far, we have discussed the changes shown by the variables of an absolute system, and have ignored the fact that all its changes occur on a background, or on a foundation, of constancies. Thus, a particular simple pendulum provides two variables which are known (S. 2/15) to be such that, if we are given a particular state of the system, we can predict correctly its ensuing behaviour; what has not been stated explicitly is that this is true only if the length of the string remains constant. The background, and these constancies, must now be considered.

Every absolute system is formed by selecting some variables out of the totality of possible variables. 'Forming a system' means dividing all possible variables into two classes: those within the system and those without. These two types of variable are in no way different in their intrinsic physical nature, but they stand in very different relations to the system.

6/2. Given a system, a variable not included in it will be described as a **parameter**. The word *variable* will, from now on, be reserved for one within the system

In general, given a system, the parameters will differ in their closeness of relation to it. Some will have a direct relation to it: their change of value would affect the system to a major degree; such is the parameter ' length of pendulum ' in its relation to the two-variable system of the previous section. Some are less closely related to it, their changes producing only a slight effect on it; such is the parameter ' viscosity of the air ' in relation to the same system. And finally, for completeness, may be mentioned the infinite number of parameters that are without detectable effect on the system; such are the brightness of the light shining on the pendulum, the events in an adjacent room, and the events in the distant nebulae. Those without detectable effect may be ignored ; but the relationship of an effective parameter to a system must be clearly understood.

Given a system, the effective parameters are usually innumerable, so that a list is bounded only by the imagination of the writer. Thus, parameters whose change might affect the behaviour of the same system of two variables are :

(1) the length of the pendulum (hitherto assumed constant),

(2) the lateral velocity of the air (hitherto assumed to be constant at zero),

(3) the viscosity of the surrounding medium (hitherto assumed constant),

(4) the position (co-ordinates) of the point of support,

(5) the force of gravity,

(6) the magnetic field in which it swings,

(7) the elastic constant of the string of the pendulum,

(8) its electrostatic charge, and the charges on bodies nearby ;

but the list has no end.

Parameter and field

6/3. The effect on an absolute system of a change of parameter-value will now be shown. Table 6/3/1 shows the results of four

Length (cm.)	Line	Variable	Time						
			0	0 05	0 10	0 15	0 20	0 25	0 30
40	1	x	0	7	14	20	25	28	29
		y	147	142	129	108	80	48	12
	2	x	14	20	25	28	29	29	27
		y	129	108	80	48	12	− 24	− 58
60	3	x	0	7	14	21	26	31	34
		y	147	144	135	121	101	78	51
	4	x	21	26	31	34	36	36	35
		y	121	101	78	51	23	− 6	− 36

TABLE 6/3/1

primary operations applied to the two-variable system mentioned above. x is the angular deviation from the vertical, in degrees ; y is the angular velocity, in degrees per second , the time is in seconds.

The first two Lines show that the lines of behaviour following the state $x = 14$, $y = 129$ are equal, so the system, as far as it has been tested, is absolute. The line of behaviour is shown solid in Figure 6/3/1. In these swings the length of the pendulum was 40 cm This parameter was then changed to 60 cm. and two further lines of behaviour were observed. On these two, the lines of behaviour following the state $x = 21$, $y = 121$ are equal, so the system is again absolute. The line of behaviour is shown dotted in the same figure. But the change of parameter-value has caused the line of behaviour from $x = 0$, $y = 147$ to change.

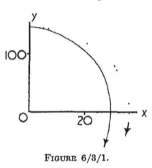

FIGURE 6/3/1.

The relationship which the parameter bears to the two variables is therefore as follows :

(1) So long as the parameter is constant, the system of x and y is absolute and has a definite field.

(2) After the parameter changes from one constant value to another, the system of x and y becomes again absolute, and has a definite field, but this field is not the same as the previous one.

The relation is general. A change in the value of an effective parameter changes the line of behaviour from each state. From this follows at once : *a change in the value of an effective parameter changes the field.*

The converse proposition is also true. Suppose we form a system's field and find it to be absolute. If our control of its surroundings has not been complete, and we test it later and find it to be again absolute but to have a changed field, then we may *deduce*, by S. 22/5, that some parameter must, in the interval, have changed from one constant value to another constant value.

6/4. The importance of distinguishing between change of a variable and change of a parameter, that is, between change of state and change of field, can hardly be over-estimated. In order to make the distinction clear I will give some examples.

In a working clock, the single variable defined by the reading of the minute-hand on the face is absolute as a one-variable system; for after some observations of its behaviour, we can predict the line of behaviour which will follow any given state. If now the regulator (the parameter) is moved to a new position, so that the clock runs at a different rate, and the system is re-examined, it will be found to be still absolute but to have a different field.

If a healthy person drinks 100 g. of glucose dissolved in water, the amount of glucose in his blood usually rises and falls as A in Figure 6/4/1. The single variable 'blood-glucose' is not absolute, for a given state (e.g. 120 mg./100 ml.) does not define the subsequent behaviour, for the blood-glucose may rise or fall. By adding a second variable, however, such as 'rate of change of blood-glucose', which may be positive or negative, we obtain a two-variable system which is sufficiently absolute for illustration. The field of this two-variable system will resemble that of A in

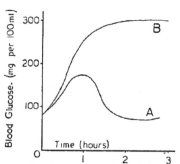

FIGURE 6/4/1 : Changes in blood-glucose after the ingestion of 100g. of glucose: (A) in the normal person, (B) in the diabetic.

Figure 6/4/2. But if the subject is diabetic, the curve of the blood-glucose, even if it starts at the same initial value, rises much higher, as B in Figure 6/4/1. When the field of this behaviour is drawn (B, Fig. 6/4/2), it is seen to be not the same as that of the normal subject. The change of value of the parameter 'degree of diabetes present' has thus changed the field.

Girden and Culler developed a conditioned reflex in a dog which was under the influence of curare (a paralysing drug). When later the animal was not under its influence, the conditioned reflex could not be elicited. But when the dog was again put under its influence, the conditioned reflex returned. We need not enquire closely into the absoluteness of the system, but we note that two characteristic lines of behaviour (two responses to the stimulus) existed, and that one line of behaviour was shown when the

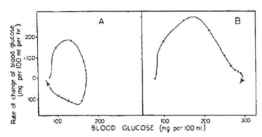

FIGURE 6/4/2 . Fields of the two lines of behaviour, *A* and *B*, from Figure 6/4/1   Cross-strokes mark each quarter-hour.

parameter ' concentration of curare in the tissues ' had a high value, and the other when the parameter had a low value.

6/5. The physicist, studying systems whose variables are all clearly marked and controllable, seldom confuses change of state with change of field.   The psychologist, however, studies systems whose variables, even in the simplest systems, are so numerous that he cannot, in practice, make an exact list of them : his grasp of the situation must be intuitive rather than explicit. In his practical work he seldom fails to distinguish between the variables he is observing and the parameters he is controlling ; it is chiefly in his theoretical work, especially when he discusses cerebral mechanisms, that he is apt to allow the distinction to become blurred.   To preserve the distinction between variable and parameter we must discuss, not the real ' machine ', with its infinite richness of variables, but a *defined* system.   The advantage to be gained will become clearer as we proceed.

Stimuli

6/6. Many stimuli may be represented adequately as a change of parameter-value, so it is convenient here to relate the physiological and psychological concept of a ' stimulus ' to our methods.
  In all cases the diagram of immediate effects is

(experimenter) $\rightarrow$ stimulator $\rightarrow$ animal $\rightarrow$ recorders.

In some cases the animal, at some resting state, is subjected to a sudden change in the value of the stimulator, and the second value is sustained throughout the observation. Thus, the pupillary reaction to light is demonstrated by first accustoming the eye to a low intensity of illumination, and then suddenly raising the illumination to a high level which is maintained while the reaction proceeds. In such cases the stimulator is parameter to the system ' animal and recorders ' ; and the physiologist's comparison of the previous control-behaviour with the behaviour after stimulation is equivalent, in our method, to a comparison of the two lines of behaviour that, starting from the same initial state, run in the two fields provided by the two values of the stimulator.

Sometimes a parameter is changed sharply and is immediately returned to its initial value, as when the experimenter applies a single electric shock, a tap on a tendon, or a flash of light. The effect of the parameter-change is a brief change of field which, while it lasts, carries the representative point away from its original position. When the parameter is returned to its original value, the original field and resting state are restored, and the representative point returns to the resting state. Such a stimulus reveals a line of behaviour leading to the resting state.

It will be necessary later to be more precise about what we mean by ' the ' stimulus. Consider, for instance, a dog developing a conditioned reflex to the ringing of an electric bell. What is the stimulus exactly ? Is it the closing of the contact switch ? The intermittent striking of the hammer on the bell ? The vibrations in the air ? The vibrations of the ear-drum, of the ossicles, of the basilar membrane ? The impulses in the acoustic nerve, in the temporal cortex ? If we are to be precise we must recognise that the experimenter controls directly only the contact switch, and that this acts as parameter to the complexly-acting system of electric bell, middle ear, and the rest.

When the ' stimulus ' becomes more complex we must generalise. One generalisation increases the number of parameters made to alter, as when a conditioned dog is subjected to combinations of a ticking metronome, a smell of camphor, a touch on the back, and a flashing light. Here we should notice that if the parameters are not all independent but change in groups, like the variables in S. 3/3, we can represent each undivided group by a single parameter and thus avoid using unnecessarily large numbers of parameters.

A more extensive generalisation is provided if we replace 'change of parameter' by 'change of initial state'. It will be shown (S. 7/7 and 21/4) that if a variable, or parameter, stays constant over some period it may, within the period, be regarded indifferently as inside or outside the system—as variable or parameter. If, therefore, a contact switch, once set, stays as the experimenter leaves it, we may, if we please, regard it as part of the system. Then what was a comparison between two lines of behaviour from two fields (of a set of variables a, b, c, say) under the change of a parameter p from p' to p'', becomes a comparison between two lines of behaviour of the four-variable system from the initial states a, b, c, p' and a, b, c, p''. 'Applying a stimulus' is now equivalent to 'releasing from a different initial state'; and this will be used as its most general representation.

Parameter and stability

6/7. We now reach the main point of the chapter. Because a change of parameter-value changes the field, and because a system's stability depends on its field, a change of parameter-value will in general change a system's stability in some way.

A simple example is given by a mixture of hydrogen, nitrogen, and ammonia, which combine or dissociate until the concentrations reach the resting state. If the mixture was originally derived from pure ammonia, the single variable 'percentage dissociated' forms a one-variable absolute system. Among its parameters are temperature and pressure. As is well known, changes in these parameters affect the position of the resting state.

Such a system is simple and responds to the changes of the parameters with only a simple shift of resting state. No such limitation applies generally. Change of parameter-value may result in any change which can be produced by the substitution of one field for another: stable systems may become unstable, resting states may be moved, single resting states may become multiple, resting states may become cycles; and so on. Figure 21/5/1 provides an illustration.

Here we need only the relationship, which is reciprocal: in

an absolute system, a change of stability can only be due to change of value of a parameter, and *change of value of a parameter causes a change in stability.*

REFERENCE

GIRDEN, E , and CULLER, E. Conditioned responses in curarized striate muscle in dogs *Journal of Comparative Psychology*, **23,** 261 , 1937.

CHAPTER 7

Step-Functions

7/1. SOMETIMES the behaviour of a variable (or parameter) can be described without reference to the cause of the behaviour · if we say a variable or system is a 'simple harmonic oscillator' the meaning of the phrase is well understood. Here we shall be more interested in the extent to which a variable displays constancy. Four types may be distinguished, and are illustrated in

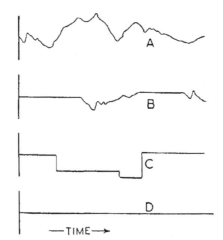

FIGURE 7/1/1 : Types of behaviour of a variable . *A*, the full-function ; *B*, the part-function ; *C*, the step-function ; *D*, the null-function.

Fig 7/1/1. (*A*) The **full-function** has no finite interval of constancy, many common physical variables are of this type · the height of the barometer, for instance. (*B*) The **part-function** has finite intervals of change and finite intervals of constancy, it will be considered more fully in S. 14/12. (*C*) The **step-function** has finite intervals of constancy separated by instantaneous jumps.

80

And, to complete the set, we need (*D*) the **null-function**, which shows no change over the whole period of observation. The four types obviously include all the possibilities, except for mixed forms. The variables of Fig. 2/10/1 will be found to be part-, full-, step-, and null-, functions respectively.

In all cases the type-property is assumed to hold only over the period of observation : what might happen at other times is irrelevant.

Sometimes physical entities cannot readily be allotted their type. Thus, a steady musical note may be considered either as unvarying in intensity, and therefore a null-function, or as represented by particles of air which move continuously, and therefore a full-function. In all such cases the confusion is at once removed if one ceases to think of the real physical object with its manifold properties, and selects that variable in which one happens to be interested.

7/2. Step-functions occur abundantly in nature, though the very simplicity of their properties tends to keep them inconspicuous. ' Things in motion sooner catch the eye than what not stirs '. The following examples approximate to the step-function, and show its ubiquity :

(1) The electric switch has an *electrical resistance* which remains constant except when it changes by a sudden jump.

(2) The *electrical resistance* of a fuse similarly stays at a low value for a time and then suddenly changes to a very high value.

(3) The *viscosity* of water, measured as the temperature passes 0° C., changes similarly.

(4) If a piece of rubber is stretched, the pull it exerts is approximately proportional to its length. The *constant of proportionality* has a definite constant value unless the elastic is stretched so far that it breaks. When this happens the constant of proportionality suddenly becomes zero, i.e. it changes as a step-function.

(5) If a trajectory is drawn through the air, a few feet above the ground and parallel to it, the *resistance* it encounters as it meets various objects varies in step-function form.

81

(6) A stone, falling through the air into a pond and to the bottom, would meet *resistances* varying similarly.

(7) The *temperature* of a match when it is struck changes in step-function form.

(8) If strong acid is added in a steady stream to an unbuffered alkaline solution, the *p*H changes in approximately step-function form.

(9) If alcohol is added slowly with mixing to an aqueous solution of protein, the *amount of protein* precipitated changes in approximately step-function form

(10) As the *p*H is changed, the *amount of adsorbed substance* often changes in approximately step-function form.

(11) By quantum principles, many *atomic* and *molecular variables* change in step-function form.

(12) The *blood flow* through the *ductus arteriosus*, when observed over an interval including the animal's birth, changes in step-function form.

(13) The *sex-hormone content* of the blood changes in step-function form as an animal passes puberty.

(14) Any variable which acts only in ' all or none ' degree shows this form of behaviour if each degree is sustained over a finite interval.

7/3. Few variables other than the atomic can change instantaneously ; a more minute examination shows that the change is really continuous : the fusing of an electric wire, the closing of a switch, and the snapping of a piece of elastic. But if the event occurs in a system whose changes are appreciable only over some longer time, it may be treated without serious error as if it occurred instantaneously. Thus, if $x = \tanh t$, it will give a graph like A in Figure 7/3/1 if viewed over the interval from $t = -2$ to $t = +2$. But if viewed over the interval from $t = -40$ to $t = +40$, it would give a graph like B, and would approximate to the step-function form.

In any experiment, some ' order ' of the time-scale is always assumed, for the investigation never records both the very quick and the very slow. Thus to study a bee's honey-gathering flights, the observer records its movements. But he ignores the movement caused by each stroke of the wing : such movements are ignored as being too rapid. Equally, over an hour's experiment he ignores the fact that the bee at the end of the hour is a little older than it was at the beginning : this change is ignored as being too slow

Such changes are eliminated by being treated as if they had their limiting values. If a single rapid change occurs, it is

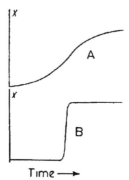

FIGURE 7/3/1 : The same change viewed : (*A*) over one interval of time, (*B*) over an interval twenty times as long

treated as instantaneous. If a rapid oscillation occurs, the variable is given its average value. If the change is very slow, the variable is assumed to be constant. In this way the concept of ' step-function ' may legitimately be applied to real changes which are known to be not quite of this form.

7/4. Behaviour of step-function form is likely to be seen whenever we observe a ' machine ' whose component parts are fast-acting. Thus, if we casually alter the settings of an unknown electronic machine we are not unlikely to observe, from time to time, sudden changes of step-function form, the suddenness being due to the speed with which the machine changes

A reason can be given most simply by reference to Figure 4/3/1. Suppose that the curvature of the surface is controlled by a parameter which makes *A* rise and *B* fall. If the ball is resting at *A*, the parameter's first change will make no difference to the ball's lateral position, for it will continue to rest at *A* (though with lessened reaction if displaced.). As the parameter is changed further, the ball will continue to remain at *A* until *A* and *B* are level. Still the ball will make no movement. But if the parameter goes on changing and *A* rises above *B*, and if gravitation is

83

intense and the ball fast-moving, then the ball will suddenly move to *B*. And here it will remain, however high *A* becomes and however low *B*. So, if the parameter changes steadily, the lateral position of the ball will tend to step-function form, approximating more closely as the passage of the ball for a given degree of slope becomes swifter.

The possibility need not be examined further, for no exact deductions will be drawn from it   The section is intended only to show that step-functions occur not uncommonly when the system under observation contains fast-acting components.   The subject will be referred to again in S. 10/5.

Critical states

7/5. In any absolute system, the behaviour of a variable at any instant depends on the values which the variable and the others have at that instant (S. 2/15). If one of the variables behaves as a step-function the rule still applies : whether the variable remains constant or undergoes a change is determined both by the value of the variable and by the values of the other variables. So, given an absolute system with a step-function at a particular value, all the states with the step-function at that value can be divided into two classes : those whose occurrence does and those whose occurrence does not lead to a change in the step-function's value. The former are its **critical states** : should one of them occur, the step-function will change value. The critical state of an electric fuse is the number of amperes which will cause it to blow. The critical state of the ' constant of proportionality ' of an elastic strand is the length at which it breaks.

An example from physiology is provided by the urinary bladder when it has developed an automatic intermittently-emptying action after spinal section. The bladder fills steadily with urine, while at first the spinal centres for micturition remain inactive. When the volume of urine exceeds a certain value the centres become active and urine is passed   When the volume falls below a certain value, the centre becomes inactive and the bladder refills. A graph of the two variables would resemble Figure 7/5/1. The two-variable system is absolute, for it has the field of Figure 7/5/2. The variable y is approximately a step-function   When it is at 0, its critical state is $x = X_2$, $y = 0$, for the occurrence of this state

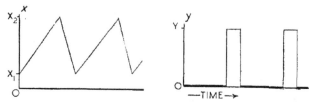

FIGURE 7/5/1 : Diagram of the changes in x, volume of urine in the bladder, and y, activity in the centre for micturition, when automatic action has been established after spinal section.

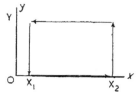

FIGURE 7/5/2 : Field of the changes shown in Figure 7/5/1.

determines a jump from 0 to Y. When it is at Y, its critical state is $x = X_1$, $y = Y$, for the occurrence of this state determines a jump from Y to 0.

7/6. A common, though despised, property of every machine is that it may 'break'. This event is in no sense unnatural, since it must follow the basic laws of physics and chemistry and is therefore predictable from its immediately preceding state. In general, when a machine 'breaks' the representative point has met some critical state, and the corresponding step-function has changed value.

As is well known, almost any machine or physical system will break if its variables are driven far enough away from their usual values. Thus, machines with moving parts, if driven ever faster, will break mechanically; electrical apparatus, if subjected to ever higher voltages or currents, will break in insulation; machines made too hot will melt—if made too cold they may encounter other sudden changes, such as the condensation which stops a steam-engine from working below 100° C.; in chemical dynamics, increasing concentrations may meet saturation, or may cause precipitation of proteins.

Although there is no rigorous law, there is nevertheless a widespread tendency for systems to show changes of step-function form if their variables are driven far from some usual value. Later (S. 10/2) it will be suggested that the nervous system is not exceptional in this respect.

Systems containing full- and null-functions

7/7. We shall now consider the properties shown by absolute systems that contain step-functions. But the discussion will be clearer and simpler if we first examine some simpler systems.

Suppose we have an absolute system composed wholly of full-functions and we ignore one of the variables. Every experimenter knows only too well what happens . the behaviour of the system becomes unpredictable. Every experimenter has spent time trying to make unpredictable experiments predictable ; he does it by identifying the unknown variable. The unknown variable may be scientifically trivial, like a loose screw, or important, like a co-enzyme in a metabolic system ; but in either case, he cannot establish a definite form of behaviour until he has identified and either controlled or observed the unknown variable. To ignore a *full*-function in an absolute system is to render the remainder non-absolute, so that no characteristic form of behaviour can be established.

On the other hand, an absolute system which includes null-functions may have the null-functions removed from it, or other null-functions added to it, and the new system will still be absolute. (The alteration is done, of course, not by interfering physically with the 'machine', but by changing the list of variables) Thus, if the two-variable system of the pendulum (S. 6/3) is absolute, and if the length of the pendulum stays constant once it is adjusted, then the system composed of the three variables

(1) length of pendulum
(2) angular deviation
(3) angular velocity)

is also absolute. A formal proof is given in S. 21/4, but it follows readily from the definitions. (The reader should first verify that every null-function is itself an absolute system.) Conversely, if three variables A, B, N, are found to form an absolute system, and N is a null-function, then the system composed of A and B is absolute.

Unlike the full-function, then, the null-function may be

omitted from a system, for its omission leaves the remainder still producing predictable behaviour.

Systems containing step-functions

7/8. Suppose that we have a system with three variables, A, B, S; that it has been tested and found absolute; that A and B are full-functions; and that S is a step-function. (Variables A and B, as in S. 21/3, will be referred to as **main** variables.) The phase-space of this system will resemble that of Figure 7/8/1 (a possible field has been sketched in). The phase-space no longer fills all three dimensions, but as S can take only discrete values, here assumed for simplicity to be a pair, the phase-space is restricted to two planes normal to S, each plane corresponding to a particular value of S. A and B being full-functions, the representative point will move on curves in each plane, describing a line of behaviour such as that drawn more heavily in the Figure. When

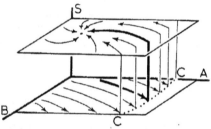

FIGURE 7/8/1 : Field of an absolute system of three variables, of which S is a step-function. The states from C to C are the critical states of the step-function.

the line of behaviour meets the row of critical states at C—C, S jumps to its other value, and the representative point continues along the heavily marked line in the upper plane. In such a field the movement of the representative point is everywhere state-determined, for the number of lines from any point never exceeds one.

If, still dealing with the same real 'machine', we ignore S, and repeatedly form the field of the system composed of A and B, S being free to take sometimes one value and sometimes the other, we shall find that we get sometimes a field like I in Figure 7/8/2, and sometimes a field like II, the one or the other appearing according to the value that S happens to have at the time.

The behaviour of the system AB, in its apparent possession of two fields, should be compared with that of the system described in S. 6/3, where the use of two parameter-values also caused the appearance of two fields. But in the earlier case the change of the field was caused by the arbitrary action of the experimenter, who forced the parameter to change value, while in this case the change of the field of AB is caused by the inner mechanisms of the 'machine' itself.

The property may now be stated in general terms. Suppose, in an absolute system, that some of the variables are step-functions, and that these are ignored while the remainder (the main variables) are observed on many occasions by having their field constructed.

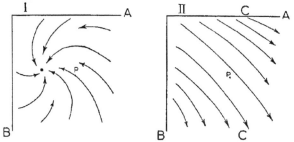

FIGURE 7/8/2 : The two fields of the system composed of A and B.
P is in the same position in each field

Then so long as no step-function changes value during the construction, the main variables will be found to form an absolute system, and to have a definite field. But on different occasions different fields may be found. *The number of different fields shown by the main variables is equal to the number of combinations of values provided by the step-functions.*

7/9.   These considerations throw light on an old problem in the theory of mechanisms.

Can a 'machine' be at once determinate and capable of spontaneous change ? The question would be contradictory if posed by one person, but it exists in fact because, when talking of living organisms, one school maintains that they are strictly determinate while another school maintains that they are capable of spontaneous change. Can the schools be reconciled ?

The presence of step-functions in an absolute system enables both schools to be right, provided that those who maintain the determination are speaking of the system which comprises *all* the variables, while those who maintain the possibility of spontaneous change are speaking of the main variables only. For the whole system, which includes the step-functions, is absolute, has one field only, and is completely state-determined (like Figure 7/8/1). But the system of main variables may show as many different forms of behaviour (like Figure 7/8/2, I and II) as the step-functions possess combinations of values. And if the step-functions are not accessible to observation, the change of the main variables from one form of behaviour to another will seem to be spontaneous. for no change or state in the main variables can be assigned as its cause.

The argument may seem plausible, but it is stronger than that. It may be proved (S. 22/5) that if a ' machine ', known to be completely isolated and therefore absolute, produces several characteristic forms of behaviour, i.e. possesses several fields, then there *must* be, interacting with the observed variables and included within the ' machine ', some step-functions.

CHAPTER 8

The Ultrastable System

8/1. Our problem, stated briefly at the end of Chapter 5, can now be stated finally. The type-problem was the kitten whose behaviour towards a fire was at first chaotic and unadapted, but whose behaviour later became effective and adapted. We have recognised (S. 5/8) that the property of being 'adapted' is equivalent to that of having the variables, both of the animal and of the environment, so co-ordinated in their actions on one another that the whole system is stable. We now know, from S. 6/3 and 7/8, that an observed system can change from one form of behaviour to another only if parameters have changed value. Since we assumed originally that no *deus ex machina* may act on it, the changes in the system must be due to step-functions acting within the whole absolute system. Our problem therefore takes the final form : *Step-functions by their changes in value are to change the behaviour of the system ; what can ensure that the step-functions shall change appropriately ?* The answer is provided by a principle, relating step-functions and fields, which will now be described.

8/2. In S. 7/8 it was shown that when a step-function changes value, the field of the main variables is changed. The process was illustrated in Figures 7/8/1 and 7/8/2. This is the action of step-function on field.

8/3. There is also a reciprocal action. Fields differ in the relation of their lines of behaviour to the critical states. Thus, if a representative point is started at random in the region to the left of the critical states in Figure 8/3/1, the proportion which will encounter critical states is, in I—1, in II—0, and in III— about a half. So, given a distribution of critical states and a distribution of initial states, a change of field will, in general,

90

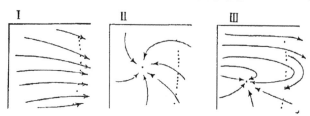

FIGURE 8/3/1 : Three fields   The critical states are dotted.

change the proportion of representative points encountering critical states.

The ultrastable system

8/4. The two factors of the two preceding sections will now be found to generate a process, for each in turn evokes the other's action. The process is most clearly shown in what I shall call an **ultrastable** system : one that is absolute and contains step-functions in a sufficiently large number for us to be able to ignore the finiteness of the number. Consider the field of its main variables after the representative point has been released from some state. If the field leads the point to a critical state, a step-function will change value and the field will be changed. If the new field again leads the point to a critical state, again a step-function will change and again the field will be changed ; and so on. The two factors, then, generate a process.

8/5. Clearly, for the process to come to an end it is necessary and sufficient that the new field should be of a form that does not lead the representative point to a critical state. (Such a field will be called **terminal.**) But the process may also be described in rather different words · if we watch the main variables only, we shall see field after field being rejected until one is retained : the process is *selective* towards fields.

As this selectivity is of the highest importance for the solution of our problem, the **principle of ultrastability** will be stated formally : *an ultrastable system acts selectively towards the fields of the main variables, rejecting those that lead the representative point to a critical state but retaining those that do not.*

This principle is the tool we have been seeking ; the previous chapters have been working towards it : the later chapters will develop it.

8/6. In the previous sections, the critical states of the step-functions were unrestricted in position ; but such freedom does not correspond with what is found in biological systems (S. 9/8), so we will examine the behaviour of an ultrastable system whose critical states are so sited that they surround a definite region in the main-variables' phase-space. (At first we shall assume that the main variables are all full-functions, though the definition makes no such restriction. Later (S. 11/8) we shall examine other possibilities.)

8/7. The simplest way to demonstrate the properties of this system is by an example. Suppose there are only two main variables, A and B, and the critical states of all the step-functions

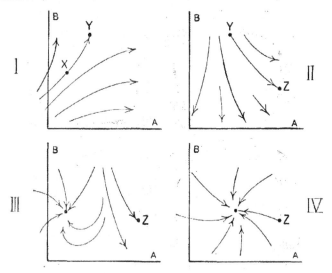

FIGURE 8/7/1 : Changes of field in an ultrastable system. The critical states are dotted.

are distributed as the dots in Figure 8/7/1. Suppose the first field is that of Figure 8/7/1 (I), and that the system is started with the representative point at X. The line of behaviour from

X is not stable in the region, and the representative point follows the line to the boundary. Here (Y) it meets a critical state and a step-function changes value; a new field, perhaps like II, arises. The representative point is now at Y, and the line from this point is still unstable in regard to the region. The point follows the line of behaviour, meets a critical state at Z, and causes a change of a step-function. a new field (III) arises The point is at Z, and the field includes a stable resting state, but from Z the line leads further out of the region. So another critical state is met, another step-function changes value, and a new field (IV) arises. In this field, the line of behaviour from Z is stable with regard to the region. So the representative point moves to the resting state and stops there. No further critical states are met, no further step-functions change value, and therefore no further changes of field take place. From now on, if the field of the main variables is examined, it will be found to be stable. *If the critical states surround a region, the ultrastable system is selective for fields that are stable within the region.*

(This statement is not rigorously true, for a little ingenuity can devise fields of bizarre type which are not stable but which are, under the present conditions, terminal. A fully rigorous statement would be too clumsy for use in the next few chapters; but the difficulty is only temporary, for S. 13/4 introduces some practical factors which will make the statement practically true.)

The Homeostat

8/8. So far the discussion of step-functions and of ultrastability has been purely logical. In order to provide an objective and independent test of the reasoning, a machine has been built according to the definition of the ultrastable system. This section will describe the machine and will show how its behaviour compares with the prediction of the previous section.

The homeostat (Figure 8/8/1) consists of four units, each of which carries on top a pivoted magnet (Figure 8/8/2, M in Figure 8/8/3). The angular deviations of the four magnets from the central positions provide the four main variables.

Its construction will be described in stages Each unit emits a D.C. output proportional to the deviation of its magnet from the central position. The output is controlled in the following

93

FIGURE 8/8/1 : The homeostat. Each unit carries on top a magnet and coil such as that shown in Figure 8/8/2. Of the controls on the front panel, those of the upper row control the potentiometers, those of the middle row the commutators, and those of the lower row the switches S of Figure 8/8/3.

FIGURE 8/8/2 : Typical magnet (just visible), coil, pivot, vane, and water potentiometer with electrodes at each end. The coil is quadruple, consisting of A, B, C and D of Figure 8/8/3.

way. In front of each magnet is a trough of water ; electrodes
at each end provide a potential gradient. The magnet carries
a wire which dips into the water, picks up a potential depending
on the position of the magnet, and sends it to the grid of the
triode. *J* provides the anode-potential at 150 V., while *H* is at
180 V. ; so *E* carries a constant current. If the grid-potential
allows just this current to pass through the valve, then no current
will flow through the output. But if the valve passes more, or
less, current than this, the output circuit will carry the difference

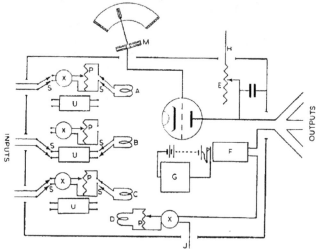

FIGURE 8/8/3 : Wiring diagram of one unit. (The letters are explained
in the text.)

in one direction or the other. So after *E* is adjusted, the output
is approximately proportional to *M*'s deviation from its central
position.

Next, the units are joined together so that each sends its
output to the other three ; and thereby each receives an input
from each of the other three.

These inputs act on the unit's magnet through the coils *A*,
B, and *C*, so that the torque on the magnet is approximately
proportional to the algebraic sum of the currents in *A*, *B*, and
C. (*D* also affects *M* as a self-feedback.) But before each
input current reaches its coil, it passes through a commutator

95

(X), which determines the polarity of entry to the coil, and through a potentiometer (P), which determines what fraction of the input shall reach the coil.

As soon as the system is switched on, the magnets are moved by the currents from the other units, but these movements change the currents, which modify the movements, and so on. It may be shown (S. 19/11) that if there is sufficient viscosity in the troughs, the four-variable system of the magnet-positions is approximately absolute To this system the commutators and potentiometers act as parameters.

When these parameters are given a definite set of values, the magnets show some definite pattern of behaviour; for the parameters determine the field, and thus the lines of behaviour. If the field is stable, the four magnets move to the central position, where they actively resist any attempt to displace them. If displaced, a co-ordinated activity brings them back to the centre. Other parameter-settings may, however, give instability; in which case a 'runaway' occurs and the magnets diverge from the central positions with increasing velocity.

So far, the system of four variables has been shown to be dynamic, to have Figure 4/12/1 (A) as its diagram of immediate effects, and to be absolute. Its field depends on the thirty-two parameters X and P. It is not yet ultrastable. But the inputs, instead of being controlled by parameters set by hand, can be sent by the switches S through similar components arranged on a uniselector (or 'stepping-switch') U. The values of the components in U were deliberately randomised by taking the actual numerical values from Fisher and Yates' Table of Random Numbers. Once built on to the uniselectors, the values of these parameters are determined at any moment by the positions of the uniselectors. Twenty-five positions on each of four uniselectors (one to each unit) provide 390,625 combinations of parameter-values. In addition, the coil G of each uniselector is energised when, and only when, the magnet M diverges far from the central position; for only at extreme divergence does the output-current reach a value sufficient to energise the relay F which closes the coil-circuit. A separate device, not shown, interrupts the coil-circuit regularly, making the uniselector move from position to position as long as F is energised.

The system is now ultrastable; its correspondence with the

definition will be shown in each of the three requirements. Firstly, the whole system, now of eight variables (four of the magnet-deviations and four of the uniselector-positions), is absolute, because the values of the eight variables are sufficient to determine its behaviour. Secondly, the variables may be divided into main variables (the four magnet-deviations), and step-functions (the variables controlled by the uniselector-positions). Thirdly, as the uniselectors provide an almost endless supply of step-function values (though not all different) we do not have to consider the possibility that the supply of step-function changes will come to an end. In addition, the critical states (those magnet-deviations at which the relay closes) are all sited at about a $45°$ deviation ; so in the phase-space of the main variables they form a ' cube ' around the origin.

It should be noticed that if only one, two, or three of the units are used, the resulting system is still ultrastable. It will have one, two, or three main variables respectively, but the critical states will be unaltered in position.

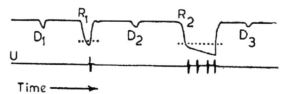

FIGURE 8/8/4 : Behaviour of one unit fed back into itself through a uniselector. The upper line records the position of the magnet, whose side-to-side movements are recorded as up and down. The lower line (U) shows a cross-stroke whenever the uniselector moves to a new position. The first movement at each D was forced by the operator, who pushed the magnet to one side to make it demonstrate the response.

Its ultrastability can now be demonstrated. First, for simplicity, is shown a single unit arranged to feed back into itself through a single uniselector coil such as A, D being shorted out. In such a case the occurrence of the first negative setting on the uniselector will give stability. Figure 8/8/4 shows a typical tracing. At first the step-functions gave a stable field to the single main variable, and the downward part of D_1, caused by the operator deflecting the magnet, is promptly corrected by the system, the magnet returning to its central position. At R_1, the operator reversed the polarity of the output-input junction, making the system unstable (S. 20/7). As a result, a runaway developed, and the magnet passed the critical state (shown by the dotted line). As a result the uniselector changed value. As it happened, the first new value provided a field which was stable, so the magnet returned to its central position. At D_2, a displacement showed that the system was now stable (though the return after R_1 demonstrated it too).

At R_2 the polarity of the join was reversed again. The value on the uniselector was now no longer suitable, the field was unstable, and a runaway occurred. This time three uniselector positions provided three fields which were all unstable : all were

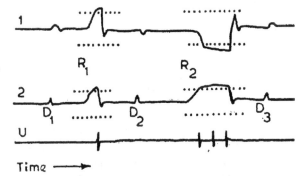

FIGURE 8/8/5 : Two units (1 and 2) interacting. (Details as in Fig. 8/8/4.)

rejected. But the fourth was stable, the magnet returned to the centre, no further uniselector changes occurred, and the single main variable had a stable field. At D_3 its stability was again demonstrated.

Figure 8/8/5 shows another experiment, this time with two units interacting. The diagram of immediate effects was $1 \rightleftarrows 2$; the effect $1 \rightarrow 2$ was hand-controlled, and $2 \rightarrow 1$ was uniselector-controlled. At first the step-function values combined to give stability, shown by the responses to D_1. At R_1, reversal of the commutator by hand rendered the system unstable, a runaway occurred, and the variables transgressed the critical states. The uniselector in Unit 1 changed position and, as it happened, gave at its first trial a stable field. It will be noticed that whereas before R_1 the upstroke of D_1 in 2 caused an *up*stroke in 1, it caused a *downstroke* in 1 after R_1, showing that the action $2 \rightarrow 1$ had been reversed by the uniselector. This reversal compensated for the reversal of $1 \rightarrow 2$ caused at R_1.

At R_2 the whole process was repeated. This time three uniselector changes were required before stability was restored. A comparison of the effect of D_3 on 1 with that of D_2 shows that compensation has occurred again.

The homeostat can thus demonstrate the elementary facts of ultrastability.

8/9. In what way does an ultrastable system differ from an ordinary stable system?

In one sense the two systems are similar. Each is assumed absolute, and if therefore we form the field of *all* its variables, each will have one permanent field. Given a region, every line of behaviour is permanently stable or unstable (see Figure 7/8/1). Viewed in this way, the two systems show no essential difference. But if we compare the variables of the stable system with only the main variables of the ultrastable, then an obvious difference appears : the field of the stable system is single and permanent, but in the ultrastable system the phase-space of the main variables shows a succession of transient fields concluded by a terminal field which is always stable. The distinction in actual behaviour can best be shown by an example. The automatic pilot is a device which, amongst other actions, keeps the aeroplane horizontal. It must therefore be connected to the ailerons in such a way that when the plane rolls to the right, its output must act on them so as to roll the plane to the left. If properly joined, the whole system is stable and self-correcting : it can now fly safely through turbulent air, for though it will roll frequently, it will always come back to the level. The homeostat, if joined in this way, would tend to do the same. (Though not well suited, it would, in principle, if given a gyroscope, be able to correct roll.)

So far they show no difference ; but connect the ailerons in reverse and compare them. The automatic pilot would act, after a small disturbance, to *increase* the roll, and would persist in its wrong action to the very end. The homeostat, however, would persist in its wrong action only until the increasing deviation made the step-functions start changing. On the occurrence of the first suitable new value, the homeostat would act to stabilise instead of to overthrow ; it would return the plane to the horizontal , and it would then be ordinarily self-correcting for disturbances.

There is therefore some justification for the name ' ultrastable ' ; for if the main variables are assembled so as to make their field unstable, the ultrastable system will change this field till it is stable. The degree of stability shown is therefore of an order higher than that of the system with a single field.

Another difference can be seen by considering the number of factors which need adjustment or specification in order to achieve stability. Less adjustment is needed if the system is ultrastable. Thus an automatic pilot must be joined to the ailerons with care, but an ultrastable pilot could safely be joined to the ailerons at random. Again, a linear system of n variables, to be made stable, needs the simultaneous adjustment of at least n parameters (S. 20/11, Ex. 3). If n is, say, a thousand, then at least a thousand parameters must be correctly adjusted if stability is to be achieved. But an ultrastable system with a thousand main variables needs, to achieve stability, the specification of about six factors ; for this is approximately the number of independent items in the specification of the system (S. 9/9). A large system, then, can be made stable with much less detailed specification if it is made ultrastable.

8/10. In S. 6/2 it was shown that every dynamic system is acted on by an indefinitely large number of parameters, many of which are taken for granted, for they are always given well-understood ' obvious ' values. Thus, in mechanical systems it is taken for granted, unless specially mentioned, that the bodies carry a zero electrostatic charge ; in physiological experiments, that the tissues, unless specially mentioned, contain no unusual drug ; in biological experiments, that the animal, unless specially mentioned, is in good health. All these parameters, however, are effective in that, had their values been different, the variables would not have followed the same line of behaviour. Clearly the field of an absolute system depends not only on those parameters which have been fixed individually and specifically, but on all the great number which have been fixed incidentally.

Now the ultrastable system proceeds to a terminal field which

is stable in conjunction with *all* the system's parameter-values
(and it is clear by the principle of ultrastability that this must be
so, for whether the parameters are at their ' usual ' values or
not is irrelevant). The ultrastable system will therefore always
produce a set of step-function values which is so related to the
particular set of parameter-values that, *in conjunction with them,*
the system is stable. If the parameters have unusual values,

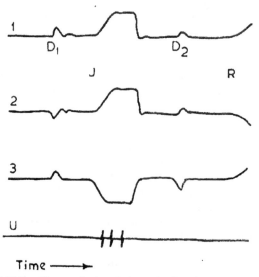

FIGURE 8/10/1 : Three units interacting. At *J*, units 1 and 2 were con-
strained to move together. New step-function values were found which
produced stability. These values give stability in conjunction with the
constraint, for when it is removed, at *R*, the system becomes unstable.

the step-functions will also finish with values that are compen-
satingly unusual. To the casual observer this adjustment of the
step-function values to the parameter-values may be surprising;
we, however, can see that it is inevitable.

The fact is demonstrable on the homeostat. After the machine
was completed, some ' unusual ' complications were imposed on
it (' unusual ' in the sense that they were not thought of till
the machine had been built), and the machine was then tested
to see how it would succeed in finding a stable field when
affected by the peculiar complications. One such test was

made by joining the front two magnets by a light glass fibre so that they had to move together. Figure 8/10/1 shows a typical record of the changes. Three units were joined together and were at first stable, as shown by the response when the operator displaced magnet 1 at D_1. At J, the magnets of 1 and 2 were joined so that they could move only together. The result of the constraint in this case was to make the system unstable. But the instability evoked step-function changes, and a new terminal field was found. This was, of course, stable, as was shown by its response to the displacement, made by the operator, at D_2. But it should be noticed that the new set of step-function values was adjusted to, or 'took notice of', the constraint and, in fact, used it in the maintenance of stability; for when, at R, the operator gently lifted the fibre away the system became unstable.

REFERENCES

Ashby, W. Ross   Design for a brain. *Electronic Engineering*, **20**, 879, 1948.
Idem   The cerebral mechanisms of intelligent behaviour, in *Perspectives in Neuropsychiatry*, edited D. Richter.   London, 1950.
Idem   Can a mechanical chess-player outplay its designer?   *British Journal for the Philosophy of Science*, 3, 44; 1952.
Fisher, R A, and Yates, F   *Statistical tables*.   Edinburgh, 1943.

CHAPTER 9

Ultrastability in the Living Organism

9/1. The principle of ultrastability has so far been treated as a principle in its own right, true or false without reference to possible applications. This separation has prevented the possibility of a circular argument; but the time for its application has now come. I propose, therefore, the thesis that the living organism uses the principle of ultrastability as an automatic means of ensuring the adaptiveness of its learned behaviour. At first I shall cite only facts in its favour, leaving all major criticisms to Chapter 11. We shall have, of course, to assume that the animal, and particularly the nervous system, contains the necessary variables behaving as step-functions : whether this assumption is reasonable will be discussed in the next chapter.

Examples of adaptive, learned behaviour are so multitudinous that it will be quite impossible for me to discuss, or even to mention, the majority of them. I can only select a few as typical and leave the reader to make the necessary modifications in other cases.

The best introduction is not an example of learned behaviour, but Jennings' classic description of the reactions of *Stentor*, a single-celled pond animalcule. I shall quote him at length :

'Let us now examine the behaviour [of *Stentor*] under conditions which are harmless when acting for a short time, but which, when continued, do interfere with the normal functions. Such conditions may be produced by bringing a large quantity of fine particles, such as India ink or carmine, by means of a capillary pipette, into the water currents which are carried to the disc of *Stentor*.

'Under these conditions the normal movements are at first not changed. The particles of carmine are taken into the pouch and into the mouth, whence they pass into the internal protoplasm. If the cloud of particles is very dense,

103

or if it is accompanied by a slight chemical stimulus, as is usually the case with carmine grains, this behaviour lasts but a short time ; then a definite reaction supervenes. The animal bends to one side . . . It thus as a rule avoids the cloud of particles, unless the latter is very large. This simple method of reaction turns out to be more effective in getting rid of stimuli of all sorts than might be expected. If the first reaction is not successful, it is usually repeated one or more times . . .

' If the repeated turning toward one side does not relieve the animal, so that the particles of carmine continue to come in a dense cloud, another reaction is tried. The ciliary movement is suddenly reversed in direction, so that the particles against the disc and in the pouch are thrown off. The water current is driven away from the disc instead of toward it. This lasts but an instant, then the current is continued in the usual way. If the particles continue to come, the reversal is repeated two or three times in rapid succession. If this fails to relieve the organism, the next reaction—contraction—usually supervenes.

' Sometimes the reversal of the current takes place before the turning away described first ; but usually the two reactions are tried in the order we have given.

' If the *Stentor* does not get rid of the stimulation in either of the ways just described, it contracts into its tube. In this way it of course escapes the stimulation completely, but at the expense of suspending its activity and losing all opportunity to obtain food. The animal usually remains in the tube about half a minute, then extends. When its body has reached about two-thirds its original length, the ciliary disc begins to unfold and the cilia to act, causing currents of water to reach the disc, as before.

' We have now reached a specially interesting point in the experiment Suppose that the water currents again bring the carmine grains. The stimulus and all the external conditions are the same as they were at the beginning. Will the *Stentor* behave as it did at the beginning ? Will it at first not react, then bend to one side, then reverse the current, then contract, passing anew through the whole series of reactions ? Or shall we find that it has become changed by the experiences it has passed through, so that it will now contract again into its tube as soon as stimulated ?

' We find the latter to be the case. As soon as the carmine again reaches its disc, it at once contracts again. This may be repeated many times, as often as the particles come to the disc, for ten or fifteen minutes. Now the animal after each contraction stays a little longer in the tube than it did at first. Finally it ceases to extend, but contracts repeatedly and violently while still enclosed in its tube. In this way the attachment of its foot to the object on which it is situated is broken and the animal is free. Now it leaves its tube and swims away. In leaving the tube it may swim forward out of the anterior end of the tube ; but if this brings it into the region of the cloud of carmine, it often forces its way backwards through the substance of the tube, and thus gains the outside. Here it swims away, to form a new tube elsewhere.

' . . . the changes in behaviour may be summed up as follows ·

(1) No reaction at first ; the organism continues its normal activities for a time.
(2) Then a slight reaction by turning into a new position.
(3) . . . a momentary reversal of the ciliary current . . .
(4) . . . the animal breaks off its normal activity completely by contracting strongly . . .
(5) . . . it abandons its tube . . . '

The behaviour of *Stentor* bears a close resemblance to the behaviour of an ultrastable system. The physical correspondences necessary would be as follows :—*Stentor* and its environment constitute an absolute system by S. 3/9 ; for Jennings, having set the carmine flowing, interferes no further. They consequently correspond to the whole ultrastable system, which is also absolute by the definition of S. 8/4. The observable (here : visible) variables of *Stentor* and its environment correspond to the main variables of the ultrastable system. In *Stentor* are assumed to be variables which behave like, and correspond to, the step-functions of the ultrastable system. The critical states of the organism's step-functions surround the region of the normal values of the organism's essential variables so that its step-functions change value if the essential variables diverge widely from their usual, normal values. These critical states must be nearer to the normal value than the extreme limits of the essential variables, for these critical states must be reached before the essential variables reach the extreme limits compatible with life.

Now compare the behaviour of the ultrastable system, described in S. 8/7, with the behaviour of organisms like *Stentor*, epitomised by Jennings in these words ·

' Anything injurious to the organism causes changes in its behaviour. These changes subject the organism to new

105

conditions. As long as the injurious condition continues, the changes of behaviour continue. The first change of behaviour may not be regulatory [what I call ' adaptive '], nor the second, nor the third, nor the tenth. But if the changes continue, subjecting the organism successively to all possible different conditions, a condition will finally be reached that relieves the organism from the injurious action, provided such a condition exists. Thereupon the changes in behaviour cease and the organism remains in the favourable situation.'

The resemblance between my statement and his is obvious. Jennings grasped the fundamental fact that *aimless* change can lead to adaptation provided that some active process rejects the bad and retains the good. He did not, however, give any physical (i.e. non-vital) reason why this selection should occur. He records only that it does occur, and that its occurrence is sufficient to account for adaptation at the primitive level.

The first example therefore suggests that, provided we are willing to assume that *Stentor* contains step-functions which (*a*) affect *Stentor's* behaviour, and (*b*) have critical states that are encountered before the essential variables reach their extreme limits, *Stentor* may well achieve its final adaptation by using the automatic process of ultrastability.

9/2. The next example includes more complicating factors but the main features are clear. Mowrer put a rat into a box with a grilled metal floor. The grill could be electrified so as to give shocks to the rat's paws. Inside the box was a pedal which, if depressed, at once stopped the shocks.

When a rat was put into the box and the electric stimulation started, the rat would produce various undirected activities such as jumping, running, squealing, biting at the grill, and random thrashing about. Sooner or later it would depress the pedal and stop the shocks. After the tenth trial, the application of the shock would usually cause the rat to go straight to the pedal and depress it. These, briefly, are the observed facts.

Consider the internal linkages in this system. We can sufficiently specify what is happening by using six variables, or sets of variables: those shown in the box-diagram below. By considering the known actions of part on part in the real system we can construct the diagram of immediate effects. Thus, the excitations in the motor cortex certainly control the rat's bodily movements, and such excitations have no direct effect on any of the other five groups of variables; so we can insert arrow 1, and know that no other arrow leaves that box. (The single arrow, of course, represents a complex channel.) Similarly, the other arrows of the diagram can be inserted. Some of the arrows, e.g. 2 and 4, represent a linkage in which there is not

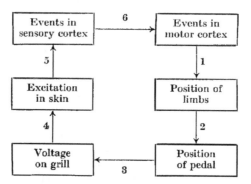

a positive physical action all the time; but here, in accordance with S. 2/3, we regard them as permanently linked though sometimes acting at zero degree.

Having completed the diagram, we notice that it forms a functional circuit. The system is complete and isolated, and may therefore be treated as absolute. To apply our thesis, we assume that the cerebral part, represented by the boxes around arrow 6, contains step-functions whose critical states will be transgressed if stimuli of more than physiological intensity are sent to the brain.

We now regard the system as straightforwardly ultrastable, and predict what its behaviour must be. It is started, by hypothesis, from an initial state at which the voltage is high. This being so, the excitation at the skin and in the brain will be high. At first the pattern of impulses sent to the muscles does not cause that pedal movement which would lower the voltage on the grill. These high excitations in the brain will cause some step-functions to change value, thus causing different patterns of body movement to occur. The step-functions act directly only at stage 6, but changes there will (S. 14/11) affect the field of all six groups of main variables. These changes of field will continue to occur as long as the high excitation in the brain persists. They will cease when, and only when, the linkages at stage 6 transform an excitation of skin receptors into such a bodily movement as will cause, through the pedal, a reduction in the excitation of the skin receptors; for only such linkages can stop further encounters with critical states. The system that is, will change until there occurs a stable field. The stability will be shown by an increase in the voltage on the grill leading to changes through skin, brain, muscles, and pedal that have the effect of *opposing* the increase in voltage. The stability, in addition, has the property that it keeps the essential variables within physiological limits; for by it the rat is protected from electrical injury, and the nervous system from exhaustion.

It will be noted that although action 3 has no direct connection, either visually in the real apparatus or functionally in the diagram of immediate effects, with the site of the changes at 6, yet the latter become adapted to the nature of the action at 3. The subject was discussed in S. 5/15.

This example shows, therefore, that if the rat and its environment formed an ultrastable system and acted purely automatically, they would have gone through the same changes as were observed by Mowrer.

9/3. The two examples have taken a known fact of animal behaviour and shown its resemblance to the behaviour of the ultrastable system. Equally, the behaviour of the homeostat, a system known to be ultrastable, shows some resemblance to that of a rudimentary nervous system. The tracings of Figures 8/8/4 and 8/8/5 show its elementary power of adaptation. In Figure 8/8/5 the reversal at R_1 might be regarded as the action of an experimenter who changed the conditions so that the ' aim ' (stability and homeostasis) could be achieved only if the ' organism ' (Unit 1) reversed its action. Such a reversal might be forced on a rat who, having learned a maze whose right fork led to food, was transferred to a maze where food was to be found only down the left fork. The homeostat, as Figure 8/8/5 shows, develops a reversed action in Unit 1, and this reversal may be compared with the reversal which is usually found to occur in the rat's behaviour.

A more elaborate reaction by the homeostat is shown in Figure 9/3/1.

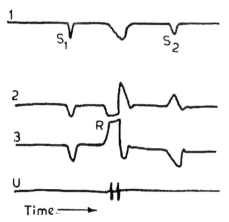

FIGURE 9/3/1 : Three units interacting. At R the effect of 2 on 3 was reversed in polarity.

The machine was arranged so that its diagram of immediate effects was

The effect $3 \rightarrow 1$ was set permanently so that a movement of 3 made 1 move in the opposite direction. The action $1 \rightarrow 2$ was uniselector-controlled, and $2 \rightarrow 3$ hand-controlled. When the tracing commenced, the actions $1 \rightarrow 2$ and $2 \rightarrow 3$ were demonstrated by the downward movement, forced by the operator, of 1 at S_1 : 2 followed 1 downward (similar movement), and 3 followed 2 downward (similar movement). 3 then forced 1 upward, opposed the original movement, and produced stability.

At R, the hand-control ($2 \rightarrow 3$) was reversed, so that 2 now forced 3 to move in the *opposite* direction to itself. This change set up a vicious circle and destroyed the stability ; but uniselector changes occurred until the stability was restored. A forced downward movement of 1, at S_2, demonstrated the regained stability.

109

The tracing, however, deserves closer study. The action $2 \rightarrow 3$ was reversed at R, and the responses of 2 and 3 at S_2 demonstrate this reversal; for while at S_1 they moved similarly, at S_2 they moved oppositely. Again, a comparison of the uniselector-controlled action $1 \rightarrow 2$ before and after R shows that whereas beforehand 2 moved similarly to 1, afterwards it moved oppositely. The reversal in $2 \rightarrow 3$, caused by the operator, thus evoked a reversal in $1 \rightarrow 2$ controlled by the uniselector. The second reversal is compensatory to the first.

The nervous system provides many illustrations of such a series of events. first the established reaction, then an alteration made in the environment by the experimenter, and finally a reorganisation within the nervous system, compensating for the experimental alteration. The homeostat can thus show, in elementary form, this power of self-reorganisation.

The necessity of ultrastability

9/4. In the previous sections a few simple examples have suggested that the adaptation of the living organism may be due to ultrastability. But the argument has not excluded the possibility that other theories might fit the facts equally well. I shall now give, therefore, evidence to show that ultrastability is not merely plausible but necessary : the organism *must* be ultrastable.

First the primary assumptions : they are such as few scientists would doubt. It is assumed that the organism and its environment form an absolute system, and that the organism sometimes changes from one regular way of behaving to another. The crucial question is whether we can prove that the organism's mechanism must contain step-functions. In S. 22/5 is given such a proof, stated in mathematical form , but its theme is simple and can be stated in plain words.

Suppose a ' machine ' or experiment behaves regularly in one way, and then suddenly changes to behaving in another way, again regularly. Suppose, for instance, a pharmacologist, testing the effect of a new drug on the frog's heart, finds at every test all through one day that it causes the pulse-rate to lessen. Next morning, taking records of the effect, he finds at every

attempt that it causes the pulse-rate to increase. He will almost
certainly ask himself ' What has changed ? '

Such facts provide valid evidence that some variable has
changed value. I need not elaborate the logic for no experimenter would question it. What has been sometimes overlooked
though, is that we are also entitled to draw the deduction that
the variable, being as it is an effective factor towards the system,
must, throughout the previous day, have remained constant ,
for otherwise the reactions observed during the day could not
have been regular. For the same reason, it must also have been
constant throughout the next morning. And further, the two
constant values cannot have been equal, for then the hearts'
behaviours would not have been changed Assembling these
inferences, we deduce that the variable must have behaved as
a step-function. Exactly the same argument, applied to the
changes of behaviour shown by Jennings' *Stentor*, leads to the
deduction that within the organism there must have been variables behaving as step-functions.

Is there any escape from this conclusion ? It rests primarily
on the simple thesis that a determinate system does not, if started
from identical states, do one thing on one day and something
else on another day. There seems to be no escape if we assume
that the systems we are discussing are determinate. Suppose,
then, that we abandon the assumption of determinism and allow
indeterminism of atomic type to affect heart, *Stentor*, or brain
to an observable extent. This would allow us to explain the
' causeless ' overnight change ; but then we would be unable to
explain the regularity throughout the previous day and the next
morning. It seems there is no escape that way. Again, we
could, with a little ingenuity, construct a hypothesis that the
pharmacologist's experiment was affected by a small group of
variables, whose joint action produced the observed result but
not one of which was a step-function ; and it might be claimed
that the theorem had been shown false. But this is really no
exception, for we are not concerned with what variables ' are '
but with how they behave, and in particular with how they
behave towards the system in question. If a group of variables
behaves towards the system as a step-function, then it *is* a step-
function , for the ' step-function ' is defined primarily as a form
of behaviour, not as a thing.

111

Once it is agreed that a system, such as that of Mowrer's rat, contains step-functions, then all it needs is that they should not be few for the system to be admitted as ultrastable.

After this, we can examine the qualifications that were added when considering *Stentor* as an ultrastable system. Are they, too, necessary ? Not with the assumptions made so far in this section, but they become so if we add the postulates that the system ' adapts ' in the sense of S. 5/8, and that it does so by ' trial and error '. In order to be definite about what ' trial and error ' implies, here is the concept defined explicitly

(1) The organism makes trials only when ' dissatisfied ' or ' irritated ' in some way.

(2) Each trial persists for a finite time.

(3) While the irritation continues, the succession of trials continues.

(4) The succeeding trial is not specially related to the preceding, nor better than it, but only different.

(5) The process stops at the first trial that relieves the irritation.

The argument goes thus. As each step-function forms part of an absolute system, its change must depend on its own and on the other variables' values ; there must, therefore, be certain states—the critical—at which it changes value. When, in the process of adaptation by trial and error, the step-function changes value, its critical states must have been encountered ; and since, by (1) above, the step-functions change value only when the organism is ' dissatisfied ' or ' irritated ', the critical states must be so related to the essential variables that only when the organism is driven from its normal physiological state does its representative point encounter the critical states. This knowledge is sufficient to place the critical states in the functional sense : they must have values intermediate between those of the normal state and those of the essential variables' limits. The qualifications introduced in S. 9/1 are thus necessary.

Training

9/5. The process of ' training ' will now be shown in its relation to ultrastability.

All training involves some use of ' punishment ' or ' reward ', and we must translate these concepts into our form. ' Punishment' is simple, for it means that some sensory organs or nerve endings have been stimulated with an intensity high enough to cause step-function changes in the nervous system (S. 7/6 and 10/2). The concept of 'reward' is more complex. It usually involves the supplying of some substance (e.g. food) or condition (e.g. escape) whose absence would act as 'punishment'. The chief difficulty is that the evidence suggests that the nervous system, especially the mammalian, contains intricate and special-ised mechanisms which give the animals properties not to be deduced from basic principles alone. Thus it has been shown that dogs with an oesophageal fistula, deprived of water for some hours, would, when offered water, drink approximately the quantity that would correct the deprivation, and would then stop drinking; they would stop although no water had entered stomach or system. The properties of these mechanisms have not yet been fully elucidated; so training by reward uses mechanisms of unknown properties. Here we shall ignore these complications. We shall assume that the training is by pain, i.e. by some change which threatens to drive the essential vari-ables outside their normal limits; and we shall assume that training by reward is not essentially dissimilar.

It will now be shown that the process of 'training' necessarily implies the existence of feedback   But first the functional rela-tionship of the experimenter to the experiment must be made clear.

The experimenter often plays a dual role. He first plans the experiment, deciding what rules shall be obeyed during it. Then, when these have been fixed, he takes part in the experi-ment and obeys these rules. With the first role we are not concerned. In the second, however, it is important to note that the experimenter is now *within* the functional machinery of the experiment. The truth of this statement can be appreciated more readily if his place is taken by an untrained but obedient assistant who carries out the instructions blindly; or better still if his place is taken by an apparatus which carries out the pre-scribed actions automatically.

When the whole training is arranged to occur automatically the feedback is readily demonstrated if we construct the diagram of immediate effects. Thus, a pike in an aquarium was separated from some minnows by a sheet of glass; every time he dashed at the minnows he struck the glass. The following immediate effects can be clearly distinguished :

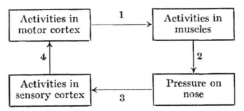

The arrow 1 represents the control exerted through spinal cord and motor nerves. Effect 2 is discontinuous but none the less clear : the experiment implies that some activities led to a high pressure on the nose while others led to a zero pressure. Effects 3 and 4 are the simple neuro-physiological results of pressures on the nose.

Although the diagram has some freedom in the selection of variables for naming, the system, regarded as a whole, clearly has feedback.

In other training experiments, the regularity of action 2 (supplied above by the constant physical properties of glass) may be supplied by an assistant who constantly obeys the rules laid down by the experimenter. Grindley, for instance, kept a guinea-pig in a silent room in which a buzzer was sounded from time to time. If and only if its head turned to the right did a tray swing out and present it with a piece of carrot ; after a few nibbles the carrot was withdrawn and the process repeated. Feedback is demonstrably present in this system, for the diagram of immediate effects is :

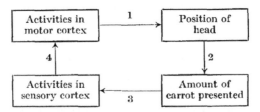

The buzzer, omitted for clarity, comes in as parameter and serves merely to call this dynamic system into functional existence ; for only when the buzzer sounds does the linkage 2 exist.

This type of experiment reveals its essential dynamic structure more clearly if contrasted with elementary Pavlovian conditioning. In the experiments of Grindley and Pavlov, both use the sequences '. . buzzer, animal's response, food . . .' In Grindley's experiment, the value of the variable ' food ' *depended on the animal's response*   if the head turned to the left, ' food ' was ' no carrot ', while if the head turned to the right, ' food ' was ' carrot given '. But in Pavlov's experiments the nature of every stimulus throughout the session was already determined *before the session commenced*. The Pavlovian experiment, therefore, allows no effect from the variable ' animal's behaviour ' to ' quantity of food given ' ; there is no functional circuit and no feedback.

It may be thought that the distinction (which corresponds to that made by Hilgard and Marquis between ' conditioning ' and ' instrumental learning ') is purely verbal. This is not so, for the description given above shows that the distinction may be made objectively by examining the structure of the experiment. Culler *et al.* performed an experiment in which feedback, at first absent, was added at an intermediate stage : as a result, the dog's behaviour changed. They gave the dog a shock to the leg and sounded a tone. The reaction to the shock was one of generalised struggling movements of the body and retraction of the leg. After a few sessions the tone produced generalised struggling and retraction of the leg. So far there had been no feedback ; but now the conditions were changed : the shock was given at the tone only if the foot was not raised. As a result the dog's behaviour changed : the response rapidly narrowed to a simple and precise flexion of the leg.

It will be seen, therefore, that the ' training ' situation necessarily implies that the trainer, or some similar device, is an integral part of the whole system, which has feedback :

We shall now suppose this system to be ultrastable, and we shall trace its behaviour on this supposition. The step-functions are, of course, assumed to be confined to the animal ; both because the human trainer may be replaced in some experiments by a device as simple as a sheet of glass (in the example of the pike); and because the rules of the training are to be decided in advance (as when we decide to punish a house-dog whenever he jumps into a chair), and therefore to be invariant throughout the process. Suppose then that jumping into a chair always results in the dog's sensory receptors being excessively stimulated. As an ultrastable system, step-function values which lead to jumps into chairs will be followed by stimulations likely to cause them to change value. But on the occurrence of a set of step-function values leading to a remaining on the ground, excessive stimulation will not occur, and the values will remain. (The cessation of punishment when the right action occurs is no less important in training than its administration after the wrong action.)

The process can be shown on the homeostat. Figure 9/5/1 provides an example. Three units were joined:

and to this system was joined a 'trainer', actually myself, which acted on the rule that if the homeostat did not respond to a forced movement of 1 by an *opposite* movement of 2, then the trainer would force 3 over to an extreme position. The diagram of immediate effects is therefore really

Part of the system's feedbacks, it will be noticed, pass through T.

At S_1, 1 was moved and 2 moved similarly. This is the 'forbidden' response; so at D_1, 3 was forced by the trainer to an extreme position. Step-functions changed value. At S_2, the homeostat was tested again: again it produced the forbidden response; so at D_2, 3 was again forced to an extreme position. At S_3, the homeostat was tested again: it moved in the desired way, so no further deviation was forced on 3. And at S_4 and S_5 the homeostat continued to show the desired reaction.

116

From S_1 onwards, T's behaviour is determinate at every instant ; so the system composed of 1, 2, 3, T, and the uniselectors, is absolute.

Another property of the whole system should be noticed. When the movement-combination ' 1 and 2 moving similarly ' occurs, T is thereby impelled, under the rules of the experiment, to force 3 outside the region bounded by the critical states. Of any inanimate system which behaved in this way we would

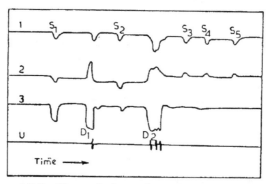

FIGURE 9/5/1 : Three units interacting. The downstrokes at S are forced by the operator. If 2 responds with a downstroke, the trainer drives 3 past its critical surface.

say, simply, that the line of behaviour from the state at which 1 and 2 started moving was unstable. So, to say in psychological terms that the ' trainer ' has ' punished ' the ' animal ' is equivalent to saying in our terms that the system has a set of step-function values that make it unstable.

In general, then, we may identify the behaviour of the animal in ' training ' with that of the ultrastable system adapting to another system of fixed characteristics.

9/6. A remarkable property of the nervous system is its ability to adapt itself to surgical alterations of the bodily structure. From the first work of Marina to the recent work of Sperry, such experiments have aroused interest and no little surprise.

Over thirty years ago, Marina severed the attachments of the internal and external recti muscles of a monkey's eyeball and re-attached them in crossed position so that a contraction of

117   I

the external rectus would cause the eyeball to turn not outwards but inwards. When the wound had healed, he was surprised to discover that the two eyeballs still moved together, so that binocular vision was preserved.

More recently Sperry severed the nerves supplying the flexor and extensor muscles in the arm of the spider monkey, and re-joined them in crossed position. After the nerves had regenerated, the animal's arm movements were at first grossly inco-ordinated but improved until an essentially normal mode of progression was re-established. The two examples are typical of a great number of experiments, and will suffice for the discussion

In S. 3/12 it was decided that the anatomical criterion for dividing the system into ' animal ' and ' environment ' is not the only possible   a functional criterion is also possible. Suppose a monkey, to get food from a box, has to pull a lever towards itself ; if we sever the flexor and extensor muscles of the arm and re-attach them in crossed position then, so far as the cerebral cortex is concerned, the change is not essentially different from that of dismantling the box and re-assembling it so that the lever has to be pushed instead of pulled. Spinal cord, peripheral nerves, muscles, bones, lever, and box—all are ' environment ' to the cerebral cortex. A reversal in the cerebral cortex will compensate for a reversal in its environment whether in spinal cord, muscles, or lever. It seems reasonable, therefore, to expect that the cerebral cortex will use the same compensatory process whatever the site of reversal.

I have already shown, in S. 8/10 and in Figure 8/10/1, that the ultrastable system arrives at a stability in which the values of the step-functions are related to those of the parameters of the system, i.e. to the surrounding fixed conditions, and that the relation will be achieved whether the parameters have values which are ' normal ' or are experimentally altered from those values. If these conclusions are applied to the experiments of Marina and Sperry, the facts receive an explanation, at least in outline. To apply the principle of ultrastability we must add an assumption that ' binocular vision ' and ' normal progression ' have neural correlates such that deviations from binocular vision or from normal progression cause an excitation sufficient to cause changes of step-function in those cerebral mechanisms that determine the actions. (The plausibility of this assumption will be discussed in S. 9/8.) Ultrastability will then automatically lead to the emergence of behaviour which produces binocular vision or normal progression. For this to be produced, the step-function values must make appropriate allowance for the particular characteristics of the environment, whether 'crossed' or 'uncrossed'. S. 8/10 and Figure 9/3/1 showed that an ultrastable system will make such allowance. The adaptation shown by Marina's monkey is therefore homologous with that shown by Mowrer's rat, for the same principle is responsible for both.

9/7. 'Learning' and 'memory' are vast subjects, and any theory of their mechanisms cannot be accepted until it has been tested against all the facts. It is not my intention to propose any such theory, since this work confines itself to the problem of adaptation. Nevertheless I must indicate briefly the relation of this work to the two concepts.

  'Learning' and 'memory' have been given almost as many definitions as there are authors to write of them. The concepts involve a number of aspects whose interrelations are by no means clear; but the theme is that a past experience has caused some change in the organism's behaviour, so that this behaviour is different from what it would have been if the experience had not occurred. But such a change of behaviour is also shown by a motor-car after an accident; so most psychologists have insisted that the two concepts should be restricted to those cases in which the later behaviour is better adapted than the earlier.

The ultrastable system shows in its behaviour something of these elementary features of 'learning'. In Figure 9/3/1, for instance, the pattern of behaviour produced at S_2 is different from the pattern at S_1. The change has occurred after the 'experience' of the instability at R. And the new field produced by the step-function change is better adapted than the previous field, for an unstable field has been replaced by a stable.

An elementary feature of 'memory' is also shown, for further responses, S_3, S_4, etc. would repeat S_2's pattern of behaviour, and thereby might be said to show a 'memory' of the reversal at R; for the later pattern is adapted to the reversal at R, and not adapted to the original setting.

The ultrastable system, then, shows rudimentary 'learning' and 'memory'. The subject is resumed in S. 11/3.

The control of aim

9/8. The ultrastable systems discussed so far, though developing a variety of fields, have sought a constant goal. The homeostat sought central positions and the rat sought zero grill-potential. In this section will be described some methods by which the goal may be varied.

If the critical states' distribution in the main-variables' phase-space is altered by any means whatever, the ultrastable system

FIGURE 9/8/1.

will be altered in the goal it seeks. For the ultrastable system will always develop a field which keeps the representative point within the region of the critical states (S. 8/7). Thus if (Figure 9/8/1) for some reason the critical states moved to surround B instead of A, then the terminal field would change from one which kept x between 0 and 5 to one which kept x between 15 and 20.

A related method is illustrated by Figure 9/8/2. An ultrastable system U interacts with a variable A. E and R represent the immediate effects which U and A have on each other ; they may be thought of as A's effectors and receptors. If A should have a marked effect on the ultrastable system, the latter will, of course, develop a field stabilising A ; at what value will depend markedly on the action of R. Suppose, for instance, that U has its critical states all at values 0 and 10, so that it always selects a field

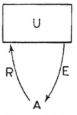

FIGURE 9/8/2.

stabilising all its main variables between these values. If R is such that, if A has some value a, R transmits to U the value $5a - 20$, then it is easy to see that U will develop a field holding A within one unit of the value 5 ; for if the field makes

A go outside the range 4 to 6, it will make U go outside the range 0 to 10, and this will destroy the field. So U becomes ' 5-seeking '. If the action of R is now changed to transmitting, not $5a - 20$ but $5a + 5$, then U will change fields until it holds A within one unit of 0 ; and U is now ' 0-seeking .' So anything that controls the b in $R = 5a + b$ controls the ' goal ' sought by U.

As a more practical example, suppose U is mobile and is ultrastable, with its critical states set so that it seeks situations of high illumination ; such would occur if its critical states resembled, in Figure 9/8/1, B rather than A. Suppose too that R is a ray of light. If in the path of R we place a red colour-filter, then green light will count as ' no light ' and the system will actively seek the red places and avoid the green. If now we merely replace the red filter by a green, the whole aim of its movements will be altered, for it will now seek the green places and avoid the red.

Next, suppose R is a transducer that converts a temperature at A into an illumination which it transmits to U. If R is arranged so that a high temperature at A is converted into a high illumination, then U will become actively goal-seeking for hot places. And if the relation within R is reversed, U will seek for cold places. Clearly, whatever controls R controls U's goal.

There is therefore in general no difficulty in accounting for the fact that a system may seek one goal at one time and another goal at another time.

Sometimes the change, of critical states or of the transducer R, may be under the control of a single parameter. When this happens we must distinguish two complexities. Suppose the parameter can take only two values and the system U is very complicated. Then the system is simple in the sense that it will seek one of only two goals, and is complicated in the sense that the behaviour with which it gets to the goal is complicated. That the behaviour is complicated is no proof, or even suggestion, that the parameter's relations to the system must be complicated , for, as was shown in S. 6/3, the number of fields is equal to the number of values the parameter can take, and has nothing to do with the number of main variables. It is this latter that determines, in general, the complexity of the goal-seeking behaviour.

These considerations may clarify the relations between the change of concentration of a sex-hormone in the blood of a mammal and its consequent sexual goal-seeking behaviour. A simple alternation between ' present ' and ' absent ', or between two levels with a threshold, would be sufficient to account for any degree of complexity in the two behaviours, for the complexity is not to be related to the hormone-parameter but to the nervous system that is affected by it. Since the mammalian nervous system is extremely complex, and since it is, at almost every point, sensitive to both physical and chemical influences, there seems to be no reason to suppose that the directiveness of the sex-hormones on the brain's behaviour is essentially different from that of any parameter on the system it controls. (That the sex-hormones evoke specifically sexual behaviour is, of course, explicable by the fact that evolution, through natural selection, has constructed specific mechanisms that react to the hormone in the specific way.)

Ultrastability and the gene-pattern

9/9. In S. 1/9 it was pointed out that although the power of adaptation shown by a species ultimately depends on its genetic endowment, yet the number of genes is, in the higher animals, quite insufficient to specify every detail of the final neuronic organisation. It was suggested that in the higher animals, the genes must establish function-rules which will look after the details automatically.

As the minimal function-rules have now been provided (S. 8/7) it is of interest to examine the specification of the ultrastable system to see how many items will have to be specified genetically if the ovum is to grow into an ultrastable organism. The items are as follows :

- (1) The animal and its environment must form an absolute system (S. 3/9) ;
- (2) The system must be actively dynamic ;
- (3) Essential variables must be defined for the species (S. 3/14);
- (4) Step-functions are to be provided (S 8/4) ;
- (5) Their critical states are all to be similar (S. 8/6) ;
- (6) The critical states are to be related in value to the limiting values' of the essential variables (S. 9/1).

From these basic rules, an ultrastable system of any size can be generated by mere repetition of parts. Thus each critical state is to have a value related to the limits of the essential variables ; but this requirement applies to all other critical states by mere repetition. The repetition needs fewer genes than would be necessary for independent specification.

It is not possible to give an exact estimate of the number of genes necessary to determine the development of an ultrastable system. But the number of items listed above is only six ; and though the number of genes required is probably a larger number, it may well be less than the number known to be available. It seems, therefore, that the requirement of S. 1/9 has been met satisfactorily.

9/10. If the higher animals are made ultrastable by their genetic inheritance, the gene-pattern must have been shaped by natural selection. Could an ultrastable system be developed by natural selection ?

Suppose the original organism had no step-functions ; such an organism would have a permanent, invariable set of reactions. If a mutation should lead to the formation of a single step-function whose critical states were such that, when the organism became distressed, it changed value *before* the essential variables transgressed their limits, and if the step-function affected in any way the reaction between the organism and the environment, then such a step-function might increase the organism's chance of survival. A single mutation causing a single step-function might therefore prove advantageous ; and this advantage, though slight, might be sufficient to establish the mutation as a species characteristic. Then a second mutation might continue the process. The change from the original system to the ultrastable can therefore be made by a long series of small changes, each of which improves the chance of survival. The change is thus possible under the action of natural selection.

REFERENCES

CULLER, E , FINCH, G., GIRDEN, E., and BROGDEN, W. Measurements of acuity by the conditioned-response technique. *Journal of General Psychology*, **12**, 223 ; 1935.

GRINDLEY, G C   The formation of a simple habit in guinea-pigs   *British Journal of Psychology*, **23**, 127 , 1932–3

HILGARD, E. R., and MARQUIS, D. G.   *Conditioning and learning.*   New York, 1940.

MARINA, A.   Die Relationen des Palaencephalons (Edinger) sind nicht fix *Neurologisches Centralblatt*, **34**, 338 , 1915.

MOWRER, O II   An experimental analogue of ' regression ' with incidental observations on ' reaction-formation '.   *Journal of Abnormal and Social Psychology*, **35**, 56 ; 1940

SPERRY, R W   Effect of crossing nerves to antagonistic limb muscles in the monkey.   *Archives of Neurology and Psychiatry*, **58**, 452 ; 1947

CHAPTER 10

Step-Functions in the
Living Organism

10/1. In S. 9/4 the existence of step-functions in the living organism was deduced from the observed facts. But so far nothing has been said, other than S. 7/6, about their physiological nature. What evidence is there of a more practical nature to support this deduction and to provide further details ?

Direct evidence of the existence of step-functions in the living organism is almost entirely lacking What evidence exists will be reviewed in this chapter. But the lack of evidence does not, of course, prove that such variables do not occur, for no one, so far as I am aware, has made a systematic search for them. Several reasons have contributed to this neglect. Their significance has not been appreciated, so if they have been mentioned in the literature they were probably mentioned only casually, and since they show a behaviour bordering on total immobility, they would usually have been regarded as uninteresting, and may not have been recorded even when observed. It is to be hoped that the recognition of the fundamental part which they play in the processes of adaptation, of integration, and of co-ordination, may lead to a fuller knowledge of their actual nature. 'The anatomical localisation', said Claude Bernard, 'is often revealed first through the analysis of the physiological process.' Here I can do no more than to indicate some possibilities.

10/2. Every cell contains many variables that might change in a way approximating to the step-function form, especially if the time of observation is long compared with the average time of cellular events. Monomolecular films, protein solutions, enzyme systems, concentrations of hydrogen and other ions, oxidation-reduction potentials, adsorbed layers, and many other constituents or processes might behave as step-functions.

If the cell is sufficiently sensitive to be affected by changes of atomic size, then such changes would usually be of step-function form, for they could change only by a quantum jump But this source of step-functions is probably unavailable, for changes of this size may be too indeterminate for the production of the regular and reproducible behaviour considered here (S. 1/10).

Round the neuron, and especially round its dendrons and axons, there is a sensitive membrane that might provide step-functions, though the membrane is probably wholly employed in the transmission of the action potential. Nerve ' fibrils ' have been described for many years, though the possibility that they are an artefact cannot yet be excluded If they are real their extreme delicacy of structure suggests that they might behave as step-functions.

The delicacy everywhere evident in the nervous system has often been remarked. This delicacy must surely imply the existence of step-functions ; for the property of being ' delicate ' can mean little other than ' easily broken ' ; and it was observed in S. 7/6 that the phenomenon of something ' breaking ' is the expression of a step-function changing value. Though the argument is largely verbal, it gives some justification for the opinion that step-functions are by no means unlikely in the nervous system

> ' The idea of a steady, continuous development ', said Jacques Loeb, ' is inconsistent with the general physical qualities of protoplasm or colloidal material. The colloidal substances in our protoplasm possess critical points. . . . The colloids change their state very easily, and a number of conditions . . . are able to bring about a change in their state. Such material lends itself very readily to a discontinuous series of changes.'

10/3. Another source of step-functions would be provided if neurons were amoeboid, so that their processes could make or break contact with other cells.

That nerve-cells are amoeboid in tissue-culture has been known since the first observations of Harrison. When nerve-tissue from chick-embryo is grown in clotted plasma, filaments grow outwards at about 0 05 mm. per hour. The filament terminates in an expanded end, about $15 \times 25 \mu$ in size, which is actively amoeboid, continually throwing out processes as though exploring the medium around Levi studied tissue-cultures by microdissection, so that individual cells could be stimulated. He found that a nerve-cell, touched with the needle-point, would sometimes throw out processes by amoeboid movement.

The conditions of tissue-culture are somewhat abnormal, and artefacts are common ; but this objection cannot be raised against the work of Speidel, who observed nerve-fibres growing into the living tadpole's tail. The ends of the fibres, like those in the tissue-culture, were actively amoeboid. Later he observed the effects of metrazol in the same way. there occurred an active retraction and, later, re-extension. More recently Carey and others have studied the motor end-plate. They found that it, too, is amoeboid, for it contracted to a ball after physical injury

To react to a stimulus by amoeboid movement is perhaps the most ancient of reactions. Reasons have been given in S. 9/1 and 9/4 suggesting that adaptation by step-functions is as old as protoplasm itself. So the hypothesis that neurons are amoeboid assumes only that they have never lost their original property. It seems possible, therefore, that step-functions might be provided in this way.

10/4. A variable which can take only the two values ' all ' or ' nothing ' obviously provides a step-function It may not always conform to the definition of a step-function, for its change is not always sustained ; but such variables may well provide changes

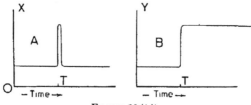

FIGURE 10/4/1.

which appear elsewhere in step-function form. Such would happen, for instance, if the change of the variable X (Figure 10/4/1 A) resulted in some accumulative change Y, which would vary as in B. Variables like X could therefore readily yield step-functions.

10/5. Step-functions could also be provided by groups of neurons acting as a whole.

Lorente de Nó has provided abundant histological evidence that neurons form not only chains but circuits. Figure 10/5/1 is taken from one of his papers. Such circuits are so common that he has enunciated a 'Law of Reciprocity of Connexions': 'if a cell-complex A sends fibres to cell or cell-complex B, then B also sends fibres to A, either direct or by means of one internuncial neuron'.

A simple circuit, if excited, would tend either to sink back to zero excitation, if the amplification-factor was less than unity, or to rise to maximal excitation if it was greater than unity. Such a circuit tends to maintain only two degrees of activity:

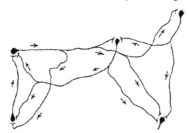

FIGURE 10/5/1 : Neurons and their connections in the trigeminal reflex arc   (Semi-diagrammatic , from Lorente de Nó.)

the inactive and the maximal. Its activity will therefore be of step-function form if the time taken by the chain to build up to maximal excitation can be neglected. Its critical states would be the smallest excitation capable of starting it to full activity, and the smallest inhibition capable of stopping it. McCulloch has referred to such circuits as 'endromes' and has studied some of their properties. The reader will notice that the 'endrome' exemplifies the principle of S. 7/4.

10/6. The definition of the ultrastable system might suggest that an almost infinite number of step-functions is necessary if the system is not to keep repeating itself; and the reader may wonder whether the nervous system can supply so large a number. In fact the number required is not large. The reason can be shown most simply by a numerical illustration.

If a step-function can take two values it can provide two fields for the main variables (Figure 7/8/1). If another step-function with two values is added, the total combinations of value are four, and each combination will, in general, produce its own field (S. 21/1). So if there are n step-functions, each capable of taking two values, the total number of fields available will be 2^n. This number would have to be lessened in practical cases for practical reasons, but even if it is only approximate, it still illustrates the main fact · the number of fields is moderate when n is moderate, but rapidly becomes exceedingly large when n increases. Ten step-functions, for instance, will provide over a thousand fields, while twenty step-functions will provide over a million. The number of fields soon becomes astronomic.

The following imaginary example emphasizes the relation between the number of fields and the number of step-functions necessary to provide them. If a man used fields at the rate of ten a second day and night during his whole life of seventy years, and if no field was ever repeated, how many two-valued step-functions would be necessary to provide them? Would the reader like to guess? The answer is that thirty-five would be ample! Quantitatively, of course, the calculation is useless; but it shows clearly that the number of step-functions can be far less than the number of fields provided. So if the human nervous system produces a very large number of fields, we need not deduce that it must have a very large number of step-functions.

REFERENCES

CAREY, E J , MASSOPUST, L C , ZEIT, W., HAUSHALTER, E., and SCHMITZ, J. Studies of ameboid motion and secretion of motor end plates : V, Experimental pathologic effects of traumatic shock on motor end plates in skeletal muscle *Journal of Neuropathology and experimental Neurology,* **4,** 134 ; 1945.

HARRISON, R G Observations on the living developing nerve fiber *Proceedings of the Society for Experimental Biology and Medicine,* **4,** 140 ; 1906–7.

LEVI. G Ricerche sperimentali sovra elementi nervosi sviluppati ' in vitro '. *Archiv fur experimentelle Zellforschung,* **2,** 244 , 1925–6

LORENTE DE NÓ, R. Vestibulo-ocular reflex arc. *Archives of Neurology and Psychiatry,* **30,** 245 ; 1933.

McCULLOCH, W S A heterarchy of values determined by the topology of nervous nets *Bulletin of mathematical Biophysics,* **7,** 89 ; 1945.

SPEIDEL, C. C. Studies of living nerves ; activities of ameboid growth cones, sheath cells, and myelin segments as revealed by prolonged observation of individual nerve fibers in frog tadpoles. *American Journal of Anatomy,* **52,** 1 ; 1933

Idem. Studies of living nerves ; VI, Effects of metrazol on tissues of frog tadpoles with special reference to the injury and recovery of individual nerve fibers. *Proceedings of the American Philosophical Society,* **83,** 349 ; 1940.

CHAPTER 11

Fully Connected Systems

11/1. In the preceding chapters all major criticisms were postponed . the time has now come to admit that the simple ultrastable system, as represented by, say, the homeostat, is by no means infallible in its attempts at adaptation.

But before we conclude that its failures condemn it, we must be clear about our aim. The designer of a new giant calculating machine and we in this book might both be described as trying to design a ' mechanical brain '. But the aims of the two designers are very different. The designer of the calculator wants something that will carry out a task of specified type, and he usually wants it to do the work *better* than the living brain can do it. Whether the machine uses methods anything like those used by the living brain is to him a side-issue. My aim, on the other hand, is simply to copy the living brain. In particular, if the living brain fails in certain characteristic ways, then I want my artificial brain to fail too ; for such failure would be valid evidence that the model was a true copy. With this in mind, it will be found that some of the ultrastable system's failures in adaptation occur in situations that are well known to be just those in which living organisms also are apt to fail.

(1) If an ultrastable system's critical surfaces are not disposed in proper relation to the limits of the essential variables (S. 9/1), the system may seek an inappropriate goal or may fail to take corrective action when the essential variables are dangerously near their limits.

In animals, though we cannot yet say much about their critical states, we can observe failures of adaptation that may well be due to a defect of this type. Thus, though animals usually react defensively to poisons like strychnine—for it has an intensely bitter taste, stimulates the taste buds strongly, and is spat out —they are characteristically defenceless against a tasteless or odourless poison : precisely because it stimulates no nerve-fibre excessively and causes no deviation from the routine of chewing and swallowing.

An even more dramatic example, showing how defenceless is the living organism if pain has not its normal effect of causing behaviour to change, is given by those children who congenitally lack the normal self-protective reflexes. Boyd and Nie have recently described such a case : a girl, aged 7, who seemed healthy and normal in all respects except that she was quite insensitive to pain. Even before she was a year old her parents noticed that she did not cry when injured. At one year of age her arm was noticed to be crooked : X-rays showed a recent fracture-dislocation The child had made no complaint, nor did she show any sign of pain when the fragments were re-set without an anaesthetic. Three months later the same injury occurred to her right elbow. At the seaside she crawled on the rocks until her hands and knees were torn and denuded of skin. At home her mother on several occasions smelt burning flesh and found the child leaning unconcernedly against the hot stove.

It seems, then, that if an imperfectly formed ultrastable system is, under certain conditions, defenceless, so may be an imperfectly formed living organism.

(2) Even if the ultrastable system is suitably arranged—if the critical states are encountered before the essential variables reach their extreme limits—it usually cannot adapt to an environment that behaves with sudden discontinuities In the earlier examples of the homeostat's successful adaptations the actions were always arranged to be continuous ; but suppose the homeostat had controlled a relay which was usually unchanging but which, if the homeostat passed through some arbitrarily selected state, would suddenly release a powerful spring that would drag the magnets away from their ' optimal ' central positions : the homeostat, if it happened to approach the special state, would take no step to avoid it and would blindly evoke the 'lethal' action. The homeostat's method for achieving adaptation is thus essentially useless when its environment contains such 'lethal' discontinuities.

The living organism, however, is also apt to fail with just the same type of environment. The pike that collided with the glass plate while chasing minnows failed at first to avoid collision precisely because of the suddenness of the transition from not seeing clear glass to feeling the impact on its nose. This flaw in the living organism's defences has, in fact, long been known and made use of by the hunter   The stalking cat's movements are such as will maintain as long as possible, for the prey, the appearance of a peaceful landscape, to be changed with the utmost possible suddenness into one of mortal threat   In the whole process the suddenness is essential   Consider too the essential features of any successful trap ; and the necessity, in poisoning vermin, of ensuring that the first dose is lethal.

If, then, the ultrastable system usually fails when attempting to adapt to an environment with sudden discontinuities, so too does the living organism.

(3) Another weakness shown by the ultrastable system's method is that success is dependent on the system's using a suitable period of delay between each trial.   Thus, the system shown in Fig. 8/7/1 must persist in Trial IV long enough for the representative point to get away from the region of the critical states. Both extremes of delay may be fatal : too hurried a change from trial to trial may not allow time for ' success ' to declare itself ; and too prolonged a testing of a wrong trial may allow serious damage to occur.   Up to now I have said nothing of this necessity for delay between one trial and the next, but there is no doubt that it is an essential part of the ultrastable system's method of adaptation.   Thus the homeostat needed a device, not shown in Fig. 8/8/3, for allowing the uniselectors to move only at about every 2–3 seconds.

In animals, little is known scientifically about the optima for such delays.   But there can be little doubt that on many occasions living organisms have missed success either by abandoning a trial too quickly, or by persisting too long with a trial that was actually useless.

The same difficulty, then, seems to confront both ultrastable system and living organism.

(4) If we grade an ultrastable system's environments according to the difficulty they present, we shall find that at the ' easy ' end are those that consist of a few variables, independent of each other, and that at the ' difficult ' end are those that contain many variables richly cross-linked to form a complex whole

The living organism, too, would classify environments in essentially the same way.   Not only does common experience show this, but the construction and use of ' intelligence tests ' has shown in endless ways that the easy problem is the one whose components are few and independent, while the difficult problem is the one with many components that form a complex whole. So when confronted with environments of various ' difficulties ', the ultrastable system and the living organism are likely to fail together.

It seems, then, that the ultrastable system's modes of failure support, rather than discredit, its claim to resemble the living brain.

11/2. Now we can turn to those features in which the simple ultra-stable system, as represented by the homeostat, differs markedly from the brain of the living organism. One obvious difference is shown by the record of Figure 8/8/4, in which the homeostat made four attempts at finding a terminal field. After its first three trials its success was zero; then, after its next trial, its success was complete. The homeostat can show no gradation in success, though this is almost universally observable in the living organism: day by day a puppy becomes steadier on its legs; year by year a child improves its education.

11/3. A second difference is seen in their powers of conservation. If the homeostat adapts to an environment A and then to an environment B, and is then returned to A again, it has no adaptation immediately ready, for its old adaptation was destroyed in the readjustments to B; it does not even start with a tendency to adapt more quickly than before: its second adaptation to A takes place as though its first adaptation had never occurred. This, of course, is not the case in living organisms, except perhaps in the extremely primitive: a child, by learning what two times three is, does not thereby destroy its acquired knowledge of what is two times two.

11/4. Although the homeostat, in adapting to B, usually destroys its adaptation to A, this is not the case necessarily, and we should notice a property. inherent in the ultrastable system, that might enable it to adapt to more than one environment. It will be described partly for its intrinsic interest, as it will be referred to later, and partly to show that it is insufficient to remove the main difficulty.

Let the homeostat be arranged so that it is partly under uni-selector-, and partly under hand-, control. Let it be started so that it works as an ultrastable system. Select a commutator switch, and from time to time reverse its polarity. This reversal provides the system with the equivalent of two environments which alternate. We can now predict that *it will be selective for fields that give adaptation to both environments*. For consider what field can be terminal: a field that is terminal for only one of the parameter-values will be lost when the parameter next changes; but the first field terminal for both will be retained. Figure 11/4/1 illustrates the process. At R_1, R_2, R_3, and R_4 the hand-

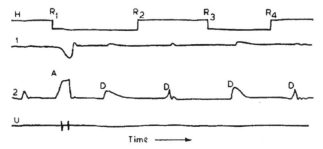

FIGURE 11/4/1 : Record of homeostat's behaviour when a commutator *H* was reversed from time to time (at the *R*'s). The first set of uniselector values which gave stability for both commutator positions was terminal.

controlled commutator *H* was reversed. At first the change of value caused a change of field, shown at *A*. But the second uniselector position happened to provide a field which gave stability with both values of *H*. So afterwards, the changes of *H* no longer caused step-function changes. The responses to the displacements *D*, forced by the operator, show that the system is stable for both values of *H*. The slight but distinct difference in the behaviour after *D* at the two values of *H* show that the two fields are different.

The ultrastable system is, therefore, selective for step-function values which give stability for both values of an alternating parameter.

11/5. Such a process would occur in a biological system if an animal had to adapt by one internal arrangement to two environments which affected the animal alternately. Such alternations do occur. A cat, for instance, must learn to catch mice, which tend to run towards corners, and birds, which tend to fly upwards ; and the diving birds alternate between aerial and submarine environments. Were the bird's nervous system like the homeostat, step-function changes would occur until there arose a set of values giving behaviour suitable to both environments, and this set would then be terminal. That such a set is not impossible is shown by the snake's mode of progression, which is suitable in both undergrowth and water.

11/6. But it is easily seen that the process cannot answer the problems of this chapter. First, the process shows, contrary to requirement, no gradation . when there occurs a set of step-function values terminal for both environments, the animal becomes adapted ; prior to that it was unadapted. The second reason is that any extensive adaptation in this way is very improbable.

This brings us to the most serious of the difficulties. A successful trial, or a terminal field, is useful for adaptation only if it occurs within some reasonable time : success at the millionth trial is equivalent to failure. Consequently, the principle of ultrastability, while it guarantees that a field of a certain type will be retained, guarantees much less than it seems to. If the delay in reaching success were slight, a general increase in the system's velocity of action might give sufficient compensation ; but in fact the delay is likely to exceed the utmost possible compensation. For definiteness, take a numerical example. Suppose that in some ultrastable system each field has a one in ten chance of being stable with any given environment, and that the chances are independent. Then the chance of a field being stable to two environments will be one in a hundred, and to N environments will be one in 10^N. The time that a system takes on the average to find a stable field is proportional to the reciprocal of the probability (S. 23/2). Suppose that when $N = 1$ the average time t taken to find a terminal field is 1 second, then

$$t = \frac{1}{10}10^N \text{ seconds}$$

Try the effect of different values of N. Three environments will require about a minute and a half. This might be tolerable.

But if N is twenty the time becomes 3,200,000,000 centuries, which for our purpose, is equivalent to 'never'. Other examples, though quantitatively different, would lead to the same general conclusion · when the number of environments is more than a few, the time taken by this method to find a field stable to all exceeds the allowable. Evidently our brains do not use this method : success by it is too improbable.

11/7. In the previous section we regarded the animal as having to adapt to a variety of environments, but we can also regard them as constituting a single ' total ' environment. This makes the number of variables in the system increase. What will be the effect of this increase on the time taken to find a terminal field ? For instance, could the homeostat adapt if it consisted of a hundred units instead of four ? The question cannot be ignored, for the human brain contains about 10,000,000,000 nerve-cells, and to this we must add the number of variables in its environment. What is the chance that a field should be terminal when it occurs in a system with this number of variables ?

If the system worked as a magnified homeostat then, although exact calculation is impossible, the evidence, reviewed in S. 20/12, is sufficient to show that, for practical purposes, there is no chance at all. If we were like homeostats, waiting till one field gave us, at a stroke, all our adult adaptation, we would wait for ever But the infant does not wait for ever , on the contrary, the probability that he will develop a full adult adaptation within twenty years is near to unity. Some extra factor must therefore be added if the large ultrastable system is to get adapted within a reasonable time.

11/8. It may seem that we have now proved that the whole solution must be wrong. But if we re-trace the argument, we find that to some extent the difficulty has been unnecessarily magnified. From S. 8/6 onwards we assumed for convenience of discussion that every main variable was in full dynamic interaction with every other main variable, so that every change in every variable at once affected every other variable This gives a system that is extremely active and that unquestionably acts as a whole, not as a collection of small parts acting independently. As an introduction it has distinct advantages, but it raises its own difficulties.

Our present difficulties are, in fact, largely due to this assumption. By modifying it we shall not only lessen the difficulties but we shall obtain a model more like the real brain.

The views held about the amount of internal connection in the nervous system—its degree of ' wholeness '—have tended to range from one extreme to the other. The ' reflexologists ' from Bell onwards recognised that in some of its activities the nervous system could be treated as a collection of independent parts. They pointed to the fact, for instance, that the pupillary reflex to light and the patellar reflex occur in their usual forms whether the other reflex is being elicited or not. The coughing reflex follows the same pattern whether the subject is standing or sitting   And the acquirement of a new conditioned reflex might leave a previously established reflex largely unaffected. On the other hand, the Gestalt school recognised that many activities of the nervous system were characterised by wholeness, so that what happened at one point was related to what was happening at other points. The two sets of facts were sometimes treated as irreconcilable

Yet Sherrington in 1906 had shown by the spinal reflexes that the nervous system was neither divided into permanently separated parts nor so wholly joined that every event always influenced every other. Rather, it showed a richer, and a more intricate picture—one in which interactions and independencies fluctuated. ' Thus, a weak reflex may be excited from the tail of the spinal dog without interference with the stepping-reflex '. . . . ' Two reflexes may be neutral to each other when both are weak, but may interfere when either or both are strong '. . . . ' But to show that reflexes may be neutral to each other in a spinal dog is not evidence that they will be neutral in the animal with its whole nervous system intact and unmutilated.' The separation into many parts and the union into a single whole are simply the two extremes on the scale of ' degree of connectedness '.

Being chiefly concerned with the origin of adaptation and co-ordination, I have tended so far to stress the connectedness of the nervous system. Yet it must not be overlooked that adaptation demands independence as well as interaction. The learner-driver of a motor-car, for instance, who can only just keep the car in the centre of the road, may find that any attempt at changing gear results in the car, apparently, trying to mount the pavement.   Later, when he is more skilled, the act of changing gear will have no effect on the direction of the car's travel   Adaptation thus demands not only the integration of related activities but the independence of unrelated activities.

We now, therefore, no longer maintain the restriction of S. 8/6 : from now on the main variables may be of any type : full-, part-, step-, or null-functions.   This freedom makes possible new types of ultrastable system, systems still ultrastable and still selective for stable fields, but no longer necessarily fully inter-connected internally.   In particular, if many of the main variables are part-functions, the system is able to avoid the earlier-mentioned difficulty in getting adapted ; it does this by developing partial, fluctuating, and temporary independencies within the whole without losing its essential wholeness.   The study of such systems will occupy the remainder of the book.

REFERENCES

BOYD, D. A., and NIE, L. W.   Congenital universal indifference to pain   *Archives of Neurology and Psychiatry*, **61**, 402 , 1949
SHERRINGTON, C. S.   *The integrative action of the nervous system.*   New Haven, 1906.

CHAPTER 12

Iterated Systems

12/1. WHEREAS in the previous chapters we studied a system whose main variables were all in intimate connection with one another, so that a disturbance applied to any one immediately disturbed all the others, we shall now study, for contrast, a system composed of the same number of main variables but divided into many parts. Each part is assumed to be wholly separated from the other parts, and to contain only a few main variables. The diagram of immediate effects might appear as in Figure 12/1/1 which shows, at A, what we have considered in Chapters 8–11, and at B what we shall be considering in this chapter. (For simplicity, the diagram shows lines instead of arrows.)

A 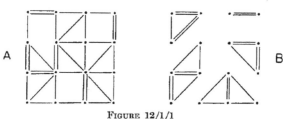 B

FIGURE 12/1/1

As before, it is assumed that each of the five systems in B consists partly of variables belonging to the animal and partly of variables belonging to the environment. The relation between animal and environment is shown more clearly in Figure 12/1/2.

Environment

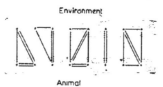

Animal

FIGURE 12/1/2 Diagrammatic representation of an animal of eight main variables interacting with its environment as five independent systems.

139

Such an arrangement would be shown by any organism that reacted to its environment by several independent reactions. In such an arrangement each system, still assumed to be ultrastable, can change its own step-functions and find its own terminal field without effect on what is happening in the others. We shall say that the whole consists of **iterated** ultrastable systems

Since each system is ultrastable it can adapt and learn independently of the others That such independent, localised learning can occur within one animal was shown by Parker in the following experiment :

> ' If a sea-anemone is fed from one side of its mouth, it will take in, by means of the tentacles on that side, one fragment of food after another If now bits of food be alternated with bits of filter paper soaked in meat juice, the two materials will be accepted indiscriminately for some eight or ten trials, after which only the meat will be taken and the filter paper will be discharged into the sea water without being brought to the mouth. If, after having developed this state of affairs on one side of the mouth, the experiment is now transferred to the opposite side, both the filter paper and the meat will again be taken in till this side has also been brought to a state of discriminating.'

12/2. If we start a set of iterated ultrastable systems, and observe the set's behaviour, noting particularly at each moment how many of the systems have arrived at a terminal field, we shall find that the set, regarded as a whole, shows the following properties.

The proportion which is adapted is no longer restricted to the two values ' all ' or ' none '. In fact, if the systems are many, the degrees of adaptation which the whole can show will be as many. A whole which consists of iterated systems will therefore show in its adaptation a *gradation* which was seen (S. 11/2) to be lacking in the fully-connected ultrastable system.

A second property is that when one system has arrived at a terminal field, the changes of the other systems will not cause the loss of the first field. In other words, while the later adaptations are being found, the earlier are conserved. A whole which consists of iterated systems will therefore show some *conservation* of adaptations.

A third property is that, as time passes, the number of systems which are adapted will increase, or may stay constant, but cannot decrease (in the conditions assumed here : more complex conditions are discussed later). If the number of stable systems is regarded as measuring, in a sense, the degree of adaptation achieved by the whole, then, in a whole which consists of iterated systems, the degree of adaptation tends always to increase. The whole will therefore show a *progression* in adaptation.

12/3. Let us now compare the two types of system, (*a*) the fully connected, and (*b*) the iterated, in the times they take, on the average, to reach terminal fields, other things, including the number of main variables, being equal. (The calculation can only be approximate but the general conclusion is unambiguous.)

We start with a system of N main variables and want to find, approximately, how long the system will take on the average to reach the condition where all N main variables belong to systems with stable fields. Three arrangements will be examined ; they are extreme in type, but they illustrate the possibilities. (1) All the N main variables belong to one system, so that to stabilise all N a field must stabilise all simultaneously. (2) Each main variable is in a system which includes it alone, and where the systems are related in such a way that only after the first is stabilised can the second start to get stabilised, and so on in succession. (3) Each system, also containing only one main variable, proceeds independently to find its own stability.

In order to calculate how long the three types will take, suppose for simplicity that each main variable has a constant and independent probability p of becoming stable in each second.

The type in which stability can occur only when all the N events are favourable simultaneously will have to wait on the average for a time given by $T_1 = \dfrac{1}{p^N}$. The type in which stability can occur only by the variables achieving stability in succession will have to wait on the average for a time given by $T_2 = N/p$. And the type in which the variables proceed independently to stability will have to wait on the average for a time which is difficult to specify but which will be of the order of $T_3 = 1/p$. These three estimates of the time taken are of interest, not for their quantitative exactness, but for the fact that they tend to have widely different values. Some numerical values will be calculated in order to demonstrate the differences. The values have not been specially selected, and if the reader will substitute some values of his own he will probably find that his values lead to essentially the same conclusions as are reached here.

Suppose that the chance of any one variable becoming stable in a given second is a half. If we are testing a system with a thousand variables, then $N = 1000$

and
$$T_1 = 2^{1000} \text{ secs.}$$
$$T_2 = \frac{1000}{2} \text{ secs.}$$
$$T_3 = \text{about } \tfrac{1}{2} \text{ sec.}$$

When these are converted to more ordinary numbers, we find that the three quantities differ widely. T_3 is about a half-second, T_2 is about 8 minutes, and T_1 is about 3×10^{291} centuries. The last number, if written in full, would consist of a 3 followed by about five lines of zeros. T_3 and T_2 are moderate, but T_1 is so vast as to be outside even astronomical duration.

This example is typical. What it means in general is that when N is large, it is not possible to get stability if all N must find some favourable feature simultaneously. The calculation confirms the statement of S. 11/7 that it is not reasonable to assume that 10^{10} neurons have formed a stable field by waiting for the fortuitous occurrence of one field which stabilises all.

12/4. The argument may also be viewed from a different angle. When the system of a thousand variables could achieve stability only by the occurrence of a field which was favourable to all at once, it had to wait, on the average, through 3×10^{291} centuries. But if its conditions were changed so that the variables could become stable in succession or independently, then the time taken dropped to a few minutes or less. In other words, what was, for all practical purposes, an impossibility under the first condition became, under the second and third conditions, a ready possibility.

It is difficult to find a real example which shows in one system the three ways of progression to stability, for few systems are constructed so flexibly. It is, however, possible to construct, by the theory of probability, examples which show the differences referred to. Thus suppose that, as the traffic passes, we note the final digit on each car's number-plate, and decide that we want to see cars go past with the final digits 0, 1, 2, 3, 4, 5, 6, 7, 8, 9, in that order. If we insist that the ten cars shall pass consecutively, then on the average we shall have to wait till about 10,000,000,000 cars have passed · for practical purposes such an event is impossible. But if we allow success to be achieved by first finding a ' 0 ', then finding a ' 1 ', and so on until a ' 9 ' is seen, then the number of cars which must pass will be about fifty, and this number makes ' success ' easily achievable.

12/5. A well-known physical example illustrating the difference is the crystallisation of a solid from solution. When in solution, the molecules of the solute move at random so that in any given interval of time there is a definite probability that a given molecule will possess a motion and position suitable for its adherence to the crystal. Now the smallest visible crystal contains billions of molecules : if a visible crystal could form only when all its molecules happened simultaneously to be properly related in position and motion to one another, then crystallisation could never occur : it would be too improbable. But in fact crystallisation can occur by succession, for once a crystal has begun to form, a single molecule which happens to possess the right position and motion can join the crystal regardless of the positions and motions of the other molecules in the solution. So the crystallisation can proceed by stages, and the time taken resembles T_2 rather than T_1

We may draw, then, the following conclusion. *A compound event that is impossible if the components have to occur simultaneously may be readily achievable if they can occur in sequence or independently.*

REFERENCE

PARKER, G. *The evolution of man* New Haven, 1922.

143

CHAPTER 13

Disturbed Systems and Habituation

13/1. WE have seen that ultrastable systems are subject to two conflicting requirements . complexity and speed. The system with abundant internal connections, though able to represent a complex and well-integrated organism and environment, requires, at least in the form so far studied, almost unlimited time for its adaptation. On the other hand, the same number of main variables, divided into many independent parts, achieves adaptation quickly, but cannot represent a complex biological system. There are, however, intermediate forms that can combine, to some extent, the advantages of these two extremes. Since the properties of the intermediate forms are somewhat subtle we shall have to proceed by small steps. As a first step I shall examine in this chapter the properties of ultrastable systems that are no longer completely isolated, as has been assumed so far, but are subject to some slight disturbance from the outside.

13/2. Before entering the subject, I must make clear a point of method that will be used frequently. In Chapter 8, the discussion of the ultrastable system necessarily paid so much attention to the process by which the terminal field was reached that some loss of proportion occurred; for the focusing of attention suggested that the system spent most of its time reaching a terminal field, whereas in the living organism this process may occupy only a few moments—a time unimportant in comparison with the remainder of the organism's life during which the terminal field will act repeatedly to keep the essential variables within limits.

From this point of view the terminal field is more important than the preceding fields simply because it is permanent while the others are transient. As we increase the time over which the system is observed, so do the transient fields become negligible. The same principle is used in the Darwinian theory of natural

144

selection where, although it is recognised that mutations and re-combinations of defective viability can occur, yet as the processes of evolution are viewed over an increasing range of time, so do these defectively adapted individuals sink into insignificance. Statistical mechanics, too, uses the same principle, for it excludes an event by proving that its occurrence is not impossible but infrequent. Sometimes we shall not be able to distinguish even the transient from the permanent, but only the lesser from the greater persistence. Nevertheless, the distinction may be important, especially if the small difference acts repeatedly and cumulatively; for what is feeble on a single action may be overwhelming on incessant repetition.

It will be suggested later (S. 16/6) that the animal's behaviour depends not on one system but on many, so that what counts is not the peculiarity of one particular field but the average properties of many. In the discussion we shall therefore notice the average properties and the tendencies rather than the individual peculiarities of the various fields.

Effects of small random disturbances

13/3. A disturbance may affect variables or parameters. If it affects the variables, the system will undergo a sudden change of state; in the phase-space the representative point would be displaced suddenly from one line of behaviour to another. If it affects a parameter, there will occur a sudden change of field: the representative point will be affected only mediately.

13/4. We shall now examine the effect on an ultrastable system of small, occasional, and random disturbances applied to the variables. I assume at first that the displacements are distributed in all directions in the phase-space.

A displacement may make the representative point meet a critical state it would not otherwise have met; then the displacement destroys the field. The three fields of Figure 13/4/1 show some of the consequences. In fields A and C the undisturbed representative points will go to, and remain at, the resting states. When they are there, a leftwards displacement sufficient to cause the representative point of A to encounter the critical states may be insufficient if applied to C; so C's field may survive

145

a displacement that destroyed A's. Similarly a displacement applied to the representative point on the resting cycle in B is more likely to change the field than if applied to C. A field like C, therefore, with its resting states compact and near the centre of the region, tends to have a higher immunity to displacement than fields whose resting states or cycles go near the edge of the

FIGURE 13/4/1 : Three fields of an ultrastable system, differing in their liability to change when the system is subjected to small random disturbances. (The critical states are shown by the dots.)

region. (A quantitative discussion of the tendency is given in S. 23/4.)

If the disturbances fall on a large number of iterated ultrastable systems, the probabilities become actual frequencies We can then predict that if iterated ultrastable systems are subjected to repeated small occasional and random disturbances, the average terminal field will tend to the form C.

13/5. How would this tendency show itself in the behaviour of the living organism ?

In S. 8/7 we noticed that a field may be terminal and yet show all sorts of bizarre features : cycles, resting states near the edge of the region, stable and unstable lines mixed, multiple resting states, multiple resting cycles, and so on. These possibilities obscured the relation between a field's being terminal and its being suitable for keeping essential variables within normal limits. But a detailed study was not necessary ; for we have just seen that all such bizarre fields tend selectively to be destroyed when the system is subjected to small, occasional, and random disturbances. Since such disturbances are inseparable from practical existence, the process of ' roughing it ' tends to cause their replacement by fields of 'normal' stability (S. 20/2) that look like C of Figure 13/4/1 and act simply to keep the representative point well away from the critical states.

Effects of repeated stimuli

13/6. So far we have studied only the effects of irregular disturbances : what of the regular ? By the argument of S. 6/6, all such can be considered as 'stimuli' and are of two types : a sudden change of parameter-value, and a sudden jump of the representative point. The two types will be considered separately.

The effect on an ultrastable system of an alternation of a parameter between two values has already been described in S. 11/4, where Figure 11/4/1 showed how the ultrastable system is automatically selective for any set of step-function values which gives stability with both the parameter-values

The facts can also be seen from another point of view. If we start alternating the parameter and observe the response of the step-functions we shall find that at first they change, and that after a time they stop changing. The responses, in other words, diminish.

13/7. Next consider the effect of repetitions of the other type of stimulus—the displacement of the representative point. Its effect can readily be found by asking what sort of field can be terminal. Suppose, for instance, that the displacement was a movement to the left through the distance shown by the arrow below Figure 13/7/1. It is easy to see that a field, to be terminal in spite of this displacement, must have its resting state within B. If the constant displacement is applied from time to time to an ultrastable system whose fields have resting states distributed over both A and B, then terminal fields with resting

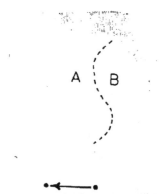

FIGURE 13/7/1 : Region of an ultrastable system The representative point must stay in B if the field is to be immune to a displacement equal and parallel to that shown by the arrow

147

state in A will be destroyed; but the first with resting state in B will be retained. The displacement will then stop causing step-function changes. So if we regard the application of the constant displacement as 'stimulus', and the step-function and main-variable changes as 'response', then we shall find that the response to the stimulus tends to diminish

13/8. This particular process cannot be shown on the homeostat, for its resting state is always at the centre, but it will demonstrate a related fact. If two fields (Figure 13/8/1) each have a

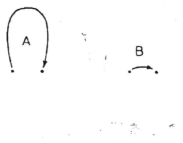

FIGURE 13/8/1.

resting state at the centre and the line of one (A) from a constant displacement returns by a long loop meeting critical states while the return path of the other (B) is more direct, then the application of the displacement will destroy A but not B. In other words, a set of step-function values which gives a large amplitude of main-variable movement after a constant displacement is more likely to be replaced than a set which gives only a small amplitude.

The process is shown in Figure 13/8/2. Two units were joined $1 \rightarrow 2$. The effect of 1 on 2 was determined by 2's uniselector, which changed position if 2 exceeded its critical states. The operator then repeatedly disturbed 2 by moving 1, at D. As often as the uniselector transmitted a large effect to 2, so often did 2 shift its uniselector. But as soon as the uniselector arrived at a position that gave a transmission insufficient to bring 2 to its critical states, that position was retained. So under constant stimulation by D the amplitude of 2's response tended to diminish.

The same process in a more complex form is shown in Figure

13/8/3. Two units are interacting : $1 \rightleftarrows 2$. Both effects go through the uniselectors, so the whole is ultrastable. At each D, the operator displaced 1's magnet through a constant distance. On the first 'stimulation', 2's response brought the system to its critical states, so the ultrastability found a new terminal

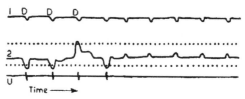

FIGURE 13/8/2 : Homeostat tracing. At each D, 1's magnet is displaced by the operator through a fixed angle. 2 receives this action through its uniselector. When the uniselector's value makes 2's magnet meet the critical states (shown dotted) the value is changed. After the fourth change the value causes only a small movement of 2, so the value is retained permanently.

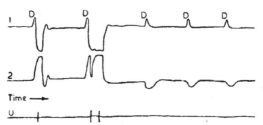

FIGURE 13/8/3 : Homeostat arranged as ultrastable system with two units interacting. At each D the operator moved 1's magnet through a fixed angle. The first field such that D does not cause a critical state to be met is retained permanently.

field. The second stimulation again evoked the process. But the new terminal field was such that the displacement D no longer caused 2 to reach its critical states ; so this field was retained. Again under constant stimulation the response had diminished.

13/9. For completeness we will now consider the effects of these disturbances in combination. The combination of repeated constant displacements with small random disturbances yields little of interest. But the combination of an alternation of parameter-value with small random disturbances is worth notice.

From S 11/4 it is known that the alternation of a parameter
p between two values, p' and p'', will result in the emergence of
two stable fields. We might get a pair like A and B of Figure
13/9/1. As the parameter p alternates between p' and p'', so

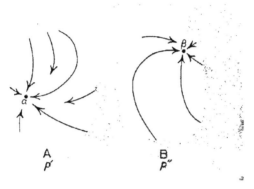

FIGURE 13/9/1 : Two possible terminal fields . A, when p has the value p'
and B, when it has the value p''. (Critical states shown as dots)

FIGURE 13/9/2 · When the parameter is constant at p', the representative
point will follow the path from β to α, when at p'' the point follows
the path from α to β

will the field of the system's main variables alternate between
A and B. If p alternates slowly in comparison with the movement of the representative point, the point will follow the circuit
of Figure 13/9/2, going from α to β when p is changed from
p' to p'', and returning to α when p is returned to p'.

Suppose now that small random disturbances are applied to

two such systems (C and D) with circuits such as are shown in Figure 13/9/3. We can predict (by S. 13/4) that a system of type D, with a short and central circuit, will have a higher immunity to random disturbance than a system of type C. Maximal immunity will be shown by systems in which α and β coalesce at the centre of the region.

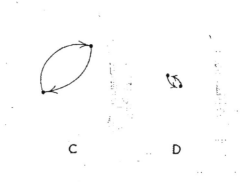

C   D

FIGURE 13/9/3.

If there are many systems like C and D, the probabilities become actual frequencies. As the less resistant fields are destroyed while the more resistant remain, the average movement of the representative point, as the parameter is alternated between p' and p'', will change from a large circuit like C towards a small central circuit like D. So both the number of step-function changes and the range of movement evoked by the stimulus p will diminish.

Habituation

13/10. Some uniformity is now discernible in the responses of an ultrastable system to repeated stimuli. There is a tendency for the response, whether measured by the number of step-functions changing or by the range of movement of the main variables, to diminish. The diminution is not due to any triviality of definition or to any peculiarity of the homeostat : it follows from the basic fact, inseparable from any delicate or ultrastable system, that large responses tend, if there is feedback, to destroy the conditions that made them large, while small responses do not destroy the conditions that made them small.

13/11. In animal behaviour the phenomenon of ' habituation ' is met with frequently : if an animal is subjected to repeated stimuli, the response evoked tends to diminish. The change has been considered by some to be the simplest form of learning. Neuronic mechanisms are not necessary, for the Protozoa show it clearly :

> ' *Amoebae* react negatively to tap water or to water from a foreign culture, but after transference to such water they behave normally.'
> ' If *Paramecium* is dropped into $\frac{1}{2}\%$ sodium chloride it at once gives the avoiding reaction . . . If the stimulating agent is not so powerful as to be directly destructive, the reaction ceases after a time, and the *Paramecia* swim about within the solution as they did before in water.' (Jennings.)

Fatigue has sometimes been suggested as the cause of the phenomenon, but in Humphrey's experiments it could be excluded. He worked with the snail, and used the fact that if its support is tapped the snail withdraws into its shell. If the taps are repeated at short intervals the snail no longer reacts. He found that when the taps were light, habituation appeared early ; but when they were heavy, it was postponed indefinitely. This is the opposite of what would be expected from fatigue, which should follow more rapidly when the heavier taps caused more vigorous withdrawals.

The nature of habituation has been obscure, and no explanation has yet received general approval. The results of this chapter suggest that it is simply a consequence of the organism's ultra-stability, a by-product of its method of adaptation.

REFERENCE

Humphrey, G   *The nature of learning.* London, 1933.

CHAPTER 14

Constancy and Independence

14/1. SEVERAL times we have used, without definition, the concept of one variable or system being ' independent ' of another. It was stated that a system, to be absolute, must be ' properly isolated '; some parameters in S. 6/2 were described as ' ineffective '; and iterated ultrastable systems were defined as ' wholly independent ' of each other. So far a simple understanding has been adequate. But as it is now intended to treat of systems that are neither wholly joined nor wholly separated, a more rigorous method is necessary.

The concept of the ' independence ' of two dynamic systems might at first seem simple : is not a lack of material connection sufficient ? Examples soon show that this criterion is unreliable. Two electrical parts may be in firm mechanical union, yet if the bond is an insulator the two parts may be functionally independent. And two reflex mechanisms in the spinal cord may be inextricably interwoven, and yet be functionally independent.

On the other hand, one system may have no material connection with another and yet be affected by it markedly : the radio receiver, for instance, in its relation to the transmitter. Even the widest separation we can conceive—the distance between our planet and the most distant nebulae—is no guarantee of functional separation, for the light emitted by those nebulae is yet capable of stirring the astronomers of this planet into controversy. The criterion of connection or separation is thus useless.

14/2. This attempted criterion obtained its data by a direct examination of the real ' machine '. The examination not only failed in its object but violated the rule of S. 2/8. What we need is a test that uses only information obtained by primary operations.

It is convenient to approach the subject by first clarifying what we mean by one system ' controlling ' or ' affecting ' another.

Our understanding has been greatly increased by the development during recent years of the science of ' cybernetics '. The word—from κυβερνήτης, a steersman—was coined by Professor Wiener to describe the science which, though really dating back to Watt and his governor for steam-engines, has developed partly as a result of the extraordinary properties of the thermionic vacuum tube, and partly as a result of the urgent demands during the last war for complex calculating and controlling machinery such as predictors for gun- and bomb-sights, automatically controlled searchlights, automatically controlled anti-aircraft guns, and electronic computors.

When a radar-installation passes information about the position of an aeroplane to a predictor, and the predictor emits instructions which determine, either manually or automatically, the laying of an anti-aircraft gun, we can write simply enough :—

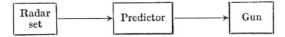

but what do the arrows mean ? what is transmitted from box to box ? Energy ? No, says cybernetics—information.

If we turn to simple machines for guidance, we will probably be misled. When my finger strikes the key of a typewriter, the movement of my finger determines the movement of the type ; and the finger also supplies the energy necessary for the type's movement. The diagram

would state, in this case, both that energy, measurable in ergs, is transmitted from A to B, and also that the behaviour of B is determined by, or predictable from, that of A. If, however, power is freely available to B, the transmission of energy from A to B becomes irrelevant to the question of the control exerted. It is easy, in fact, to devise a mechanism in which the flow of both energy and matter is from B to A and yet the control is exerted by A over B. Thus, suppose B contains a compressor which pumps air at a constant rate into a cylinder creating a pressure that is shown on a dial. From the cylinder a pipe goes to A, where there is a tap which can allow air to escape and can cause the pressure in the cylinder to fall. Now suppose a stranger comes along; he knows nothing of the internal mechanism, but tests the relations between the two variables: A, the position of the tap, and B, the reading on the dial. By direct testing he soon finds that A controls B, but that B has no effect on A. The direction of control has thus no necessary relation to the direction of flow of either energy or matter when the system is such that all parts are supplied freely with energy.

14/3. The factual content of the concept of one variable 'controlling' another is now clear. A 'controls' B if B's behaviour depends on A, while A's does not depend on B. But first we need a definition of 'independence'. *Given a system that includes two variables A and B, and two lines of behaviour whose initial states differ only in the values of B, A is* **independent** *of B if A's behaviours on the two lines are identical.* The definition can be illustrated on the data in Table 14/3/1. On the two lines of

		Variable	Time				
			0	1	2	3	4
Line	1	A	12	19	33	49	55
		B	46	39	31	21	14
		C	18	22	28	37	47
	2	A	12	19	33	49	55
		B	25	18	12	7	4
		C	18	21	20	17	5

TABLE 14/3/1. Two lines of behaviour of a three-variable absolute system.

behaviour the initial states are equal except for the values of B. The subsequent behaviours of A on the two lines are identical. So A is independent of B. (Independence within the range covered by the table in no way restricts what may happen outside it.) By the definition, C is not independent of B.

By 'dependent' will be meant simply 'not independent'.

The definition is given primarily by reference to two lines of behaviour, for only in this form is the result of the criterion always unambiguous. Other criteria might be confused by some of the fields that ingenuity can construct. But often a simple uniformity holds. Two variables may be independent over all such pairs of initial states; and sometimes all variables of one set may be independent of all variables of another set : *a system R is* **independent** *of a system S if every variable in R is independent of every variable in S, all possible pairs being considered.* Some region of the field is understood to be given before the test is applied.

14/4. To illustrate the definition's use, and to show that its answers accord with common experience, here are some examples.

If a bacteriologist wishes to test whether the growth of a micro-organism is affected by a chemical substance, he prepares two tubes of nutrient medium containing the chemical in different concentrations but with all other constituents equal; he seeds them with equal numbers of organisms; and he observes how the increasing numbers of organisms compare in the two tubes from hour to hour. Thus he is observing the numbers of organisms after two initial states that differed only in the concentrations of chemical.

To test whether an absolute system is dependent on a parameter, i.e. to test whether the parameter is 'effective ', we observe the system's behaviour on two occasions when the parameter has different values. Thus, to test whether a thermostat is really affected by its regulator one sets the regulator at some value, checks that the temperature is at its usual value, and records the subsequent behaviour of the temperature; then one returns the temperature to its previous value, changes the position of the regulator, and observes again. A change of behaviour implies an effective regulator. (Here we have used the fact that by S. 21/4 we can take a null-function into the system without altering its absoluteness, for the change is only formal.)

Finally, an example from animal behaviour   Parker tested the sea-anemone to see whether the behaviour of a tentacle was independent of its connection with the body.

> 'When small fragments of meat are placed on the tentacles of a sea-anemone, these organs wind around the bits of food and, by bending in the appropriate direction, deliver them to the mouth.'

156

(He has established that the behaviour is regular, and that the system of tentacle-position and food-position is approximately absolute. He has described the line of behaviour following the initial state : tentacle extended, food on tentacle.)

> ' If, now, a distending tentacle on a quiet and expanded sea-anemone is suddenly seized at its base by forceps, cut off and held in position so that its original relations to the animal as a whole can be kept clearly in mind, the tentacle will still be found to respond to food brought in contact with it and will eventually turn toward that side which was originally toward the mouth.'

(He has now described the line of behaviour that follows an initial state identical with the first except that the null-function ' connection with the body ' has a different value. He observed that the two behaviours of the variable ' tentacle-position ' are identical.) He draws the deduction that the tentacle-system is, in this aspect, independent of the body-system :

> ' Thus the tentacle has within itself a complete neuro-muscular mechanism for its own responses.'

The definition, then, agrees with what is usually accepted. Though clumsy in simple cases, it has the advantage in complex cases of providing a clear and precise foundation. By its use the independencies within a system can be proved by primary operations only.

14/5. In an absolute system it is not generally possible to assign the dependencies and independencies arbitrarily. For if x is dependent on y, and y is dependent on z, then x must necessarily be dependent on z. This is evident, for when z's initial state is changed, y's behaviour is changed ; and these changed values of y, acting in an absolute system, will cause x's behaviour to change. So the observer will find that a change in z's initial state is followed by a change in x's behaviour. (A formal proof is given in S. 24/11.)

14/6. We can now see that the method for testing an immediate effect, described in S. 4/12, is simply a test for independence applied when all the variables but two are held constant. The relation can be illustrated by an example. Suppose three real machines are linked so that their diagram of immediate effects is

$$z \longrightarrow y \longrightarrow x.$$

The system's responses to tests for independence will show that y is independent of x, and that z is independent of both. The same set of independencies would be found if we tested the three machines when their linkages were

The distinction appears when we test the immediate effect between z and x. For if in both cases we fix y, we shall find in the first that x is independent of z, but in the second that x is not independent of z.

Given a system's diagram of immediate effects, its **diagram of ultimate effects** is formed by adding to every pair of arrows joined tail to head a third arrow going from tail to head, like $z \longrightarrow x$ above, and by repeating this process until no further additions are possible. Thus, the diagram of immediate effects I in Figure 14/6/1 would yield the diagram of ultimate effects II.

FIGURE 14/6/1.

The diagram of ultimate effects shows directly and completely the independencies in the system. Thus, from II of the figure we see that variable 1 is independent of 2, 3, and 4, and that the latter three are dependent on all the others.

14/7. If, in a system, some of the variables are independent of the remainder, while the remainder are not independent of the first set, then the first set **dominates** the remainder. Thus, in Figure 14/6/1, variable 1 dominates 2, 3, and 4. And in the diagram of S. 6/6 the animal dominates the recorders

The effects of constancy

14/8. So far the independencies have been assumed permanent: we now study the conditions under which they can alter.

Suppose an absolute system of eight variables has the diagram of immediate effects shown in Figure 14/8/1. What properties must the three variables B have if the systems A and C are to become independent and absolute ? The question has not only theoretical but practical importance. Many experiments require that one system be shielded from effects coming from others Thus, a system using magnets may have to be shielded from the effects of the earth's magnetism ; or a thermal system may have to be shielded from the effects of changes in the atmospheric tem-

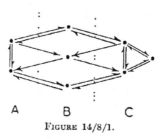

FIGURE 14/8/1.

perature ; or the pressure which drives blood through the kidneys may have to be kept independent of changes in the pulse-rate.

A first suggestion might be that the three variables B should be removed. But this conceptual removal corresponds to no physical reality : the earth's magnetic field, the atmospheric temperature, the pulse-rate cannot be ' removed '. In fact the answer is capable of proof (S. 24/15): *that A and C should be independent and absolute it is necessary and sufficient that the variables B should be null-functions.* In other words, A and C must be separated by a wall of constancies.

14/9. Here are some illustrations to show that the theorem accords with common experience.

(a) If A (of Figure 14/8/1) is a system in which heat-changes are being studied, B the temperatures of the parts of the container, and C the temperatures of the surroundings, then for A to be isolated from C and absolute, it is necessary and sufficient for the B's to be kept constant. (b) Two electrical systems joined by an insulator are independent, if varying slowly, because electrically the insulator is unvarying. (c) The centres in the spinal cord are often made independent of the activities in the brain by a transection of the cord ; but a break in physical con-

tinuity is not necessary : a segment may be poisoned, or anaes-
thetised, or frozen ; what is necessary is that the segment should
be unvarying.

Physical separation, already noticed to give no certain independence, is sometimes effective because it sometimes creates an
intervening region of constancy.

14/10. The example of Figure 14/8/1 showed one way in which
the constancy of a set of variables could affect the independencies
within a system. The range of ways is, however, much greater.

To demonstrate the variety we need a rule by which we can
make the appropriate modifications in the diagram of ultimate
effects when one or more of the variables are held constant. The
rule is proved in S. 24/14 :—Take the diagram of immediate
effects. If a variable V is constant, remove all arrows whose
heads are at V ; then, treating this modified diagram as one of
immediate effects, complete the diagram of ultimate effects, using

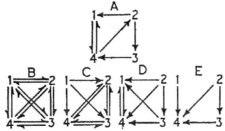

FIGURE 14/10/1 : If a four-variable system has the diagram of immediate
effects A, and if 1 and 2 are part-functions, then its diagram of ultimate
effects will be B, C, D or E as none, 1, 2, or both 1 and 2 become
inactive, respectively.

the rule of S. 14/6. The resulting diagram will be that of the
ultimate effects, and therefore of the independencies, when V is
constant. (It will be noticed that the effect of making V constant
cannot be deduced from the diagram of ultimate effects alone.)
Thus, if the system of Figure 14/10/1 has the diagram of immediate effects A, then the diagram of ultimate effects will be B, C,
D or E according as none, 1, 2, or both 1 and 2 are constant,
respectively.

It can be seen that with only four variables, and with only
two of the four possibly becoming constant, the patterns of

independence show a remarkable variety. Thus, in *C*, 1 dominates 3; but in *D*, 3 dominates 1. As the variables become
more numerous so does the variety increase rapidly.

The multiplicity of inter-connections possible in a telephone
exchange is due primarily to the widespread use of temporary
constancies. The example serves to remind us that 'switching'
is merely one of the changes producible by a re-distribution of

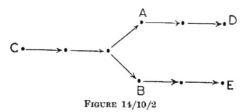

FIGURE 14/10/2

constancies. For suppose a system has the diagram of immediate effects shown in Figure 14/10/2. If an effect coming from
C goes down the branch *AD* only, then, for the branch *BE* to
be independent, *B* must be constant. How the constancy is
obtained is here irrelevant. When the effect from *C* is to be
'switched' to the *BE* branch, *B* must be freed and *A* must
become constant. Any system with a 'switching' process must
use, therefore, an alterable distribution of constancies. Conversely, *a system whose variables can be sometimes fluctuating and
sometimes constant is adequately equipped for switching.*

14/11. At this point it is convenient to consider what degree
of independence is shown in a system if some part is not directly
affected by some other part. To take an extreme case, to what
extent are two parts joined functionally if they have only a

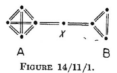

FIGURE 14/11/1.

single variable in common—the parts *A* and *B* in Figure 14/11/1,
for instance, which share only the variable *x*? It is shown in
S. 24/17 that if *x* is a full-function capable of unrestricted variation, then the two parts *A* and *B* are as effectively joined as if

they had many more direct effects bridging the gap. Construction of the diagram of ultimate effects provides a simple proof. The explanation is that each system affects, and is affected by, not only x's value but also x's first, second, and higher derivatives with respect to time. These act to provide a richness of functional connection that is not evident at first glance.

Part-functions

14/12. In S. 14/8 we saw that if a whole system is to be divided into independent parts some intervening variables must become constant. It follows that if the independence is to be temporary, being sometimes present and sometimes absent, the intervening variables must be sometimes constant and sometimes varying: they must, in short, be part-functions. This class of variable will therefore now be considered.

A part-function was defined in S. 7/1 as a variable which, over some interval of observation, was constant over some finite intervals and fluctuated over some finite intervals. It is not implied that the constant values are all equal. The definition refers solely to the variable's observed behaviour, making no reference to any cause for such behaviour; though there will usually be some definite physical reason to account for this way of behaving. A part-function will be said to be 'active', or 'inactive', at a given moment according to whether it is, or is not, varying. As the amount of time spent active tends to 'all', or 'none', so does the part-function tend to full-, or step-, function form. The part-function thus fills the gap between the two types, and may be expected to have intermediate properties.

14/13. Here are some examples. Like the step-function, it is met with much more commonly in the real world than in books. —The pressure on the brake-pedal during a car journey. The current flowing through a telephone during the day. The position co-ordinates of an animal, such as a frog or grasshopper, that moves intermittently. The pressure on the sole of the foot during walking. The activity of pain receptors, if they are activated only intermittently. The rate of secretion of saliva in an experiment on the conditioned reflex. The rate at which water is being swallowed (ml./sec.) by a land animal observed over several days. The sexual activities of a stag during the twelve months. The activity in the mechanisms responsible for reflexes which act only intermittently. vomiting, sneezing, shivering.

14/14. The property of ' threshold ' leads often to behaviour of part-function form. For if x dominates y, and if, when x is less than some value, y remains constant, while if, when x is greater than the value, y fluctuates as some function of x, then, if x is a full-function and fluctuates across the threshold, y will behave as a part-function. In the nervous system, and in living matter generally, threshold properties are widespread ; part-functions may therefore be expected to be equally widespread.

Systems containing part-functions

14/15. Having earlier examined the properties of systems containing null-functions (S. 7/7), and step-functions (S. 7/8 *et seq.*), we will now examine the properties of systems containing part-functions. It is convenient to suppose at first that the system is composed of them exclusively.

Even when not at a resting state, some of such a system's variables may be constant. If the system is composed of part-functions which are active for most of the time, the system will show little difference in behaviour from one composed wholly of full-functions. But if the part-functions are active only at infrequent intervals then, as the system traverses some line of behaviour, inspection will show that only some of the variables are changing, the remainder being constant. Further, if observed on two lines of behaviour, the set of variables which were active on the first line will in general be not the same as the set active on the second. That this may be so can be seen by considering its field.

The field of an absolute system which contains part-functions has the peculiarity that the lines of behaviour often run in a sub-space. Thus, over an interval when all the variables but one are inactive, the line will run in a straight line parallel to the axis of the active variable. If all but two are inactive, the line will run in a plane parallel to that which contains the axes of the two active variables; and so on. If all the variables are inactive, the line becomes a point. Thus a three-variable

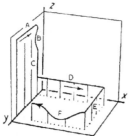

system might give the line of behaviour shown in Figure 14/15/1.

An absolute system composed of part-functions has also the property that if a variable changes from inactive to active, then amongst the variables which affect that variable directly there must, at that moment, have been at least one which was active. One might say, more vividly but less accurately, that activity in one variable can be obtained only from activity in others. A proof is given in S. 24/16, but the reason is not

FIGURE 14/15/1. In the different stages the active variables are: *A, y; B, y* and *z; C, z; D, x; E, y; F, x* and *z*.

difficult to see. Suppose for simplicity that a variable *A* is directly affected only by *B* and *C*, so that the diagram of immediate effects is

Suppose that over a finite interval of time all three have been constant, and that the whole is absolute. If *B* and *C* remain at these constant values, and if *A* is started at the same value as before, then by the absoluteness *A*'s behaviour must be the same as before, i.e. *A* must stay constant. The property has nothing to do with energy or its conservation; nor does it attempt to dogmatise about what real 'machines' can or cannot do; it simply says that if *B* and *C* remain constant and *A* changes from inactive to active, then the system cannot be absolute—in other words, it is not completely isolated.

The sparks which wander in charred paper give a vivid picture of this property: they can spread, one can become multiple, or several can converge; but no spark can arise in an unburning region.

14/16. Part-functions were introduced primarily in the hope that they would provide a system more readily stabilised than one of full-functions. It can now be shown that this is so.

164

First, what do we mean by 'difficulty of stabilisation'? Consider an engineer designing, on the bench, an electronic system. He has before him an apparatus which he wants to be stable at some particular state. The apparatus contains a number of adjustable constants, parameters, and he has to find a combination of values that will give him what he wants. The 'difficulty' of stabilisation may be defined as, and measured by, the proportion of all possible parameter-values that fail to give the required stability. The definition has the advantage that it is directly applicable to the homeostat and any similar mechanism that has to search through combinations of values

With this definition it can be shown that if a system of N part-functions has on the average k of its variables active, then its difficulty of stabilisation is the same, other things being equal, as that of a system of k full-functions.

The proof is given in S. 24/18, but the theorem is clearly plausible. When a system of part-functions is in a region of the phase-space where k variables are active and where all the other variables are constant, the k variables form a system which is absolute and which is not essentially different from any other absolute system of k variables. The fact that *we* have been thinking of it differently does not affect the intrinsic nature of the situation. Equally, whenever we have postulated an absolute system, we have assumed that its surrounding variables are constant, at least for the duration of the experiment or observation. Yet these surrounding variables are usually not constant for ever. So our 'absolute system' was quite commonly only a portion of a larger system of part-functions. There is therefore no intrinsic difference between an absolute system of k full-functions and a subsystem of k active variables within a larger system of part-functions. That being so, there is no reason to expect any difference in their difficulties of stabilisation.

The theorem is of great importance to us, for it means that the time taken to stabilise a system of N part-functions will, very roughly, be more like T_2 of S. 12/3 than T_1; so the change to part-functions may change the stabilisation from 'impossible' to 'possible'. The subject will be developed in S. 17/3.

CHAPTER 15

Dispersion

15/1. Systems of part-functions have the fundamental property that each line of behaviour may leave some of the variables inactive. **Dispersion** occurs when the set of variables made active by one line of behaviour differs from the set made active by another. We will begin to consider the physiological applications of this fact.

First consider a system of full-functions. Suppose we record a few of its variables' behaviours while it traverses first one line of behaviour and then another. The records would show the variables always fluctuating, and the two records would differ only in their patterns of fluctuation. Now suppose we have a system of part-functions. Again we record some of the variables' behaviours. It may happen that from one initial state the line of behaviour leaves all the recorded variables inactive, while the line from another shows some activity. Since, by S. 6/6, the change of initial state corresponds to ' applying a stimulus ', a by-standing physiologist would describe the affair as a simple case of a mechanism ' responding ' to a stimulus. Since living organisms' responses to stimuli have been sometimes offered as proof that the organism has some power not possessed by mechanisms, we must examine these reactions more closely.

In S. 6/6 we saw that the most general representation of a ' stimulus ' was a change from one initial state to another. Now in general, even though the system is absolute, the course of the line of behaviour from one initial state puts no restriction on the course from another initial state. From this lack of restriction follow several consequences.

15/2. The first consequence is that, in a system known only to be complex, however small the difference between the initial states—however slight or simple the stimulus—we can put no limit to the greatness of the difference between the subsequent

166

lines of behaviour. Thus Pavlov conditioned a dog so that it gave no salivary response when subjected to the compound stimulus of:

the experimental room, the harness, the feeding apparatus, the sound of a metronome beating at 104 per minute, and the sound of a No. 16 organ pipe,

but gave a positive salivary response when subjected to:

the experimental room, the harness, the feeding apparatus, the sound of a metronome beating at 104 per minute, and the sound of a No. 15 organ pipe.

Such a 'discrimination' has been considered by some to be beyond the powers of mechanism, but this is not so: all that is necessary is that the system should be complex and should contain part-functions.

15/3. The same point of view helps to make clear the physiological concept of 'adding' stimuli. In the simple case it is easy enough to see what is meant by the 'addition' of two stimuli. If a dog has developed one response to a flashing light and another to a ticking metronome, it is easy to apply simultaneously the flashes and the ticks and to regard this stimulation as the 'sum' of the two stimuli. But the application of such 'sums' was found in many cases to lead to no simple addition of responses · a dog could easily be conditioned to salivate to flashes and to ticks and yet to give no salivation when both were applied simultaneously. Some physiologists have been surprised that this could happen. Let us view the events in phase-space. Suppose our system has variables a, b, c, . . . and that the basal, 'control', behaviour follows the initial state $a_0, b_0, c_0, \ldots$ Suppose the effect of stimulus A corresponds to the line of behaviour from the initial state $a_1, b_0, c_0, \ldots$, and that of stimulus B to the line from $a_0, b_1, c_0, \ldots$ Then the behaviour after the initial state $a_1, b_1, c_0, \ldots$ would correspond to the response to the simultaneous presentation of A and B. If we know the behaviours after A and after B separately, what can we predict of the behaviour after their presentation simultaneously? The possibility is illustrated in Figure 15/3/1, which shows at once that the lines of behaviour from H and J in no way restrict that from K, which represents, in this scheme, the 'sum' response.

It will be seen, therefore, that in a complex system, every group of stimuli will have a holistic quality, in that the response to the whole group will not be predictable from the responses to the separate stimuli, or even to sub-groups. The dog that

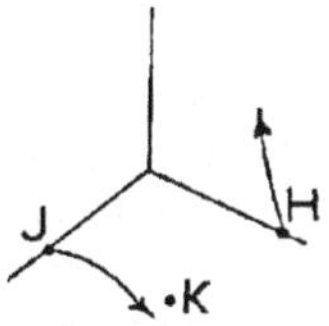

FIGURE 15/3/1.

salivated to each of two stimuli but not to the two together is therefore behaving in no way surprisingly, and such behaviour is no evidence of any ' supra-mechanistic ' power. In complex systems such non-additive compoundings are to be expected.

15/4. Another variation in stimulus-giving occurs when a pattern is varied in some mode of presentation without the pattern itself being changed, as when an equilateral triangle is shown both erect and inverted   The same argument as before prevents us from expecting any necessary relation between the two evoked responses.

In some cases the two evoked responses are found to be the same, and to be characteristic of the particular pattern even though its presentation may have been much changed : an object may be recognised though its image falls on a part of the retina never before stimulated by it. This power of *Gestalt*-recognition was also sometimes thought to demand ' supra-mechanistic ' powers. But in 1947 Pitts and McCulloch showed that any mechanism can show such recognition provided it can form an invariant over the group of equivalent patterns. As the formation of such invariants demands nothing that cannot be supplied by ordinary mechanism, the subject need not be discussed further here.

To sum up, these examples have shown that no matter how small the difference between stimuli, or initial states, we can, in general, if the system is complex, put no limits to the difference that may occur between the subsequent lines of behaviour. From this we may deduce that if the system is one with many part-functions, we can put no limit to the difference there may be between the two sets of variables made active in the two responses ; or in other words, there is, in general, no limit to the degree of dispersion that may occur other than that imposed by the finiteness of the mechanism

15/5. It will be proposed later that dispersion is used widely in the nervous system. First we should notice that it is used widely in the sense-organs. The facts are well known, so I can be brief.

The fact that the sense-organs are not identical enforces an initial dispersion. Thus if a beam of radiation of wave-length $0.5\,\mu$ is directed to the face, the eye will be stimulated but not the skin ; so the optic nerve will be excited but not the trigeminal. But if the wave-length is increased beyond $0.8\,\mu$, the excitation changes from the optic nerve to the trigeminal   Dispersion has occurred because a change in the stimulus has moved the excitation (activity) from one set of anatomical elements (variables) to another.

The sense of taste depends on four histologically-distinguishable types of receptors each sensitive to only one of the four qualities of salt, sweet, sour, and bitter. If change from one solution to another changes the excitation from one type of receptor to another, then dispersion has occurred.

In the skin are histologically-distinguishable receptors sensitive to touch, pain, heat, and cold. If a needle on the skin is changed from lightly touching it to piercing it, the excitation is shifted from the ' touch ' to the ' pain ' type of receptor ; i.e. dispersion occurs.

In the cochlea, sounds differing in pitch vibrate different parts of the basilar membrane. As each part has its own sensitive cells and its own nerve-fibres, a change in pitch will shift the excitation from one set of fibres to another

The three semicircular canals are arranged in planes mutually at right-angles, and each has its own sensitive cells and nerve-fibres. A change in the plane of rotation of the head will therefore shift the excitation from one set of fibres to another.

Whether a change in colour of a stimulating light changes the excitation from one set of elements in the retina to another is at present uncertain. But dispersion clearly occurs when the light changes its position in space ; for, if the eyeball does not move, the excitation is changed from one set of elements to another. The lens is, in fact, a device for ensuring that dispersion occurs : from the primitive light-spot of a Protozoon dispersion cannot occur.

It will be seen therefore that a considerable amount of dispersion is enforced before the effects of stimuli reach the central nervous system : the different stimuli not only arrive at the central nervous system different in their qualities but they often arrive by different paths, and excite different groups of cells.

15/6. The sense organs evidently have as an important function the achievement of dispersion   That it occurs or is maintained in the nervous system is supported by two pieces of evidence.

The fact that cerebral processes, especially those of cellular magnitude, frequently show threshold, the fact that this property generates part-functions (S. 14/14), and the fact that part-functions cause dispersion (S. 14/15) have already been treated   The deduction that dispersion must occur within the nervous system can hardly be avoided

More direct evidence is provided by the fact that, in such cases as are known, the tracts from sense-organ to cortex at least maintain such dispersion as has occurred in the sense organ. The point-to-point representation of the retina on the visual cortex, for instance, ensures that the dispersion achieved in the retina will at least not be lost. Similarly the point-to-point representation now known to be made by the projection of the auditory nerve on the temporal cortex ensures that the dispersion due to pitch will also not be lost.   There are therefore strong reasons for believing that dispersion plays an important part in the nervous system.   What that part is will be discussed in the next three chapters.

REFERENCE

PITTS, W., and McCULLOCH, W S   How we know universals : the perception of auditory and visual forms   *Bulletin of mathematical Biophysics*, 9, 127 ; 1947.

CHAPTER 16

The Multistable System

16/1. THE systems discussed in the previous chapter contained no step-functions, and the effect of ultrastability on their properties was not considered   In this chapter, ultrastability will be re-introduced, so we shall now consider what properties will be found in systems which show both ultrastability and dispersion.

To study the interactions of these two properties we might start by examining the properties of an ultrastable system whose main variables are all part-functions. But it has been found simpler to start by considering a system defined thus : a **multistable** *system consists of many ultrastable systems joined main variable to main variable, all the main variables being part-functions.*

The restriction to part-functions is really slight, for the part-function ranges all the way from the full- to the step-function. It will further be noticed that, as the ultrastable, or 'sub-', systems are joined main variable to main variable only, each step-function will now be restricted in two ways. The critical states which determine whether a particular step-function shall change value depend only on those main variables that belong to the same subsystem.   And when a step-function has changed value, the immediate effect is confined to that subsystem to which it belongs   In the definition of the ultrastable system (S. 8/6) no such limitation was imposed.

This type of system has been defined, not because it is the only possible type, but because the exactness of its definition makes possible an exact discussion.   When we have established its properties, we will proceed on the assumption that other systems, far too varied for individual study, will, if they approximate to the multistable system in construction, approximate to it in behaviour.

171

16/2. The multistable system is itself ultrastable. The proposition may be established by considering the class of 'all ultrastable systems'. Such a class will include every system not incompatible with the definition of S. 8/6. It will, for instance, contain systems whose main variables are all full-functions, systems some of whose main variables are part-functions, and systems whose main variables are all part-functions (S. 11/8). Further, the class will include both those whose step-functions are wide in their immediate effects and those whose step-functions act directly on only a few main variables. The class will therefore include those systems defined as 'multistable'.

From this fact it follows that all the properties possessed generally by the ultrastable system will be possessed by the multistable. In particular, the multistable system will reject all unstable fields of its main variables but will retain the first occurring stable field. In other words, the multistable system will 'adapt' just as will any other ultrastable system.

On the other hand, the faults discussed in Chapter 11 were due to the fact that the systems considered before that chapter had main variables which were all full-functions. Now that the main variables have become all part-functions we shall find, in this and the next two chapters, that the faults have been reduced or eliminated.

16/3. In a multistable system, if no step-function changes in value, the main variables, being all part-functions, will form a system identical with that discussed in S. 14/15. In particular, it will show dispersion : two lines of behaviour will make active two sets of variables ; the two sets will usually not be identical, and may perhaps have no common member.

16/4. It is now possible to deduce the conditions that must hold if a system, multistable or not, is to be able to acquire a second adaptation without losing a first

We may view the process in two ways, which are really equivalent. First, I will suppose that we have an ultrastable system which can be connected to either of two environments (as Units 3 and 4 of the homeostat, representing the adapting system, might be joined to either Unit 1 or Unit 2, representing the two environments). Suppose that the system has been joined to environment α, has adapted to it, and has thus reached a terminal field. To record this 'first adaptation', we disturb α slightly in various ways and record the system's responses. Give the variables activated in these responses the generic label A. Next, remove α, join on environment β, and allow ultrastability to establish a 'second adaptation'. Give the generic label S to all step-functions that were changed by this process. Finally, remove β, restore α, and again test the system's responses to small disturbances applied to α; compare these responses with those first recorded to see whether the first adaptation has been retained or lost. *For the responses to be unchanged—for the first adaptation to be retained—it is necessary and sufficient that during the responses there should be a wall of null-functions between the variables A and the step-functions S.* The condition is necessary, for if an S is not so separated from an A, then at least one A's behaviour will be changed. It is also sufficient, for if the wall of constancies is present, then by S. 14/8 the A's are independent of the S's, and the S's changes will not affect the A's responses.

(The other way of viewing the process is to allow a parameter P to affect the ultrastable system, the two environments being represented by two values P' and P''. The 'disturbance from α' becomes a transient variation in the value of P. The reader can verify that this view leads to the same conclusion.)

The necessary wall of constancies can be obtained in more than one way. Thus, if the system really consisted of two permanently unconnected parts, one of which was joined to α and the other to β, then the addition of a second adaptation would be possible; so the present discussion includes the case of the iterated ultrastable systems. More interesting now is the possibility that the constancies have been provided by part-functions, for this enables the connections to be temporary and conditional. The multistable system is certainly not incapable of so acquiring a second adaptation. The facts that set A will often be only a fraction of the whole, that part-functions are ubiquitous, and that all step-functions are only local in their effects makes the separation of A and S readily possible.

16/5. As a further step towards understanding the multistable system, suppose that we are observing two of the subsystems, that their main variables are directly linked so that changes of either immediately affects the other, and that for some reason all the other subsystems are inactive.

The first point to notice is that, as the other subsystems are inactive, their presence may be ignored; for they become like the ' background ' of S. 6/1. Even if some are active, they can still be ignored if the two observed subsystems are separated from them by a wall of inactive subsystems (S. 14/8).

The next point to notice is that the two subsystems, regarded as a unit, form a whole which is ultrastable. This whole will therefore proceed, through the usual series of events, to a terminal field. Its behaviour will not be essentially different from that recorded in Figure 8/8/5. If, however, we regard the same series of events as occurring, not within one ultrastable whole, but as interactions between two subsystems, then we shall observe behaviours homologous with those observed when interaction occurs between ' animal ' and ' environment '. In other words, *within a multistable system, subsystem adapts to subsystem in exactly the same way as animal adapts to environment.* Trial and error will appear to be used; and, when the process is completed, the activities of the two parts will show co-ordination to the common end of maintaining the variables of the double system within the region of its critical states.

Exactly the same principle governs the interactions between three subsystems. If the three are in continuous interaction, they form a single ultrastable system which will have the usual properties.

As illustration we can take the interesting case in which two of them, A and C say, while having no immediate connection with each other, are joined to an intervening system B, intermittently but not simultaneously. Suppose B interacts first with A : by their ultrastability they will arrive at a terminal field. Next let B and C interact. If B's step-functions, together with those of C, give a stable field to the main variables of B and C, then that set of B's step-function values will persist indefinitely ; for when B rejoins A the original stable field will be re-formed. But if B's set with C's does not give stability, then it will be changed to another set. It follows that B's step-functions will stop changing when, and only when, they have a set of values which forms fields stable with both A and C. (The identity in principle with the process described in S. 11/4 should be noted.)

The process can be illustrated on the homeostat. Three units were connected so that the diagram of immediate effects was $2 \rightleftarrows 1 \rightleftarrows 3$ (corresponding to A, B, and C respectively). To separate the effects of 2 and 3 on 1, bars were placed across the potentiometer dishes (Figure 8/8/2) of 2 and 3 so that they could move only in the direction recorded as downwards in Figure 16/5/1, while 1 could move either upwards or downwards. If 1 was above the central line (shown broken), 1 and 2 interacted, and 3 was independent; but if 1 was below the central line, then 1 and 3 interacted, and 2 was independent. 1 was

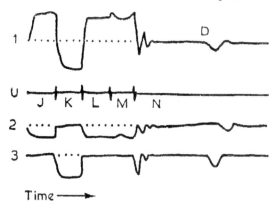

Time ⟶

FIGURE 16/5/1 : Three units of the homeostat interacting. Bars in the central positions prevent 2 and 3 from moving in the direction corresponding here to upwards. Vertical strokes on U record changes of uniselector position in unit 1.

set to act on 2 negatively and on 3 positively, while the effects $2 \rightarrow 1$ and $3 \rightarrow 1$ were uniselector-controlled.

When switched on, at J, 1 and 2 formed an unstable system and the critical state was transgressed. The next uniselector connections (K) made 1 and 2 stable, but 1 and 3 were unstable. This led to the next position (L) where 1 and 3 were stable but 1 and 2 became again unstable. The next position (M) did not remedy this; but the following position (N) happened to provide connections which made both systems stable. The values of the step-functions are now permanent ; 1 can interact repeatedly with both 2 and 3 without loss of stability.

It has already been noticed that if A, B and C should form from time to time a triple combination, then the step-functions of all three parts will stop changing when, and only when, the triple combination has a stable field. But we can go further than that. If A, B and C should join intermittently in various ways, sometimes joining as pairs, sometimes as a triple, and sometimes remaining independent, then their step-functions will stop changing when, and only when, they arrive at a set of values which gives stability to all the arrangements.

Clearly the same line of reasoning will apply no matter how many subsystems interact or in what groups or patterns they join. Always we can predict that *their step-functions will stop changing when, and only when, the combinations are all stable.* Ultrastable systems, whether isolated or joined in multistable systems, act always selectively towards those step-function values which provide stability ; for the fundamental interaction between step-function and stability, the principle of ultrastability described in S. 8/5, still rules the process.

16/6. At the beginning of the preceding section it was assumed, for simplicity, that the process of dispersion was suspended, for we assumed that the two subsystems interacting remained the same two during the whole process. What modifications must be made when we allow for the fact that in the multistable system the number and distribution of subsystems active at each moment fluctuates ?

It is readily seen that the principle of ultrastability holds equally whether dispersion is absent or present ; for the proof of Chapter 8 was independent of special assumptions about the type of variable. The chief effect of dispersion is to destroy the individuality of the subsystems considered in the previous section. There two subsystems were pictured as going through the complex processes of ultrastability, their main variables being repeatedly active while those of the surrounding subsystems remained inactive. This permanence of individuality can hardly occur when dispersion is restored. Thus, suppose that a multistable system's field of all its main variables is stable, and that its representative point is at a resting state R. If the representative point is displaced to a point P, or to Q, the lines from these points will lead it back to R. As the point travels back from P to R, subsystems will come into action, perhaps singly, perhaps in combination, becoming active and inactive in kaleidoscopic variety and apparent confusion. Travel along the other line, from Q to R, will also activate various combinations of subsystems ; and the set made active in the second line may be very different from that made active by the first.

In such conditions it is no longer profitable to observe particular subsystems when a multistable system adapts. What will happen is that instability, and consequent step-function change, will cause combination after combination of subsystems to become active. So long as instability persists, so long will new combinations arise. But when a stable field arises not causing step-functions to change, it will, as usual, be retained. If now the multistable system's adaptation be tested by displacements of its representative point, the system will be found to respond by various activities of various subsystems, all co-ordinated to the common end   But though co-ordinated in this way, there will, in general, be no simple relation between the actions of subsystem on subsystem : knowing which subsystems were activated on one line of behaviour, and how they interacted, gives no certainty about which will be activated on some other line of behaviour, or how they will interact.

Later I shall refer again to ' subsystem A adapting to, or interacting with, subsystem B ', but this will be only a form of words, convenient for description : it is to be understood that what is A and what is B may change from moment to moment.

16/7. In S. 12/4 it was shown that the division of a system into parts reduced markedly the time necessary for adaptation. The multistable system, being able to adapt by parts (S. 16/5), can adapt by this quicker method. But no reason has yet been given why this quicker method should be taken if offered. There is, however, a well-known principle which ensures this.

When changes can occur by two processes which differ in their speeds of achievement, the faster process, by depriving the slower of material, will convert more material than the slow ; and if we imagine the material marked in some way according to its mode of change, then the major part of the material will bear the mark of the faster process. If the difference between the speeds is great, then for practical purposes the slow process may not be in evidence at all. The important fact here is that we can predict *a priori* that if the change be examined, it will

be found to occur by the fast process; and we can make this
prediction without any reference to the particular physical or
chemical details of the particular change.

The principle is well known in chemical dynamics. Thus there
is a reaction whose initial and final states are described by the
equation

$$6FeCl_2 + KClO_3 + 6HCl = 6FeCl_3 + KCl + 3H_2O.$$

There are at least two processes leading from the initial to the
final states : one corresponding to the reaction (of the thirteenth
order) as written above, and one composed of a series of reactions
of low order of which the slowest is the reaction (of the third
order)

$$2FeCl_2 + Cl_2 = 2FeCl_3.$$

The first is slow, for it has to wait for an appropriate collision
of thirteen molecules, while the second is fast. We can predict
that the fast will be preferred; and direct testing has shown that
the reaction occurs by the second, and not the first, process.

From this we may draw several deductions. First, the multistable system will similarly tend to adapt by its fast rather than
by its slow process   Secondly, since the fast process, by S. 12/4,
is that of adaptation by a series of small independent parts, any
multistable system will behave as if it 'preferred' to adapt by
many small independent adaptations rather than by a few complex adaptations : it 'prefers' to adapt piecemeal if this is
possible. Finally, by using the fast process, the time it takes
in getting adapted will tend to the moderate T_2 (of S. 12/3)
rather than to the immoderate T_1. It is therefore at least partly
free from the fault of excessive slowness described in S. 11/7.

CHAPTER 17

Serial Adaptation

17/1. WE have now reached a stage where we must distinguish more clearly between the organism and its environment, for the concept of the ' multistable ' system clearly refers primarily to the nervous system. From now on we shall develop the theme that the nervous system is approximately multistable, and that it is joined to, or interacts with, an environment. But before discussing the events in the nervous system we must be clear on what we mean by an ' environment '. So far we have left the meaning very open : now we want to know what we mean exactly. The question occurs in its most urgent form to the designer of a ' mechanical brain ', for if he has designed this successfully he still has to decide with what it shall interact : having made a model of the brain, he must confront it with a model of the environment. What model could represent the environment adequately in principle ?

It seems clear that we can, in general, put no limit to what may confront the organism. The last century's discoveries have warned us that the universe may be inexhaustible in surprises, so we should not attempt to define the environment by some formula such as ' that which obeys the law of conservation of energy ', for the formula may be obsolete before it is in print. In general, therefore, the nature of the environment must be left entirely open.

On the other hand, we may obtain a partial definition of some practical use by noticing that the living organism on this earth adapts not to the whole universe but to some part of it. It is often not unlike the homeostat, adapting to a unit or two within its immediate cognisance and ignoring the remainder of the world around it. Yet, given a particular organism, especially if human, we cannot with certainty point to a single variable in the universe and say ' this variable will never affect this organism '. This possibility makes the homeostat unrepresentative; for a man does not, like a prince in a fairy tale, pass instantaneously from one world to another, but has rather a series of environments that are interrelated, neither wholly separate nor wholly continuous. We are, in fact, led again to consider the properties of a system whose connections are fluctuating and conditional—the type encountered before in S. 11/8, and therefore treatable by the same method. I suggest, therefore, that many of the environments encountered on this earth by living organisms contain many part-functions Conversely, a system of part-functions adequately represents a very wide class of commonly occurring environments.

As a confirmatory example, here is Jennings' description of an hour in the life of *Paramecium*, with the part-functions indicated as they occur.

(It swims upwards and) '. . . thus reaches the surface film.'

The effects of the surface, being constant at zero throughout the depths of the pond, will vary as part-functions. A discontinuity like a surface will generate part-functions in a variety of ways.

' Now there is a strong mechanical jar—someone throws a stone into the water perhaps.'

Intermittent variations of this type will cause variations of part-function form in many variables.

(The *Paramecium* dives) '. . . thus soon brings it into water that is notably lacking in oxygen.'

The content of oxygen will vary sometimes as part-, sometimes as full-, function, depending on what range is considered. Jennings, by not mentioning the oxygen content before, was evidently assuming its constancy.

'. . . it approaches a region where the sun has been . . . heating the water.'

Temperature of the water will behave sometimes as part-, sometimes as full-, function.

(It wanders on) '. . . into the region of a fresh plant stem which has lately been crushed. The plant-juice, oozing out, alters markedly the chemical constitution of the water.'

Elsewhere the concentration of these substances is constant at zero.

' Other *Paramecia* . . often strike together ' (collide).

180

The pressure on the *Paramecium's* anterior end varies as a part-function.

'The animal may strike against stones.'

Similar part-functions.

'Our animal comes against a decayed, softened, leaf.'

More part-functions.

'. . . till it comes to a region containing more carbon dioxide than usual.'

Concentration of carbon dioxide, being generally uniform with local increases, will vary as a part-function.

'Finally it comes to the source of the carbon dioxide—a large mass of bacteria, embedded in zoogloea.'

Another part-function due to contact.

It is clear that the ecological world of *Paramecium* contains many part-functions, and so too do the worlds of most living organisms.

A total environment, or universe, that contains many part-functions will show dispersion, in that the set of variables active at one moment will often be different from the set active at another. The pattern of activity will therefore tend, as in S. 14/15, to be fluctuating and conditional rather than invariant. As an animal interacts with its environment, the observer will see that the activity is limited now to this set, now to that. If one set persists active for a long time and the rest remains inactive and inconspicuous, the observer may, if he pleases, call the first set 'the' environment. And if later the activity changes to another set he may, if he pleases, call it a 'second' environment. It is the presence of part-functions and dispersion that makes this change of view reasonable.

An organism that tries to adapt to an environment composed largely of part-functions will find that the environment is composed of subsystems which sometimes have individuality and independence but which from time to time show linkage. The alternation is shown clearly when one learns to drive a car. The beginner has to struggle with several subsystems : he has to learn to control the steering-wheel and the car's relation to pavement and pedestrian ; he has to learn to control the accelerator and its relation to engine-speed, learning neither to race the engine nor to stall it ; and he has to learn to change gear, neither burning the clutch nor stripping the cogs. On an open, level, empty road he can ignore accelerator and gear and can study steering as if the other two systems did not exist ; and at the bench he can learn to change gear as if steering did not exist. But on an ordinary journey the relations vary For much of the time the three systems

> driver + steering wheel + . . .
> driver + accelerator + .
> driver + gear lever + . . .

could be regarded as independent, each complete in itself. But from time to time they interact. Not only may any two use common variables in the driver (in arms, legs, brain) but some linkage is provided by the machine and the world around. Thus, any attempt to change gear must involve the position of the accelerator and the speed of the engine ; and turning sharply round a corner should be preceded by a slowing down and by a change of gear. The whole system thus shows that temporary and conditional division into subsystems that is typical of the whole that is composed largely of part-functions.

17/2. Before supposing that the nervous system, in its construction and function, resembles the multistable, we may ask to what extent the supposition is necessary. S. 9/4 showed the necessity for ultrastability ; is the hypothesis of multistability equally necessary ?

Our basic facts and assumptions are now as follows :
  (1) the nervous system adapts by the process of ultrastability (S. 9/4),
  (2) it can retain one adaptation during the acquisition of another (S. 11/3),
  (3) this independence is not achieved by a division of the nervous system into permanently separate parts (S. 11/8),
  (4) no special mechanism is to be postulated for special environmental conditions (S. 1/9) : if possible, the variables are to be statistically homogeneous.

Given these, what can be deduced ?

In the system, label the main variables M and the step-functions S. Call those variables immediately affected by the first environment, M_1; those immediately affected by the second, M_2; those step-functions which changed during the second adaptation, S_2; and those main variables that S_2 directly affects, M_3. It is not assumed that the M-classes are exclusive.

After the step-functions S_2 have changed value, the behaviours of the variables M_1 are unchanged, by postulate 2; so M_1 is independent of S_2 (S. 14/3). But S_2 affects M_3; so M_1 must be independent of M_3 (S. 14/5). There must therefore be a wall of constancies between them (S. 14/8), which must be only temporary, by postulate 3. We can deduce therefore that *some of the main variables must be part-functions.*

Since M_1 is independent of S_2, it follows that the step-functions S_2 can have no immediate effect on the main variables M_1. In other words, some of the step-functions' immediate effects are restricted to a few of the main variables.

If we now use the fourth postulate, that these particular main variables and step-functions are typical, it follows that part-functions must be common, and step-functions must usually be restricted in the variables they immediately affect. We conclude, therefore, that if the nervous system is to show the listed properties, the main features of the multistable system are *necessary.*

17/3. We can now start to examine the thesis that the nervous system is approximately multistable. We assume it to be joined to an environment that contains many part-functions, and we ask to what extent the thesis can explain not only elementary adaptation of the type considered earlier but also the more complex adaptations of the higher animals, found earlier to be beyond the power of a simple system like the homeostat.

We may conveniently divide the discussion into stages according to the complexity of the environment. First there is the environment that, though perhaps extensive, is really simple, for it consists of many parts that are independent, so that they can be adapted to separately. Such an environment was sketched in Figure 12/1/2. It will be considered in this section. Then there is the environment that has some connection between its parts but where the adaptation can proceed from one part to another, perhaps in some order. It will be considered in the remainder of this chapter. Then there is the environment that is richly interconnected but in which there is still some transient subdivision into parts, where there are many subsystems, some simple, some complex, acting sometimes independently and sometimes in conjunction, where an adaptation produced for one part of the environment may conflict with an adaptation produced for another part, and where the adaptations themselves have to be woven into more complex patterns if they are to match the complex demands of the environment. It will be considered in Chapter 18. Beyond this, for completeness, are the environments of extreme complexity; but they hardly need discussion, for at the limit they go beyond any possibility of being adapted to— at least, in the present state of our knowledge.

The environment of the first type, that composed of independent parts, would, if joined to a multistable system, form an ultrastable whole (S. 16/2). Adaptation will, therefore, tend to occur. But as the whole is also multistable the process will show modifications. Dispersion will occur, so that at each moment only some of the whole system's variables will be active. This allows the possibility that though the whole may contain a great number of variables yet little subsystems may occur containing only a few. A subsystem may become stable before all the rest are stable. By the usual rule such stable subsystems will tend to be self-preserving. There is therefore the possibility that the multistable system will adapt piecemeal, its final adaptation resembling that of a collection of iterated ultrastable systems, like that of Figure 12/1/2. The present system will, however, differ in that the constancies that divide subsystem from subsystem are not unalterable but conditional.

Such a multistable system, having arranged itself as a set of iterated systems, will show the features previously noticed (S. 12/2): its adaptation will be graduated; it can conserve its old adaptations while developing new; and, most important, the time taken before all its variables become stabilised will be reduced from the impossibly long to the reasonably short (S. 12/4).

This is what may happen; but will it actually occur? The tendency to adaptation may be persistent, but why should the process take the favourable course? First we notice that as adaptation in some form or other is inevitable the only question is what form it will take. For simplicity, consider an eight-variable environment that can be stabilised either in two independent parts of four variables each or in one of eight. During the random changes of trial and error, a field stabilising one of the sets of four will occur many times more frequently than will a field stabilising all eight (S. 20/12). Such a four, once stabilised, will retain its field leaving only the other four to find a stable field. Consequently, before the process starts we can predict that the eight-variable system is much more likely to arrive at stability by a sequence of four and four than by a simultaneous eight. The fast process is the more probable (S. 16/7).

We can predict, therefore, that in general if a multistable system adapts to an environment composed of P independent parts it will tend to develop P independent subsystems, each reacting to one part. The nervous system, if multistable, will thus tend to adapt to a fragmented environment by a fragmented set of reactions, each complete in itself and having no relation to the other reactions. It will do this, not because this way is the best but because it must. But even though unavoidable, the method is by no means unsuitable. It has the great advantage of speed—it reduces to a minimum the dangerous period of error-making—and there is no point in the nervous system's attempting to integrate the reactions when no integration is required.

17/4. The second degree of complexity occurs when the environment is neither divided into independent parts nor united into a whole, but is divided into parts that can be adapted to individually provided that they are taken in a suitable order and that the earlier adaptations are used to promote adaptation later. Such environments are of common occurrence. A puppy can learn how to catch rabbits only after it has learned how to run : the environment does not allow the two reactions to be learned in the opposite order. A great deal of learning occurs in this way. Mathematics, for instance, though too vast and intricate for one all-comprehending flash, can be mastered by stages. The stages have a natural articulation which must be respected if mastery is to be achieved. Thus, the learner can proceed in the order ' Addition, long multiplication, . . . ' but not in the order ' Long multiplication, addition, . . . ' Our present knowledge of mathematics has in fact been reached only because the subject contains such stage-by-stage routes.

As a clear illustration of such a process I quote from Lloyd Morgan on the training of a falcon

> ' She is trained to the lure—a dead pigeon . . .—at first with the leash.   Later a light string is attached to the leash, and the falcon is unhooded by an assistant, while the falconer, standing at a distance of five to ten yards, calls her by shouting and casting out the lure.   Gradually day after day the distance is increased, till the hawk will come thirty yards or so without hesitation ; then she may be trusted to fly to the lure at liberty, and by degrees from any distance, say a thousand yards   This accomplished, she should learn to stoop to the lure. . . .   This should be done at first only once, and then progressively until she will stoop backwards and forwards at the lure as often as desired.   Next she should be entered at her quarry . . . '

The same process has also been demonstrated more formally. Wolfe and Cowles, for instance, taught chimpanzees that tokens could be exchanged for fruit : the chimpanzees would then learn to open problem boxes to get tokens ; but this way of getting fruit (the ' adaptive ' reaction) was learned only if the procedure for the exchange of tokens had been well learned first.   In other words, the environment was beyond their power of adaptation if presented as a complex whole—they could not get the fruit— but if taken as two stages in a particular order, could be adapted to.

'. . . the growing child fashions day by day, year by year, a complex concatenation of acquired knowledge and skills, adding one unit to another in endless sequence ', said Culler.   I need not further emphasise the importance of serial adaptation.

17/5.   To what process in the multistable system does serial adaptation correspond ?   It is sufficient if we examine the relation of a second adaptation to a first, for a series consists only of this primary relation repeated.

We assume then that the multistable system has learned one reaction and that it is now faced with an environment that can be adapted to only by the system developing some new reaction that uses the old.   It is convenient, for simplicity, to assume here that the first reaction is no longer able to be disrupted by subsequent events.   The assumption demands little, for in the next chapter we shall examine the contrary assumption ; and there is, in fact, some evidence to suggest that, in the mammalian brain, step-functions that were once labile may become fixed. Duncan, for instance, let rats run through a maze, and at various times after the run gave them a convulsion by giving an electric shock to the brain. He found that if the shock was given within about half an hour of the run, all memory of the maze seemed to be lost ; but if the shock was given later, the memory was retained In his words : ' It is suggested that newly learned material undergoes a period of consolidation or perseveration. Early in this period a cerebral electroshock may practically wipe out the effect of learning. The material becomes more resistant to such disruption ; at the end of an hour no retroactive effect was found.' Such a consolidation could easily occur in the animal brain : many proteins, for instance, if kept in unusual ionic conditions undergo irreversible changes. But with the details we are hardly concerned : we simply assume the possibility.

If, then, the first learned reaction is unbreakable, the whole system becomes simple, at least in principle, for as it is an ultrastable system adapting to a system not subject to step-function change (i.e. to the complex of environment and first reaction-system acting together), the situation is homologous with that already treated in Chapter 9—the adaptation and ' training ' of an ultrastable system by an environment. It is therefore not playing with words, but expressing a fundamental parallelism to say that, in serial learning, the first reaction-system and the environment together ' train ' the second. They train it by not allowing the second to follow lines of behaviour incompatible with their own requirements.

To see the process in more detail, consider the following example. A young animal has already learned how to move about the world without colliding with objects. (Though this learning is itself complex, it will serve for illustration, and has the advantage of making the example more vivid.) This learning process was due to ultrastability : it has established a set of step-function values which give a field such that the system composed of eyes, muscles, skin-receptors, some parts of the brain, and hard external objects is stable and always acts so as to keep within limits the mechanical stresses and pressures caused by objects in contact with the skin-receptors (S. 5/4). The diagram of immediate effects will therefore resemble Figure 17/5/1. This system will be referred to as part *A*, the ' avoiding ' system.

As the animal must now get its own food, the brain must develop a set of step-function values that will give a field in which the brain and the food-supply occur as variables, and which is stable so that it holds the blood-glucose concentration within

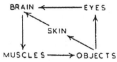

FIGURE 17/5/1 : Diagram of immediate effects of the ' avoiding ' system. Each word represents many variables.

normal limits (S. 5/6).   (This system will be referred to as part B, the ' feeding ' system.)   This development will also occur by ultrastability ; but while this is happening the two systems will interact.

The interaction will occur because, while the animal is making trial-and-error attempts to get food, it will repeatedly meet objects with which it might collide.   The interaction is very obvious when a dog chases a rabbit through a wood.   Further, there is the possibility that the processes of dispersion may allow the two reactions to use common variables   When the systems interact, the diagram of immediate effects will resemble Figure 17/5/2.

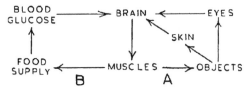

FIGURE 17/5/2.

As the ' avoiding ' system A is not subject to further step-function changes, its field will not alter, and it will at all times react in its characteristic way.   So the whole system is equivalent to an ultrastable system B interacting with an ' environment ' A. B will therefore change its step-function values until the whole has a field which is stable and which holds within limits the variable (blood-glucose concentration) whose extreme deviations cause the step-functions to change.   We know from S. 8/10 that, whatever the peculiarities of A, B's terminal field will be adapted to them.

It should be noticed that the seven sets of variables (Figure 17/5/2) are grouped in one way when viewed anatomically and in a very different way when viewed functionally. The anatomical point of view sees five sets in the animal's body and two sets in the outside world. The functional point of view sees the whole as composed of two parts : an ' adapting ' part B, to which A is ' environment '.

It is now possible to predict how the system will behave after the above processes have occurred. Because part A, the ' avoiding ' system, is unchanged, the behaviour of the whole will still be such that collisions do not occur ; and the reactions to the food supply will maintain the blood-glucose within normal limits. But, in addition, because B became adapted to A, the getting of food will be modified so that it does not involve collisions, for all such variations will have been eliminated.

If, next, the second reaction becomes unbreakable, by mere repetition third and subsequent reactions can similarly be added.

The multistable system will thus show the phenomenon of serial adaptation, not only in its seriality but in the proper adaptation of each later acquisition to the earlier.

REFERENCES

COWLES, J. T. Food-tokens as incentives for learning by chimpanzees. *Comparative Psychology Monographs*, 14, No. 71 ; 1937–8.
CULLER, E A. Recent advances in some concepts of conditioning *Psychological Review*, 45, 134 , 1938.
DUNCAN, C. P The retroactive effect of electroshock on learning. *Journal of comparative and physiological Psychology*, 42, 32 , 1949.
WOLFE, J. B. Effectiveness of token-rewards for chimpanzees. *Comparative Psychology Monographs*, 12, No. 60 , 1935–6.

CHAPTER 18

Interaction between Adaptations

18/1. At this stage it is convenient to consider in more detail the question of ' localisation ' in a multistable system : how will the pattern of activity be distributed within it ? In treating the brain as a multistable system we followed the incoming sensory stimuli through the sense-organs to the sensory cortex (S. 15/5 and 15/6) ; we have now to consider what happens in the areas of ' association ', not of course in detail but sufficiently to develop a clear picture of what we would expect to see there.

Some functions in the cortex are, of course, unquestionably localised : the reception of retinal stimuli at the *area striata* for instance. With such I shall not be concerned. I shall consider only the localisation of learned reactions, especially of those to situations, such as puzzle-boxes containing food, for which the organism has no detailed inborn preparation. In such a case the simplest hypothesis, the one to be tried first, is that the dispersion occurs at random. By this I mean that at each elementary point, at each synapse perhaps, the functional details are determined by factors of only local significance and action : whether two *pieds terminaux* make contact or three, whether the nucleus happens to be on this side of the cell or that, whether five dendrons converge or seven (I use these examples only as illustrations of my meaning) Such details have been determined by primary genetic factors modified by merely local incidents in embryological development and perhaps by local incidents in past learning.

But though the local details were once decided by some trifling local event, I assume that they persist with some tenacity; for learned behaviour can, in the absence of disruptive factors, persist for many years. I will quote a single example. By differential reinforcement with food, Skinner trained twenty young pigeons to peck at a translucent key when it was illuminated with a complex visual pattern. They were then transferred to the

190

usual living quarters where they were used for no further experiments but served simply as breeders. Small groups were tested from time to time for retention of the habit.

> ' The bird was fed in the dimly-lighted experimental apparatus in the absence of the key for several days, during which emotional responses to the apparatus disappeared. On the day of the test the bird was placed in the darkened box. The translucent key was present but not lighted. No responses were made. When the pattern was projected upon the key, all four birds responded quickly and extensively. . . . This bird struck the key within two seconds after presentation of a visual pattern that it had not seen for four years, and at the precise spot upon which differential reinforcement had previously been based '

I assume, therefore, that the system's behaviour is locally regular, in the sense of S. 2/14.

How will responses be localised in such a system? Understanding is easier if we first consider the distribution over a town of the chimneys that ' smoke ' when the wind blows from a given direction. The smoking or not of a particular chimney will be locally determinate; for a wind of a particular force and direction, striking the chimney's surroundings from a particular angle, will regularly produce the same eddies, which will regularly determine the smoking or not of the chimney. But geographically the smoking chimneys are distributed more or less at random; for if we mark a plan of the town with a black dot for every chimney that smokes in a west wind, and a red dot for every one that smokes in a north wind, and then examine the plan, we shall find the black and red dots intermingled and scattered irregularly. The phenomenon of ' smoking ' is thus localised in detail yet distributed geographically at random.

Such is the ' localisation ' shown by the multistable system. We are thus led to expect that the cerebral cortex will show a ' localisation ' of the following type. The events in the environment will provide a continuous stream of information which will pour through the sense organs into the nervous system. The set of variables activated at one moment will usually differ from the set activated at a later moment; for in this system there is nothing to direct all the activities of one reaction into one set of variables and all those of another reaction into another set. On the contrary, the activity will spread and wander with as

191

little orderliness as the drops of rain that run, joining and separating, down a window-pane. But though the wanderings seem disorderly, the whole is regular ; so that if the same reaction is started again later, the same initial stimuli will meet the same local details, will develop into the same patterns, which will interact with the later stimuli as they did before, and the behaviour will consequently proceed as it did before.

This type of system would be affected by removals of material in a way not unlike that demonstrated by many workers on the cerebral cortex   The works of Pavlov and of Lashley are typical. Pavlov established various conditioned reflexes in dogs, removed various parts of the cerebral cortex, and observed the effects on the conditioned reflexes. Lashley taught rats to run through mazes and to jump to marked holes, and observed the effects of similar operations on their learned habits. The results were complicated, but certain general tendencies showed clearly. Operations involving a sensory organ or a part of the nervous system first traversed by the incoming impulses are usually severely destructive to reactions that use that sensory organ. Thus, a conditioned reflex to the sound of a bell is usually abolished by destruction of the cochleae, by section of the auditory nerves, or by ablation of the temporal lobes.   Equally, reactions involving some type of motor activity are apt to be severely upset if the centre for this type of motor activity is damaged.   But it was found that the removal of cerebral cortex from other parts of the brain gave vague results.   Removal of almost any part caused some disturbance, no matter from where it was removed or what type of reflex or habit was being tested ; and no part could be found whose removal would destroy the reflex or habit specifically.

These results have offered great difficulties to many theories of cerebral mechanisms, but are not incompatible with the theory put forward here.   For in a large multistable system the whole reaction will be based on step-functions and activations that are both numerous and widely scattered.   And, while any exact statement would have to be carefully qualified, we can see that, just as England's paper-making industry is not to be stopped by 'the devastation of any single county, so a reaction based on numerous and widely scattered elements will tend to have more immunity to localised injury than one whose elements are few and compact.

18/2. Lashley had noticed this possibility in 1929, remarking that the memory-traces might be localised individually without conflicting with the main facts, provided there were many traces and that they were scattered widely over the cerebral cortex, unified physiologically but not anatomically. He did not, however, develop the possibility further; and the reason is not far to seek when one considers its implications.

Such a localisation would, of course, be untidy; but mere untidiness as such matters little. Thus, in a car factory the spare parts might be kept so that rear lamps were stored next to radiators, and ash-trays next to grease guns; but the lack of obvious order would hardly matter if in some way every item could be produced when wanted. More serious in the cortex are the effects of adding a second reaction; for merely random dispersion provides no means for relating their locations. It not only allows related reactions to activate widely separated variables, but it has no means of keeping unrelated reactions apart: it even allows them to use common variables We cannot assume that unrelated reactions will always differ sufficiently in their sensory forms to ensure that the resulting activations stay always apart, for two stimuli may be unrelated yet closely similar. Nor is the differentiation trivial, for it includes the problem of deciding whether a few vertical stripes in a jungle belong to some reeds or to a tiger.

Not only does dispersion lead to the intermingling of sub-systems, with abundant chances of random interaction and confusion, but even more confusion is added with every fresh act of learning. Even if some order has been established among the previous reactions, each addition of a new reaction is preceded by a period of random trial and error which will necessarily cause the changing of step-functions which were already adjusted to previous reactions, which will be thereby upset. At first sight, then, such a system might well seem doomed to fall into chaos. Nevertheless, I hope to show that there are good reasons for believing that its tendency will actually be towards ever-increasing adaptation.

18/3. Before considering these reasons we should notice that the tendency for new learning to upset old is by no means unknown in psychology; and an examination of the facts shows that the details are strikingly similar to those that would be expected to

193

occur if the nervous system were multistable. Pavlov, for instance, records that '. . . the addition of new positive, and especially of new negative, reflexes exercises, in the great majority of cases, an immediate, though temporary, influence upon the older reflexes'. And in experimental psychology 'retroactive inhibition' has long been recognised. The evidence is well known and too extensive to be discussed here, so I will give simply a typical example. Muller and Pilzecker found that if a lesson were learned and then tested after a half-hour interval, those who passed the half-hour idle recalled 56 per cent of what they had learned, while those who filled the half-hour with new learning recalled only 26 per cent. Hilgard and Marquis, in fact, after reviewing the evidence, consider that the phenomenon is sufficiently ubiquitous to justify its elevation to a ' principle of interference '. There can therefore be no doubt that the phenomenon is of common occurrence. New learning does tend to destroy old.

In this the nervous system resembles the multistable , but the resemblance is even closer. In a multistable system, the more the stimuli used in new learning resemble those used in previous learning, the more will the new tend to upset the old ; for, by the method of dispersion assumed here, the more similar are two stimuli the greater is the chance that the dispersion will lead them to common variables and to common step-functions. In psychological experiments it has repeatedly been found that the more the new learning resembled the old the more marked was the interference. Thus Robinson made subjects learn four-figure numbers, perform a second task, and then attempt to recall the numbers ; he found that maximal interference occurred when the second task consisted of learning more four-figure numbers. Similarly Skaggs found that after learning five-men positions on the chessboard, the maximal failure of memory was caused by learning other such arrangements. The multistable system's tendency to be disorganised by new reactions is thus matched by a similar tendency in the nervous system.

18/4. One factor tending always to lessen the amount of interaction between subsystems is ' habituation ', already shown in Chapter 13 to be an inevitable accompaniment of an ultrastable system's activities. There it was shown that an ultrastable system, coupled to a source of disturbance, tends to change its step-functions to such values as will render it independent of the source. Such a change must also occur if one part of a multistable system is repeatedly disturbed by another part ; for the reacting system possesses the essential properties, and the origin of the disturbance is irrelevant. A subsystem is safe from such disturbance when and only when its variables are independent of all the other variables in the system. There is no necessity for me to repeat the evidence here, for it is identical with that of Chapter 13. It can therefore be predicted that as the various subsystems of a multistable system act on one another, the tendency will be, as time goes on, for the various subsystems to upset each other less and less.

If the nervous system is multistable it would show the same tendency. It would thus show habituation twice : once in its interactions with its environment and again between its various component subsystems. Such 'intracerebral' habituation will tend to lessen the disturbing actions of part on part, and it will therefore contribute to lessening the chaos described in S. 18/2. But such a process will not always lead to complete adaptation ; for its tendency, being always to remove interaction, is to divide the whole into many independent parts. With some simple environments such subdivision may be sufficient, as was noticed in S. 17/3 ; but it contributes nothing towards the co-ordination of reactions when a complex environment can be controlled only by an intricate co-ordination in the nervous system.

18/5. In the turbulence of many subsystems interacting, the principle of ultrastability still holds and still acts persistently in the direction of tending to improve the organism's adaptation to its environment. It will still act selectively towards the useful interactions. Suppose first that two subsystems interact in such a way that, though individually adaptive, their compounded reactions are non-adaptive. A kitten, for instance, has already learned that when it is cold it should go right up to the warmth of its mother, and that when it is hungry it should go right up to the redness of a piece of meat. If later, when it is both cold and hungry, it sees a fire, it would probably tend, in the absence of other factors, to go right up to it. But the very fact that the interaction leads to non-adaptive behaviour provides the cause for its own correction · step-functions change value, and that particular form of interaction is destroyed. Then the step-functions' new values provide new forms of interaction, which are again tested against the environment. The process can stop when and only when the step-functions have values that, acting with the environment, give behaviour that keeps the essential variables within normal limits. Interactions are thus as subject to the requirements of ultrastability as are the other characteristics of behaviour.

Ultrastability thus works in all ways towards adaptation. The only question that remains is whether it is sufficiently effective.

18/6. Is the principle of ultrastability really sufficient to overcome the tendency to chaos ? Is it really sufficient to co-ordinate the activities of, say, 10^{10} neurons when they interact with an extremely complicated environment ? Let me admit at once that the problem will require a great deal of further study before a final answer can be given. The mathematical study of such systems has yet hardly begun, so no rigorous proof can be given. The available physiological evidence is slight, and the physiologist who tries to get direct evidence will encounter formidable difficulties. Nevertheless, we are not wholly without evidence on the subject.

Consider first the spinal reflexes. If we examine a mammal's reflexes, examining them in relation to its daily life, we shall usually find, not only that each individual reflex is adapted to the environment but that the various reflexes are so co-ordinated in their interactions that they work together harmoniously. Nor is this surprising, for species whose reflexes are badly co-ordinated have an obviously diminished chance of survival. The principle of natural selection has thus been *sufficient* to produce not only well-constructed reflexes but co-ordination between them.

A second example is given by the many complex biochemical processes that must be co-ordinated successfully if an organism is to live. Not only must a complicated system like the Krebs' cycle, involving a dozen or more reactions, be properly co-ordinated within itself, but it must be properly co-ordinated into all the other cycles and processes with which it may interact. Biochemists have already demonstrated something of the complexity of these systems and the future will undoubtedly reveal more. Yet in the normal organism natural selection has been *sufficient* to co-ordinate them all.

If now from the principle of natural selection we remove all reference to its cytological details, there remains a process strikingly similar in the abstract to that impelled by the principle of ultrastability. Thus natural selection co-ordinates the reflexes by repeated application of the two operations:

(1) test the organism against the environment; if harmful interactions occur, remove that organism;

(2) replace it by new organisms, differing randomly from the old.

And it is known that in general these rules are sufficient, given time, to achieve the co-ordination. Similarly, the principle of ultrastability leads to the repeated application of the two operations:

(1) test the organism against the environment; if a harmful interaction occurs, change the values of the step-functions responsible for it;

(2) let the new values provide new forms of behaviour, differing randomly from the old.

The analogy between genes and step-functions is most interesting and could be developed further; but it must not distract us now The point at issue is: if natural selection's method of action is sufficient to account for the co-ordination between spinal reflexes, may not ultrastability's method of action also be sufficient to account for the co-ordination between cerebral responses, considering that the two processes are abstractly almost identical?

It may be objected that the spinal reflexes do not have to fear disorganisation by new learning; but the objection will not stand. We are comparing the ontogenetic progress of the cerebral responses with the phylogenetic progress of the spinal reflexes. As the species evolves, its environment changes and new reflexes have to be developed to suit the new conditions. Each new reflex, though suitable in itself, may cause difficulties if it compounds badly with the pre-existing reflexes. Thus, a bird that developed a new reflex for pecking at a new type of white, round, edible fungus might be in danger of using the same reflex on its eggs. Evolution has thus often had to face the difficulty that a harmonious set of reflexes will be disorganised if an extra reflex is added. Again, consider the biochemical systems. As most, if not all, genes have biochemical effects, the acquisition of many a new favourable mutation has meant that a harmonious set of biochemical reactions has had to be reorganised to allow the incorporation of the new reaction.

Evolution has thus had to cope, phylogenetically, with all the difficulties of integration that beset the individual ontogenetically. The tendency to ' chaos ', described in S. 18/2, thus occurs in the species as well as in the individual. In the species, the co-ordinating power of natural selection has shown itself stronger than the tendency to chaos.

Natural selection is effective in proportion to the number of times that the selection occurs : in a single generation it is negligible, over the ages irresistible. And if the unrepeated action of ultrastability seems feeble, might it not become equally irresistible if the nervous system was subjected to its action on an equally great number of occasions ?

How often does it act in the life of, say, the average human being ? I suggest that in those reactions where interaction is important and extensive, the total duration of the learning process is often of ' geological ' duration when compared with the duration of a single incident, in that the total number of incidents contributing to the final co-ordination is very large. I will give a single example. Consider the adult's ability to make a prescribed movement without hitting a given object—to put the cap on a fountain-pen, say, without damaging the nib This skill demands co-ordinated activity, but the co-ordination has not been developed by a single experience. Here are some of the incidents that will probably have contributed to this particular skill :

Putting the finger into the mouth (without hitting lips or teeth) ; putting the finger into the handle of a cup (without striking the handle) , dipping pen into inkwell (without striking the rim) ; putting button into button-hole ; passing a shoe-lace through its hole ; inserting a collar-stud into the neck-band , putting pen-nib into pen ; making a knot by passing an end through a loop ; replacing the cork in a bottle ; putting a key into a key-hole , threading a needle , placing a gramophone record on the turntable's central pin ; putting the finger into a ring ; inserting a funnel into a flask ; putting a cigarette into a holder ; putting a cuff-link into a cuff; inserting a pipe-cleaner ; putting a screw into a nut ; and so on.

Not only could the list be extended almost indefinitely, but each item is itself representative of a great number of incidents, carried out on a variety of occasions in a variety of ways. The total number of incidents contributing to the adult's skill may thus be very large.

So by the time a human being has developed an adult's skill and knowledge, he has been subjected to the action of ultrastability repetitively to a degree which may be comparable with that to which an established species has been subjected to natural selection. If this is so, it is not impossible that ultrastability can account fully for the development of adaptive behaviour, even when the adaptation is as complex as that of Man.

REFERENCES

ASHBY, W. ROSS.   Statistical machinery.   *Thalès*, **7**, 1 , 1951.

LASHLEY, K S   Nervous mechanisms in learning.   *The foundations of experimental psychology*, edited C. Murchison.   Worcester, 1929

MULLER, G E , and PILZECKER, A.   Experimentelle Beitrage zur Lehre vom Gedächtniss.   *Zeitschrift fur Psychologie und Physiologie der Sinnesorgane*, Ergänzungsband No 1 , 1900.

ROBINSON, E. S.   Some factors determining the degree of retroactive inhibition.   *Psychological Monographs*, **28**, No 128 ; 1920.

SKAGGS, E. B   Further studies in retroactive inhibition   *Psychological Monographs*, **34**, No. 161 , 1923.

SKINNER, B F.   Are theories of learning necessary?   *Psychological Review*, **57**, 193 ; 1950.

APPENDIX

CHAPTER 19

The Absolute System

(Some of the definitions already given are repeated here for convenience)

19/1. A **system** of n variables will usually be represented by $x_1, \ldots, x_n$, or sometimes more briefly by x. n will be assumed finite; a system with an infinite number of variables (e g. that of S. 19/23), where x_i is a continuous function of i, will be replaced by a system in which' i is discontinuous and n finite, and which differs from the original system by some negligible amount.

19/2. Each variable x_i is a function of the time t; it will sometimes be written as $x_i(t)$ for emphasis. It must be single-valued, but need not be continuous. A constant may be regarded as a variable which undergoes zero change.

19/3. The **state** of a system at a time t is the set of numerical values of $x_1(t), \ldots, x_n(t)$. Two states are ' equal ' if n equalities exist between the corresponding pairs.

19/4. A **line of behaviour** is specified by a succession of states and the time-intervals between them. Two lines of behaviour which differ only in the absolute times of their initial states are equal.

19/5. A geometrical co-ordinate space with n axes $x_1, \ldots, x_n$, and a dynamic system with variables $x_1, \ldots, x_n$ provide a one-one correspondence between each point of the space (within some region) and each state of the system. The region is the system's ' phase-space '.

19/6. A **primary operation** discovers the system's behaviour by

finding how it behaves after being released from an initial state
$x_1^0, \ldots, x_n^0$. It generates one line of behaviour.

The **field** of a system is its phase-space filled with such lines
of behaviour.

19/7. If, on repeatedly applying primary operations to a
system, it is found that all the lines of behaviour which follow
an initial state S are equal, and if a similar equality occurs after
every other initial state S', S'', . . . then the system is **regular**.

Such a system can be represented by equations of form

$$\left.\begin{aligned} x_1 &= F_1(x_1^0, \ldots, x_n^0;\ t) \\ &\cdots\cdots\cdots \\ x_n &= F_n(x_1^0, \ldots, x_n^0;\ t) \end{aligned}\right\}$$

Obviously, if the initial state is at $t = 0$, we must have

$$F_i(x_1^0, \ldots, x_n^0;\ 0) = x_i^0 \qquad (i = 1, \ldots, n).$$

The equations are the written form of the lines of behaviour;
and the forms F_i define the field. They are obtained directly
from the results of the primary operations.

19/8. If, on repeatedly applying primary operations to a system,
it is found that all lines of behaviour which follow a state S
are equal, no matter how the system arrived at S, and if a
similar equality occurs after every other state S', S'', . . . then
the system is **absolute**.

19/9. A system is 'state-determined' if the occurrence of a
particular state is sufficient to determine the line of behaviour
which follows. Reference to the preceding section shows that
absolute systems are state-determined, and vice versa.

The equations of an absolute system form a group

19/10. *Theorem.* That the equations

$$x_i = F_i(x_1^0, \ldots, x_n^0;\ t) \qquad (i = 1, \ldots, n)$$

should be those of an absolute system, it is necessary that, regarded as a substitution converting $x_1^0, \ldots, x_n^0$ to $x_1, \ldots, x_n$,

they should form a finite continuous (Lie) group of order one with t as parameter.

(1) The system is assumed absolute. Let the initial state of the variables be x^0, where the single symbol represents all n, and let time t' elapse so that x^0 changes to x'. With x' as initial

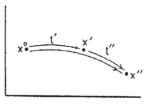

FIGURE 19/10/1.

state let time t'' elapse so that x' changes to x''. As the system is absolute, the same line of behaviour will be followed if the system starts at x^0 and goes on for time $t' + t''$. So

$$x_i'' = F_i(x_1', \ldots, x_n'; \ t'') = F_i(x_1^0, \ldots, x_n^0; \ t' + t'')$$
$$(i = 1, \ldots, n)$$

but $x_i' = F_i(x_1^0, \ldots, x_n^0; \ t')$ $(i = 1, \ldots, n)$

giving

$$F_i\{F_1(x^0; \ t'), \ldots, F_n(x^0; \ t'); \ t''\}$$
$$= F_i\{x_1^0, \ldots, x_n^0; \ t' + t''\} \qquad (i = 1, \ldots, n)$$

for all values of x^0, t' and t'' over some given region. The equation is known to be one way of defining a one-parameter finite continuous group.

(2) The group property is not, however, sufficient to ensure absoluteness. Thus consider $x = (1 + t)x^0$; the times do not combine by addition, which has just been shown to be necessary.

Example: The system with lines of behaviour given by

$$\left.\begin{array}{l} x_1 = x_1^0 + x_2^0 t + t^2 \\ x_2 = x_2^0 + 2t \end{array}\right\}$$

is absolute, but the system with lines given by

$$\left.\begin{array}{l} x_1 = x_1^0 + x_2^0 t + t^2 \\ x_2 = x_2^0 + t \end{array}\right\}$$

is not.

The canonical equations of an absolute system

19/11.   *Theorem :* That a system $x_1, \ldots, x_n$ should be absolute it is necessary and sufficient that the x's, as functions of t, should satisfy differential equations

$$\left. \begin{aligned} \frac{dx_1}{dt} &= f_1(x_1, \ldots, x_n) \\ &\quad \ldots \ldots \\ \frac{dx_n}{dt} &= f_n(x_1, \ldots, x_n) \end{aligned} \right\} \qquad . \qquad . \qquad . \quad (1)$$

where the f's are single-valued, but not necessarily continuous, functions of their arguments; in other words, the fluxions of the set $x_1, \ldots, x_n$ can be specified as functions of that set and of no other functions of the time, explicit or implicit.

(The equations will be written sometimes as shown, sometimes as $dx_i/dt = f_i(x_1, \ldots, x_n)$ $(i = 1, \ldots, n)$. (2) and sometimes abbreviated to $\dot{x} = f(x)$), where each letter represents the whole set, when the context indicates the meaning sufficiently.)

(1) Start the absolute system at $x_1^0, \ldots, x_n^0$ at time $t = 0$ and let it change to $x_1, \ldots, x_n$ at time t, and then on to $x_1 + dx_1, \ldots, x_n + dx_n$ at time $t + dt$. Also start it at $x_1, \ldots, x_n$ at time $t = 0$ and let time dt elapse. By the group property (S. 19/10) the final states must be the same. Using the same notation as S. 19/10, and starting from x_i^0, x_i changes to $F_i(x^0 ; \ t + dt)$ and starting at x_i it gets to $F_i(x ; \ dt)$. Therefore

$$F_i(x^0 ; \ t + dt) = F_i(x ; \ dt) \qquad (i = 1, \ldots, n).$$

Expand by Taylor's theorem and write $\frac{\partial}{\partial b} F_i(a ; \ b)$ as $F_i'(a ; \ b)$.

Then

$$F_i(x^0 ; \ t) + dt \cdot F_i'(x^0 ; \ t) = F_i(x ; \ 0) + dt \cdot F_i'(x ; \ 0)$$
$$(i = 1, \ldots, n)$$

But both $F_i(x^0 ; \ t)$ and $F_i(x ; \ 0)$ equal x_i.

Therefore $F_i'(x^0 ; \ t) = F_i'(x ; \ 0)$ $(i = 1, \ldots, n)$. (3)

But $x_i = F_i(x^0 ; \ t)$ $(i = 1, \ldots, n)$

so $$\frac{dx_i}{dt} = \frac{\partial}{\partial t} F_i(x^0 ; \ t)$$

$$= F_i'(x^0 , \ t)$$

so, by (3), $\dfrac{dx_i}{dt} = F'_i(x ; \; 0)$ $(i = 1, \ldots, n)$

which proves the theorem, since $F'_i(x ; \; 0)$ contains t only in $x_1, \ldots, x_n$ and not in any other form, either explicit or implicit.

Example 1 : The absolute system of S. 19/10, treated in this way, yields the differential equations

$$\left. \begin{aligned} \frac{dx_1}{dt} &= x_2 \\ \frac{dx_2}{dt} &= 2 \end{aligned} \right\}$$

The second system may not be treated in this way as it is not absolute and the group property does not hold.

Corollary :

$$f_i(x_1, \ldots, x_n) \equiv \left[\frac{\partial}{\partial t} F_i(x_1, \ldots, x_n ; \; t)\right]_{t=0} \qquad (i = 1, \ldots, n)$$

(2) Given the differential equations, they may be written

$$dx_i = f_i(x_1, \ldots, x_n) . dt \qquad (i = 1, \ldots, n)$$

and this shows that a given set of values of $x_1, \ldots, x_n$, i.e. a given state of the system, specifies completely what change dx_i will occur in each variable x_i during the next time-interval dt. By integration this defines the line of behaviour from that state. The system is therefore absolute.

Example 2 : By integrating

$$\left. \begin{aligned} \frac{dx_1}{dt} &= x_2 \\ \frac{dx_2}{dt} &= 2 \end{aligned} \right\}$$

the group equations of the example of S. 19/10 are regained

Example 3 . The equations of the homeostat may be obtained thus :—If x_i is the angle of deviation of the ith magnet from its central position, the forces acting on x_i are the momentum, proportional to x_i, the friction, also proportional to $\dot{x}_i$, and the four currents in the coil, proportional to x_1, x_2, x_3 and x_4. If linearity is assumed, and if all four units are constructionally identical, we have

$$\frac{d}{dt}(m\dot{x}_i) = - k\dot{x}_i + l(p - q)(a_{i1}x_1 + \ldots + a_{i4}x_4)$$

$$(i = 1, 2, 3, 4)$$

where p and q are the potentials at the ends of the trough, l depends on the valve, k depends on the friction at the vane, and m depends on the moment of inertia of the magnet. If $h = \dfrac{l(p-q)}{m}$, $\jmath = \dfrac{k}{m}$ then the equations can be written

$$\left.\begin{aligned}
\frac{dx_i}{dt} &= \dot{x}_i \\
\frac{d\dot{x}_i}{dt} &= h(a_{i1}x_1 + \ldots + a_{i4}x_4) - \jmath \dot{x}_i
\end{aligned}\right\} \quad (i = 1,\, 2,\, 3,\, 4)$$

which shows the 8-variable system to be absolute.

They may also be written

$$\left.\begin{aligned}
\frac{dx_i}{dt} &= \dot{x}_i \\
\frac{d\dot{x}_i}{dt} &= \frac{k}{m}\left\{\frac{l(p-q)}{k}(a_{i1}x_1 + \ldots + a_{i4}x_4) - \dot{x}_i\right\}
\end{aligned}\right\} (i = 1,\, 2,\, 3,\, 4)$$

Let $m \to 0$. $d\dot{x}_i/dt$ becomes very large, but not dx_i/dt. So x_i tends rapidly towards

$$\frac{l(p-q)}{k}(a_{i1}x_1 + \ldots + a_{i4}x_4)$$

while the x's, changing slowly, cannot alter rapidly the value towards which $\dot{x}_i$ is tending. In the limit,

$$\frac{dx_i}{dt} = x_i = \frac{l(p-q)}{k}(a_{i1}x_1 + \ldots + a_{i4}x_4) \qquad (i = 1,\, 2,\, 3,\, 4)$$

Change the time-scale by $\tau = \dfrac{l(p-q)}{k}t$;

$$\frac{dx_i}{d\tau} = a_{i1}x_1 + \ldots + a_{i4}x_4 \qquad (i = 1,\, 2,\, 3,\, 4)$$

showing the system $x_1, \ldots, x_4$ to be absolute and linear. The a's are now the values set by the hand-controls of Figure 8/8/3.

19/12. That a system should be absolute, it is necessary and sufficient that at no point of the field should a line of behaviour bifurcate. The statement can be verified from the definition or from the theorem of S. 19/11. The statement does not prevent lines of behaviour from running together.

19/13. The theorems of the previous four sections show that the following properties, collected for convenience, in a system $x_1, \ldots, x_n$, are all equivalent in that the possession of any one of them implies the others :

(1) From any point in the field departs only one line of behaviour (S. 19/8) ;

(2) the system is state-determined (S. 19/9) ;

(3) the system has lines of behaviour whose equations specify a finite continuous group of order one ;

(4) the system has lines of behaviour specified by differential equations of form

$$\frac{dx_i}{dt} = f_i(x_1, \ldots, x_n) \qquad (i = 1, \ldots, n)$$

where the right-hand side contains no functions of t except those whose fluxions are given on the left.

19/14. From the experimental point of view the simplest test for absoluteness is to see whether the lines of behaviour are state-determined. An example has been given in S. 2/15. It will be noticed that experimentally one cannot *prove* a system to be absolute—one can only say that the evidence does not disprove the possibility. On the other hand, one value may be sufficient to prove that the system is not absolute.

19/15. A simple example of a system which is regular but not absolute is given by the following apparatus. A table top is altered so that instead of being flat, it undulates irregularly but gently like a putting-green (Figure 19/15/1). Looking down on it from above, we can mark across it a rectangular grid of lines to act as co-ordinates If we place a ball at any point and then release it, the ball will roll, and by marking its position at, say, every one-tenth second we can determine the lines of behaviour of the two-variable system provided by the two co-ordinates.

If the table is well made, the lines of behaviour will be accurately reproducible and the system will be regular. Yet the experimenter, if he knew nothing of forces, gravity, or momenta, would find the system unsatisfactory. He would establish that the ball, started at A, always went to A'; and started at B it always went to B'. He would find its behaviour at C difficult to explain. And if he tried to clarify the situation by starting the ball at C itself, he would find it went to D! He would say that he could make nothing of the system; for although each

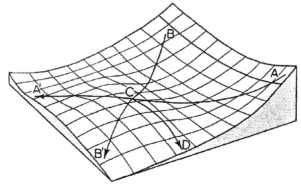

FIGURE 19/15/1.

line of behaviour is accurately reproducible, the different lines of behaviour have no relation to one another.

This lack of relation means that they do not form a ' group '. But whether the experimenter agrees with this or not, he will, in practice, reject this 2-variable system and will not rest till he has discovered, either for himself or by following Newton, a system that *is* state-determined. In my theory I insist on the systems being absolute because I agree with the experimenter who, in his practical work, is similarly insistent.

19/16. That the field of a system should not vary with time, it is necessary and sufficient that the system be regular. The proof is obvious.

19/17. One reason why a system's absoluteness is important is because the system is thereby shown to be adequately *isolated* from other unknown and irregularly varying parameters. This demonstration is obviously fundamental in the experimental study of a dynamic system, for the proof of isolation comes, not from an examination of the material substance of the system (S. 14/1), which may be misleading and in any case presupposes that we know beforehand what makes for isolation and what does not, but from a direct test on the behaviour itself.

Closely related to this in a fundamental way is the fact that Shannon's concept of a 'noiseless transducer' is identical in definition with my definition of an absolute system. Thus he defines such a transducer as one that, having states α and an input x, will, if in state α_n and given input x_n, change to a new state α_{n+1} that is a function only of x_n and α_n:

$$\alpha_{n+1} = g(x_n, \alpha_n)$$

Though expressed in a superficially different form, this equation is identical with my 'canonical' equation, for it says simply that if the parameters x and the state of the system are given, then the system's next step is determined. Thus the communication engineer, if he were to observe the physicist and the psychologist for the first time, would say that they seem to prefer to work with noiseless systems. His remark would not be as trite as it seems, for from it flow far-reaching consequences and the possibilities of rigorous deduction.

19/18. A second feature which makes absoluteness important is that its presence establishes, by appeal only to the behaviour, that the system of variables is *complete*, i.e. that it includes *all* the variables necessary for the specification of the system.

19/19. When we assemble a machine, we usually know the canonical equations directly If, for instance, certain masses, springs, magnets, be put together in a certain way the mathematical physicist knows how to write down the differential equations specifying the subsequent behaviour.

His equations are not always in our canonical form, but they can *always* be converted to this form provided that the system is isolated, i.e. not subjected to arbitrary interference, and is determinate.

19/20. In general there are two methods for studying a dynamic system. One method is to know the properties of the parts and the pattern of assembly. With this knowledge the canonical equations can be written down, and their integration predicts the behaviour of the whole system. The other method is to study the behaviour of the whole system empirically. From this knowledge the group equations are obtained : differentiation of the functions then gives the canonical equations and thus the relations between the parts.

Sometimes systems that are known to be isolated and complete are treated by some method not identical with that used here. In those cases some manipulation may be necessary to convert the other form into ours. Some of the possible manipulations will be shown in the next few sections.

19/21. Systems can sometimes be described better after a change of co-ordinates. This means changing from the original variables $x_1, \ldots, x_n$ to a new set $y_1, \ldots, y_n$, equal in number to the old and related in some way

$$y_i = \phi_i(x_1, \ldots, x_n) \qquad (i = 1, \ldots, n)$$

If we think of the variables as being represented by dials, the change means changing to a new set of dials each of which indicates some function of the old. It is easily shown that such a change of co-ordinates does not change the absoluteness.

19/22. In the 'homeostat' example of S. 19/11 a derivative was treated as an independent variable. I have found this treatment to be generally advantageous · it leads to no difficulty or inconsistency, and gives a beautiful uniformity of method.

For example, if we have the equations of an absolute system we can write them as

$$\dot{x}_i - f_i(x_1, \ldots, x_n) = 0 \qquad (i = 1, \ldots, n)$$

treating them as n equations in $2n$ algebraically independent variables $x_1, \ldots, x_n, \dot{x}_1, \ldots, \dot{x}_n$. Now differentiate all the equations q times, getting $(q + 1)n$ equations with $(q + 2)n$ variables and derivatives. We can then select n of these variables arbitrarily, and noticing that we also want the next higher derivatives of these n, we can eliminate the other qn variables, using up qn equations. If the variables selected were $z_1, \ldots, z_n$ we now have n equations, in $2n$ variables, of type

$$\Phi_i(z_1, \ldots, z_n, z_1, \ldots, z_n) = 0 \qquad (i = 1, \ldots, n)$$

These have only to be solved for $z_1, \ldots, \dot{z}_n$ in terms of $z_1, \ldots, z_n$ and the equations are in canonical form. So the new system is also absolute.

This transformation implies that *in an absolute system we can avoid direct reference to some of the variables provided we use derivatives of the remaining variables to replace them.*

Example .
$$\left.\begin{array}{l} \dot{x}_1 = x_1 - x_2 \\ \dot{x}_2 = 3x_1 + x_2 \end{array}\right\}$$

can be changed to omit direct reference to x_2 by using $\dot{x}_1$ as a new independent variable. It is easily converted to

$$\left.\begin{array}{l} \dfrac{dx_1}{dt} = \qquad\qquad \dot{x}_1 \\[2mm] \dfrac{d\dot{x}_1}{dt} = -4x_1 + 2x_1 \end{array}\right\}$$

which is in canonical form in the variables x_1 and $\dot{x}_1$.

19/23. Systems which are isolated but in which effects are transmitted from one variable to another with some finite delay may be rendered absolute by adding derivatives as variables. Thus, if the effect of x_1 takes 2 units of time to reach x_2, while x_2's effect takes 1 unit of time to reach x_1, and if we write $x(t)$ to show the functional dependence,

then
$$\frac{dx_1(t)}{dt} = f_1\{x_1(t),\ x_2(t-2)\}$$

$$\frac{dx_2(t)}{dt} = f_2\{x_1(t-1),\ x_2(t)\}.$$

This is not in canonical form; but by expanding $x_1(t-1)$ and $x_2(t-2)$ in Taylor's series and then adding to the system as many derivatives as are necessary to give the accuracy required, we can obtain an absolute system which resembles it as closely as we please.

19/24. If a variable depends on some accumulative effect so that, say, $\dot{x}_1 = f\left\{\displaystyle\int_a^t \phi(x_2)dt\right\}$, then if we put $\displaystyle\int_a^t \phi(x_2)dt = y$, we get the equivalent form

$$\frac{dx_1}{dt} = f(y)$$

$$\frac{dy}{dt} = \phi(x_2)$$

$$\frac{dx_2}{dt} = \ldots \text{ etc.}$$

which is in canonical form.

19/25. If a variable depends on velocity effects so that, for instance

$$\frac{dx_1}{dt} = f_1\left(\frac{dx_2}{dt}, \; x_1, \; x_2\right)$$

$$\frac{dx_2}{dt} = f_2(x_1, \; x_2)$$

then if we substitute for $\frac{dx_2}{dt}$ in $f_1(\ldots)$ we get the canonical form

$$\left.\begin{array}{l} \dfrac{dx_1}{dt} = f_1\{f_2(x_1,x_2), \; x_1, \; x_2\} \\[2ex] \dfrac{dx_2}{dt} = f_2(x_1, \; x_2) \end{array}\right\}$$

19/26. If one variable changes either instantaneously or fast enough to be so considered without serious error, then its value can be given as a function of those of the other variables; and it can therefore be eliminated from the system.

19/27. Explicit solutions of the canonical equations

$$dx_i/dt = f_i(x_1, \ldots, x_n) \qquad (i = 1, \ldots, n)$$

will seldom be needed in our discussion, but some methods will be given as they will be required for the examples.

(1) A simple symbolic solution, giving the first few terms of x_i as a power series in t, is given by

$$x_i = e^{tX}x_i^0 \qquad (i = 1, \ldots, n) \qquad . \qquad . \qquad (1)$$

where X is the operator

$$f_1(x_1^0, \ldots, x_n^0)\frac{\partial}{\partial x_1^0} + \ldots + f_n(x_1^0, \ldots, x_n^0)\frac{\partial}{\partial x_n^0} . \qquad (2)$$

and $\qquad e^{tX} = 1 + tX + \dfrac{t^2}{2!}X^2 + \dfrac{t^3}{3!}X^3 + \ldots \qquad . \qquad (3)$

It has the important property that any function $\Phi(x_1, \ldots, x_n)$ can be shown as a function of t, if the x's start from $x_1^0, \ldots, x_n^0$,

by
$$\Phi(x_1, \ldots, x_n) = e^{tX}\Phi(x_1^0, \ldots, x_n^0) \qquad . \quad (4)$$

(2) If the functions f_i are linear so that

$$\left.\begin{aligned}\frac{dx_1}{dt} &= a_{11}x_1 + a_{12}x_2 + \ldots + a_{1n}x_n + b_1\\[6pt]& \qquad \ldots \quad \ldots\\[6pt]\frac{dx_n}{dt} &= a_{n1}x_1 + a_{n2}x_2 + \ldots + a_{nn}x_n + b_n\end{aligned}\right\} \qquad . \quad (5)$$

then if the b's are zero (as can be arranged by a change of origin) the equations may be written in matrix form as

$$\dot{x} = Ax \qquad . \qquad . \qquad . \qquad . \quad (6)$$

where $\dot{x}$ and x are column vectors and A is the square matrix $[a_{ij}]$ In matrix notation the solution may be written

$$x = e^{tA}x^0 \qquad . \qquad . \qquad . \qquad . \quad (7)$$

(3) Most convenient for actual solution of the linear form is the recently developed method of the Laplace transform. The standard text-books should be consulted for details.

19/28.   Any comparison of an absolute system with the other types of system treated in mechanics and in thermodynamics must be made with caution.   Thus, it should be noticed that the concept of the absolute system makes no reference to energy or its conservation, treating it as irrelevant.   It will also be noticed that the absolute system, whatever the ' machine ' providing it, is essentially irreversible. This can be established either by examining the group equations of S. 19/10, the canonical equations of S. 19/11, or, in a particular case, by examining the field of the common pendulum in Figure 2/15/1.

REFERENCE

SHANNON, C E. A mathematical theory of communication   *Bell System technical Journal*, **27**, 379-423, 623-56 , 1948.

CHAPTER 20

Stability

20/1. ' STABILITY ' is defined primarily as a relation between a line of behaviour and a region in phase-space because only in this way can we get a test that is unambiguous in all possible cases. Given an absolute system and a region within its field, a line of behaviour from a point within the region is **stable** if it never leaves the region.

20/2. If all the lines within a given region are stable from all points within the region, and if all the lines meet at one point, the system has ' normal ' stability.

20/3. A **resting state** can be defined in several ways. In the field it is a terminating point of a line of behaviour. In the group equations of S. 19/10 the resting state $X_1, \ldots, X_n$ is given by the equations

$$X_i = \operatorname*{Lim}_{t \to \infty} F_i(x^0 ; \ t) \qquad (i = 1, \ldots, n) \qquad . \quad (1)$$

if the n limits exist. In the canonical equations the values satisfy

$$f_i(X_1, \ldots, X_n) = 0 \qquad (i = 1, \ldots, n) \qquad . \quad (2)$$

A resting state is an invariant of the group, for a change of t does not alter its value.

If the Jacobian of the f's, i.e. the determinant $\left| \dfrac{\partial f_i}{\partial x_j} \right|$, which will be symbolised by J, is not identically zero, then there will be isolated resting states. If $J \equiv 0$, but not all its first minors are zero, then the equations define a curve, every point of which is a resting state. If $J \equiv 0$ and all first minors but not all second minors are zero, then a two-way surface exists composed of resting states; and so on.

20/4. *Theorem :* If the f's are continuous and differentiable, an absolute system tends to the linear form (S. 19/27) in the neighbourhood of a resting state.

Let the system, specified by
$$dx_i/dt = f_i(x_1, \ldots, x_n) \qquad (i = 1, \ldots, n)$$
have a resting state $X_1, \ldots, X_n$, so that
$$f_i(X_1, \ldots, X_n) = 0 \qquad (i = 1, \ldots, n)$$
Put $x_i = X_i + \xi_i$ $(i = 1, \ldots, n)$ so that x_i is measured as a deviation ξ_i from its resting value. Then
$$\frac{d}{dt}(X_i + \xi_i) = f_i(X_1 + \xi_1, \ldots, X_n + \xi_n) \qquad (i = 1, \ldots, n)$$

Expanding the right-hand side by Taylor's theorem, noting that $dX_i/dt = 0$ and that $f_i(X) = 0$, we find, if the ξ's are infinitesimal, that
$$\frac{d\xi_i}{dt} = \frac{\partial f_i}{\partial \xi_1}\xi_1 + \ldots + \frac{\partial f_i}{\partial \xi_n}\xi_n \qquad (i = 1, \ldots, n)$$

The partial derivatives, taken at the point $X_1, \ldots, X_n$, are numerical constants. So the system is linear.

20/5. In general the only test for stability is to observe or compute the given line of behaviour and to see what happens as $t \to \infty$. For the linear system, however, there are tests that do not involve the line of behaviour explicitly. Since, by the previous section, many systems approximate to the linear within the region in which we are interested, the methods to be described are widely applicable.

Let the linear system be
$$\frac{dx_i}{dt} = a_{i1}x_1 + a_{i2}x_2 + \ldots + a_{in}x_n \qquad (i = 1, \ldots, n) \quad (1)$$
or, in the concise matrix notation (S. 19/27)
$$\dot{x} = Ax \qquad . \qquad . \qquad . \qquad . \quad (2)$$
Constant terms on the right-hand side make no difference to the stability and can be ignored. If the determinant of A is not zero, there is a single resting state. The determinant
$$\begin{vmatrix} a_{11}-\lambda & a_{12} & \ldots & a_{1n} \\ a_{21} & a_{22}-\lambda & \ldots & a_{2n} \\ \ldots & \ldots & \ldots & \ldots \\ a_{n1} & a_{n2} & \ldots & a_{nn}-\lambda \end{vmatrix}$$
when expanded gives a polynomial in λ of degree n which, when equated to 0, gives the **characteristic equation** of the matrix A:
$$\lambda^n + m_1\lambda^{n-1} + m_2\lambda^{n-2} + \ldots + m_n = 0.$$

20/6. Each coefficient m_i is the sum of all i-rowed principal (co-axial) minors of A, multiplied by $(-1)^i$. Thus,

$$m_1 = -(a_{11} + a_{22} + \ldots + a_{nn}); \quad m_n = (-1)^n |A|.$$

Example : The linear system

$$\begin{aligned}
dx_1/dt &= -5x_1 + 4x_2 - 6x_3 \\
dx_2/dt &= 7x_1 - 6x_2 + 8x_3 \\
dx_3/dt &= -2x_1 + 4x_2 - 4x_3
\end{aligned}\Bigg\}$$

has the characteristic equation

$$\lambda^3 + 15\lambda^2 + 2\lambda + 8 = 0.$$

20/7. Of this equation the roots $\lambda_1, \ldots, \lambda_n$ are the **latent roots** of A. The integral of the canonical equations gives each x_i as a linear function of the exponentials $e^{\lambda_1 t}, \ldots, e^{\lambda_n t}$. For the sum to be convergent, no real part of $\lambda_1, \ldots, \lambda_n$ must be positive, and this criterion provides a test for the stability of the system.

Example : The equation $\lambda^3 + 15\lambda^2 + 2\lambda + 8 = 0$ has roots -14.902 and $-0.049 \pm 0.729\sqrt{-1}$, so the system of the previous section is stable.

20/8. A test which avoids finding the latent roots is Hurwitz' : a necessary and sufficient condition that the linear system is stable is that the series of determinants

$$m_1, \quad \begin{vmatrix} m_1 & 1 \\ m_3 & m_2 \end{vmatrix}, \quad \begin{vmatrix} m_1 & 1 & 0 \\ m_3 & m_2 & m_1 \\ m_5 & m_4 & m_3 \end{vmatrix}, \quad \begin{vmatrix} m_1 & 1 & 0 & 0 \\ m_3 & m_2 & m_1 & 1 \\ m_5 & m_4 & m_3 & m_2 \\ m_7 & m_6 & m_5 & m_4 \end{vmatrix}, \text{ etc.}$$

(where, if $q > n$, $m_q = 0$), are all positive.

Example : The system with characteristic equation

$$\lambda^3 + 15\lambda^2 + 2\lambda + 8 = 0$$

yields the series

$$+15, \quad \begin{vmatrix} 15 & 1 \\ 8 & 2 \end{vmatrix}, \quad \begin{vmatrix} 15 & 1 & 0 \\ 8 & 2 & 15 \\ 0 & 0 & 8 \end{vmatrix}.$$

These have the values $+15$, $+22$, and $+176$. So the system is stable, agreeing with the previous test.

20/9. If the coefficients in the characteristic equation are not all positive the system is unstable. But the converse is not true. Thus the linear system whose matrix is

$$\begin{bmatrix} 1 & \sqrt{6} & 0 \\ -\sqrt{6} & 1 & 0 \\ 0 & 0 & -3 \end{bmatrix}$$

has the characteristic equation $\lambda^3 + \lambda^2 + \lambda + 21 = 0$; but the latent roots are $+1 \pm \sqrt{-6}$ and -3; so the system is unstable.

20/10. Another test, related to Nyquist's, states that a linear system is stable if, and only if, the polynomial

$$\lambda^n + m_1\lambda^{n-1} + m_2\lambda^{n-2} + \ldots + m_n$$

changes in amplitude by $n\pi$ when λ, a complex variable ($\lambda = a + bi$ where $i = \sqrt{-1}$), goes from $-i\infty$ to $+i\infty$ along the b-axis in the complex λ-plane.

Nyquist's criterion of stability is widely used in the theory of electric circuits and of servo-mechanisms. It, however, uses data obtained from the response of the system to persistent harmonic disturbance. Such disturbance renders the system non-absolute and is therefore based on an approach different from ours.

20/11. Some further examples will illustrate various facts relating to stability.

Example 1 : If a matrix $[a]$ of order $n \times n$ has latent roots $\lambda_1, \ldots, \lambda_n$, then the matrix, written in partitioned form,

$$\left[\begin{array}{c|c} 0 & I \\ \hline a & 0 \end{array} \right]$$

of order $2n \times 2n$, where I is the unit matrix, has latent roots $\pm\sqrt{\lambda_1}, \ldots, \pm\sqrt{\lambda_n}$. It follows that the system

$$\frac{d^2x_i}{dt^2} = a_{i1}x_1 + a_{i2}x_2 + \ldots + a_{in}x_n \qquad (i = 1, \ldots, n)$$

of common physical occurrence, must be unstable.

Example 2 : The diagonal terms a_{ii} represent the intrinsic stabilities of the variables, for if all variables other than x_i are held constant, the linear system's i-th equation becomes

$$dx_i/dt = a_{ii}x_i + c,$$

where c is a constant, showing that under these conditions x_i will converge to $-c/a_{ii}$ if a_{ii} be negative, and will diverge without limit if a_{ii} be positive.

If the diagonal terms a_{ii} are much larger in absolute magnitude than the others, the roots tend to the values of a_{ii}. It follows that if the diagonal terms take extreme values they determine the stability.

Example 3 : If the terms a_{ij} in the first $n-1$ rows (or columns) are given, the remaining n terms can be adjusted to make the latent roots take any assigned values

Example 4 : The matrix of the homeostat equations of S. 19/11 is

$$
\begin{bmatrix}
\cdot & \cdot & \cdot & \cdot & 1 & \cdot & \cdot & \cdot \\
\cdot & \cdot & \cdot & \cdot & \cdot & 1 & \cdot & \cdot \\
\cdot & \cdot & \cdot & \cdot & \cdot & \cdot & 1 & \cdot \\
\cdot & \cdot & \cdot & \cdot & \cdot & \cdot & \cdot & 1 \\
a_{11}h & a_{12}h & a_{13}h & a_{14}h & -j & \cdot & \cdot & \cdot \\
a_{21}h & a_{22}h & a_{23}h & a_{24}h & \cdot & -j & \cdot & \cdot \\
a_{31}h & a_{32}h & a_{33}h & a_{34}h & \cdot & \cdot & -j & \cdot \\
a_{41}h & a_{42}h & a_{43}h & a_{44}h & \cdot & \cdot & \cdot & -j
\end{bmatrix}
$$

If $j = 0$, the system must be unstable (by Example 1 above). If the matrix has latent roots $\mu_1, \ldots, \mu_8$, and if $\lambda_1, \ldots, \lambda_4$ are the latent roots of the matrix $[a_{ij}h]$, and if $j \neq 0$, then the λ's and μ's are related by $\lambda_p = \mu_q^2 + j\mu_q$. As $j \to \infty$ the 8-variable and the 4-variable systems are stable or unstable together.

Example 5 : In a stable system, fixing a variable may make the system of the remainder unstable. For instance, the system with matrix

$$
\begin{bmatrix}
6 & 5 & -10 \\
-4 & -3 & -1 \\
4 & 2 & -6
\end{bmatrix}
$$

is stable. But if the third variable is fixed, the system of the first two variables has matrix

$$
\begin{bmatrix}
6 & 5 \\
-4 & -3
\end{bmatrix}
$$

and is unstable.

Example 6 : Making one variable more stable intrinsically

(Example 2 of this section) may make the whole unstable. For instance, the system with matrix

$$\begin{bmatrix} -4 & -3 \\ 3 & 2 \end{bmatrix}$$

is stable. But if a_{11} becomes more negative, the system becomes unstable when a_{11} becomes more negative than $-4\frac{1}{2}$.

Example 7: In the $n \times n$ matrix

$$\left[\begin{array}{c|c} a & b \\ \hline c & d \end{array}\right]$$

in partitioned form, $[a]$ is of order $k \times k$. If the k diagonal elements a_{ii} become much larger in absolute value than the rest, the latent roots of the matrix tend to the k values a_{ii} and the $n - k$ latent roots of $[d]$. Thus the matrix, corresponding to $[d]$,

$$\begin{bmatrix} 1 & -3 \\ 1 & 2 \end{bmatrix}$$

has latent roots $+1\cdot5 \pm 1\cdot658\iota$, and the matrix

$$\begin{bmatrix} -100 & -1 & 2 & 0 \\ -2 & -100 & -1 & 2 \\ 0 & -3 & 1 & -3 \\ 2 & -1 & 1 & 2 \end{bmatrix}$$

has latent roots $-101\cdot39$, $-98\cdot62$, and $+1\cdot506 \pm 1\cdot720\iota$.

Corollary: If system $[d]$ is unstable but the whole 4-variable system is stable, then making x_1 and x_2 more stable intrinsically will eventually make the whole unstable.

Example 8: The holistic nature of stability is well shown by the system with matrix

$$\begin{bmatrix} -3 & -2 & 2 \\ -6 & -5 & 6 \\ -5 & 2 & -4 \end{bmatrix}$$

in which each variable individually, and every pair, is stable; yet the whole is unstable.

The probability of stability

20/12. The probability that a system should be stable can be made precise by the point of view of S. 14/16. We consider an *ensemble* of absolute systems

$$dx_i/dt = f_i(x_1, \quad . \quad , x_n ; \ \alpha_1, \ . \ . \ ) \qquad (i = 1, \ldots, n)$$

with parameters α_j, such that each combination of α-values gives an absolute system. We nominate a point Q in phase-space, and then define the ' probability of stability at Q ' as the proportion of α-combinations (drawn as samples from known distributions) that give both (1) a resting state at Q, and (2) stable equilibrium at that point. The system's general ' probability of stability ' is the probability at Q averaged over all Q-points. As the probability will usually be zero if Q is a point, we can consider instead the infinitesimal probability dp given when the point is increased to an infinitesimal volume dV.

The question is fundamental to our point of view ; for, having decided that stability is necessary for homeostasis, we want to get a system of 10^{10} nerve-cells and a complex environment stable by some method that does not demand the improbable. The question cannot be treated adequately without some quantitative study. Unfortunately, the quantitative study involves mathematical difficulties of a high order. Non-linear systems cannot be treated generally but only individually. Here I shall deal only with the linear case. It is not implied that the nervous system is linear in its performance or that the answers found have any quantitative application to it. The position is simply that, knowing nothing of what to expect, we must collect what information we can so that we shall have at least some fixed points around which the argument can turn.

The applicability of the concept of linearity is considerably widened by the theorem of S. 20/4.

The problem may be stated as follows : A matrix of order $n \times n$ has elements which are real and are random samples from given distributions. Find the probability that all the latent roots have non-positive real parts.

This problem seems to be still unsolved even in the special cases in which all the elements have the same distributions, selected to be simple, as the ' normal ' type e^{-x^2}, or the ' rectangular ' type, constant between $- a$ and $+ a$. Nevertheless, some answer is desirable, so the ' rectangular ' distribution (integers evenly distributed between $- 9$ and $+ 9$) was tested empirically. Matrices were formed from Fisher and Yates' Table of Random

Numbers, and each matrix was then tested for stability by Hurwitz'
rule (S. 20/8 and S. 20/9). Thus a typical 3×3 matrix was

$$\begin{bmatrix} -1 & -3 & -8 \\ -5 & 4 & -2 \\ -4 & -4 & -9 \end{bmatrix}$$

In this case the second determinant is -86, so it need not be
tested further as it is unstable by S 20/9. The testing becomes
very time-consuming when the matrices exceed 3×3, for the time
taken increases approximately as n^5. The results are summarised
in Table 20/12/1.

Order of matrix	Number tested	Number found stable	Per cent stable
2×2	320	77	24
3×3	100	12	12
4×4	100	1	1

TABLE 20/12/1

The main feature is the rapidity with which the probability
tends to zero The figures given are compatible ($\chi^2 = 4\cdot53$,
$P = 0\cdot10$) with the hypothesis that the probability for a matrix
of order $n \times n$ is $1/2^n$. That this may be the correct expression
for this particular case is suggested partly by the fact that it
may be proved so when $n = 1$ and $n = 2$, and partly by the
fact that, for stability, the matrix has to pass all of n tests.
And in fact about a half of the matrices failed at each test.
If the signs of the determinants in Hurwitz' test are statistically
independent, then $1/2^n$ would be the probability.

In these tests, the intrinsic stabilities of the variables, as
judged by the signs of the terms in the main diagonal, were
equally likely to be stable or unstable. An interesting variation,
therefore, is to consider the case where the variables are all
intrinsically stable (all terms in the main diagonal distributed
uniformly between 0 and -9).

The effect is to increase their probability of stability. Thus
when n is 1 the probability is 1 (instead of $\frac{1}{2}$); and when n is

223

2 the probability is 3/4 (instead of 1/4). Some empirical tests gave the results of Table 20/12/2.

Order of matrix	Number tested	Number found stable	Per cent stable
2 × 2	120	87	72
3 × 3	100	55	55

TABLE 20/12/2.

The probability is higher, but it still falls as n is increased.

A similar series of tests was made with the homeostat. Units were allowed to interact with settings determined by the uni-selectors, and the percentage of stable combinations found when the number of units was two; the percentage was then found for the same general conditions except that three units interacted;

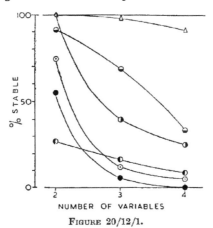

NUMBER OF VARIABLES

FIGURE 20/12/1.

and then four. The general conditions were then changed and a new triple of percentages found. And this was repeated six times altogether. As the general conditions sometimes encouraged, sometimes discouraged, stability, some of the triples were all high, some all low; but in every case the per cent stable fell as the number of interacting units was increased. The results are given in Figure 20/12/1.

These results prove little ; but they suggest that the probability of stability is small in large systems assembled at random. It is suggested, therefore, that large systems should be assumed unstable unless evidence to the contrary can be produced.

REFERENCES

ASHBY, W. Ross   The effect of controls on stability. *Nature*, 155, 242 , 1945

Idem.   Interrelations between stabilities of parts within a whole dynamic system. *Journal of comparative and physiological Psychology*, 40, 1 ; 1947.

Idem   The stability of a randomly assembled nerve-network. *Electroencephalography and clinical neurophysiology*, 2, 471 ; 1950

FRAZER, R. A , and DUNCAN, W. J.   On the criteria for the stability of small motions. *Proceedings of the Royal Society*, A, 124, 642 ; 1929

HURWITZ, A.   Über die Bedingungen, unter welchen eine Gleichung nur Wurzeln mit negativen reellen Teilen besitzt   *Mathematische Annalen*, 46, 273 ; 1895.

NYQUIST, H.   Regeneration theory. *Bell System technical Journal*, 11, 126 ; 1932

CHAPTER 21

Parameters

21/1. WITH canonical equations

$$\frac{dx_i}{dt} = f_i(x_1, \ldots, x_n) \qquad (i = 1, \ldots, n),$$

the form of the field is determined by the functional forms f_i regarded as functions of $x_1, \ldots, x_n$. If parameters $a_1, a_2, \ldots,$ are taken into consideration, the system will be specified by equations

$$\frac{dx_i}{dt} = f_i(x_1, \ldots, x_n; a_1, a_2, \ldots) \qquad (i = 1, \ldots, n).$$

If the parameters are constant, the x's continue to form an absolute system. If the a's can take m combinations of values, then the x's form m different absolute systems, and will show m different fields. If a parameter can change continuously (in value, not in time), no limit can be put to the number of different fields which can arise.

If a parameter affects only certain variables directly, it will appear only in the corresponding f's. Thus, if it affects only x_1 directly, so that the diagram of immediate effects is

$$a \rightarrow x_1 \rightleftarrows x_2,$$

then a will appear only in f_1:

$$dx_1/dt = f_1(x_1, x_2; a)$$
$$dx_2/dt = f_2(x_1, x_2).$$

But it will in general appear in all the F's of the integrals (S. 19/10). The subject is developed further in Chapter 24.

Change of parameters can represent *every* alteration which can be made on an absolute system, and therefore on any physical or biological ' machine '. It includes every possibility of experimental interference. Thus if a set of variables that are joined to form the system $\dot{x} = f(x)$ are changed in their relations so that they form the system $\dot{x} = \phi(x)$, then the change can equally

226

well be represented as a change in the single system $\dot{x} = \psi(x\,;\,\alpha)$. For if α can take two values, 1 and 2 say, and if

$$f(x) \equiv \psi(x\,;\,1)$$
$$\phi(x) \equiv \psi(x\,;\,2)$$

then the two representations are identical.

As example of its method, the action of S. 8/10, where the two front magnets of the homeostat were joined by a light glass fibre and so forced to move from side to side together, will be shown so that the joining and releasing are equivalent in the canonical equations to a single parameter taking one of two values.

Suppose that units x_1, x_2 and x_3 were used, and that the magnets of 1 and 2 were joined. Before joining, the equations were (S. 19/11)

$$\left.\begin{array}{l} dx_1/dt = a_{11}x_1 + a_{12}x_2 + a_{13}x_3 \\ dx_2/dt = a_{21}x_1 + a_{22}x_2 + a_{23}x_3 \\ dx_3/dt = a_{31}x_1 + a_{32}x_2 + a_{33}x_3 \end{array}\right\}$$

After joining, x_2 can be ignored as a variable since x_1 and x_2 are effectively only a single variable. But x_2's output still affects the others, and its force still acts on the fibre. The equations therefore become

$$\left.\begin{array}{l} dx_1/dt = (a_{11} + a_{12} + a_{21} + a_{22})x_1 + (a_{13} + a_{23})x_3 \\ dx_3/dt = \qquad\qquad (a_{31} + a_{32})x_1 + \qquad a_{33}x_3 \end{array}\right\}$$

It is easy to verify that if the full equations, including the parameter b, were :

$$\left.\begin{array}{l} dx_1/dt = \{a_{11} + b(a_{12} + a_{21} + a_{22})\}x_1 + (1 - b)a_{12}x_2 \\ \qquad\qquad\qquad\qquad\qquad\qquad + (a_{13} + ba_{23})x_3 \\ dx_2/dt = \qquad\qquad\qquad a_{21}x_1 \qquad + a_{22}x_2 + \quad a_{23}x_3 \\ dx_3/dt = \qquad\qquad (a_{31} + ba_{32})x_1 + (1 - b)a_{32}x_2 + \quad a_{33}x_3 \end{array}\right\}$$

then the joining and releasing are identical in their effects with giving b the values 1 and 0 respectively. (These equations are sufficient but not, of course, necessary)

21/2. A variable x_k behaves as a 'null-function' if it has the following properties, which are easily shown to be necessary and sufficient for each other :

(1) As a function of the time, it remains at its initial value x_k^0.

(2) In the canonical equations, $f_k(x_1, \ldots, x_n)$ is identically zero.

(3) In the group equations, $F_k(x_1^0, \ldots, x_n^0, t) \equiv x_k^0$.

(Some region of the phase-space is assumed given.)

Since we usually consider absolute systems, we shall usually require the parameters to be held constant. Since null-functions also remain constant, the properties of the two will often be similar. (A fundamental distinction by definition is that parameters are outside, while null-functions may be inside, the given system.)

21/3. In an absolute system, the variables other than the step- and null-functions will be referred to as **main variables**.

21/4. *Theorem :* In an absolute system, the system of the main-variables forms an absolute subsystem provided no step-function changes from its initial value.

Suppose $x_1, \ldots, x_k$ are null- and step-functions and the main-variables are $x_{k+1}, \ldots, x_n$. The canonical equations of the whole system are

$$
\left.
\begin{aligned}
&dx_1/dt = 0 \\
&\cdots\cdots\cdots \\
&dx_k/dt = 0 \\
&dx_{k+1}/dt = f_{k+1}(x_1, \ldots, x_k, x_{k+1}, \ldots, x_n) \\
&\cdots\cdots\cdots \\
&dx_n/dt = f_n(x_1, \ldots, x_k, x_{k+1}, \ldots, x_n)
\end{aligned}
\right\}
$$

The first k equations can be integrated at once to give $x_1 = x_1^0$, $\ldots$, $x_k = x_k^0$. Substituting these in the remaining equations we get :

$$
\left.
\begin{aligned}
&dx_{k+1}/dt = f_{k+1}(x_1^0, \ldots, x_k^0, x_{k+1}, \ldots, x_n) \\
&\cdots\cdots\cdots \\
&dx_n/dt = f_n(x_1^0, \ldots, x_k^0, x_{k+1}, \ldots, x_n)
\end{aligned}
\right\}
$$

The terms $x_1^0, \ldots, x_k^0$ are now constants, not effectively functions of t at all. The equations are in canonical form, so the system is absolute over any interval not containing a change in $x_1^0, \ldots, x_k^0$.

Usually the selection of variables to form an absolute system is rigorously determined by the real, natural relationships existing in the real ' machine ', and the observer has no power to alter them without making alterations in the ' machine ' itself. The theorem, however, shows that without affecting the absoluteness we may take null-functions into the system or remove them from it as we please.

It also follows that the statements: 'parameter a was held constant at a^0', and 'the system was re-defined to include a, which, as a null-function, remained at its initial value of a^0' are merely two ways of describing the same facts.

21/5. The fact that the field is changed by a change of parameter implies that the stabilities of the lines of behaviour are changed. For instance, consider the system

$$dx/dt = -x + ay, \quad dy/dt = x - y + 1$$

where x and y have been used for simplicity instead of x_1 and x_2. When $a = 0$, 1, and 2 respectively, the system has the three fields shown in Figure 21/5/1.

FIGURE 21/5/1 : Three fields of x and y when a has the values (left to right) 0, 1, and 2.

When $a = 0$ there is a stable resting state at $x = 0$, $y = 1$; when $a = 1$ there is no resting state; when $a = 2$ there is an unstable resting state at $x = -2$, $y = -1$.

The system has as many fields as there are values to a.

21/6. The simple physical act of joining two machines has, of course, a counterpart in the equations, shown more simply in the canonical than in the group equations.

One could, of course, simply write down equations in all the variables and then simply let some parameter a have one value when the parts are joined and another when they are separated. This method, however, gives no insight into the real events in 'joining' two systems. A better method is to equate parameters in one system to variables in the other. When this is done, the second dominates the first. If parameters in each are equated to variables in the other, then a two-way interaction occurs. For instance, suppose we start with the 2-variable system

$$\left.\begin{aligned} dx/dt &= f_1(x,\ y\ ;\ a) \\ dy/dt &= f_2(x,\ y) \end{aligned}\right\} \text{and the 1-variable system } dz/dt = \phi(z\ ;\ b)$$

then the diagram of immediate effects is

$$a \longrightarrow x \rightleftarrows y \qquad b \longrightarrow z$$

If we put $a = z$, the new system has the equations

$$\left.\begin{aligned} dx/dt &= f_1(x,\ y\ ;\ z) \\ dy/dt &= f_2(x,\ y) \\ dz/dt &= \phi(z\ ;\ b) \end{aligned}\right\}$$

and the diagram of immediate effects becomes

$$b \longrightarrow z \longrightarrow x \rightleftarrows y.$$

If a further join is made by putting $b = y$, the equations become

$$\begin{aligned} dx/dt &= f_1(x,\ y\ ;\ z) \\ dy/dt &= f_2(x,\ y) \\ dz/dt &= \phi(z\ ;\ y) \end{aligned}$$

and the diagram of immediate effects becomes

In this method each linkage uses up one parameter. This is reasonable; for the parameter used by the other system might have been used by the experimenter for arbitrary control. So the method simply exchanges the experimenter for another system

This method of joining does no violence to each system's internal activities : these proceed as before except as modified by the actions coming in through the variables which were once parameters.

21/7. The stabilities of separate systems do not define the stability of the system formed by joining them together.

In the general case, when the f's are unrestricted, this proposition is not easily given a meaning. But in the linear case (to which all continuous systems approximate, S. 20/4) the meaning is clear.   Several examples will be given.

Example 1 · Two systems may be stable if joined one way, and unstable if joined another.   Consider the 1-variable systems $dx/dt = x + 2p_1 + p_2$ and $dy/dt = -2r - 3y$.   If they are joined by putting $r = x$, $p_1 = y$, the system becomes

$$\left.\begin{aligned} dx/dt &= x + 2y + p_2\\ dy/dt &= -2x - 3y \end{aligned}\right\}$$

The latent roots of its matrix are -1, -1; so it is stable.   But if they are joined by $r = x$, $p_2 = y$, the roots become $+0\,414$ and $-2\,414$: and it is unstable.

Example 2: Several systems, all stable, may be unstable when joined.   Join the three systems

$$dx/dt = -x - 2q - 2r$$
$$dy/dt = -2p - y + r$$
$$dz/dt = p + q - z$$

all of which are stable, by putting $p = x$, $q = y$, $r = z$.   The resulting system has latent roots $+1$, -2, -2.

Example 3: Systems, each unstable, may be joined to form a stable whole.   Join the 2-variable system

$$\left.\begin{aligned} dx/dt &= 3x - 3y - 3p\\ dy/dt &= 3x - 9y - 8p \end{aligned}\right\}$$

which is unstable, to $dz/dt = 21q + 3r + 3z$, which is also unstable, by putting $q = x$, $r = y$, $p = z$.   The whole is stable.

Example 4. If a system

$$dx_i/dt = f_i(x_1, \ \ldots, \ x_n; \ a_1, \quad .) \qquad (i = 1, \ldots, \ n)$$

is joined to another system, of y's, by equating various a's and y's, then the resting states that were once given by certain combinations of x and a will still occur, so far as the x-system is concerned, when the y's take the values the a's had before.   The zeros of the f's are thus invariant for the operations of joining and separating.

CHAPTER 22

Step-Functions

22/1. A variable behaves as a **step-function** over some given period of observation if it changes value at only a finite number of discrete instants, at which it changes value instantaneously. The term ' step-function ' will also be used, for convenience, to refer to any physical part whose behaviour is typically of this form.

22/2. An example of a step-function in a system will be given to establish the main properties.

Suppose a mass m hangs downwards suspended on a massless strand of elastic. If the elastic is stretched too far it will break and the mass will fall. Let the elastic pull with a force of k dynes for each centimetre increase from its unstretched length, and, for simplicity, assume that it exerts an opposite force when compressed. Let x, the position of the mass, be measured vertically downwards, taking as zero the position of the elastic when there is no mass.

If the mass is started from a position vertically above or below the point of rest, the movement will be given by the equation

$$\frac{d}{dt}\left(m\frac{dx}{dt}\right) = gm - kx \quad . \quad . \quad . \quad (1)$$

where g is the acceleration due to gravity. This equation is not in canonical form, but may be made so by writing $x = x_1$, $dx/dt = x_2$, when it becomes

$$\left.\begin{array}{l} \dfrac{dx_1}{dt} = x_2 \\[2mm] \dfrac{dx_2}{dt} = g - \dfrac{k}{m}x_1 \end{array}\right\} . \quad . \quad . \quad (2)$$

232

If the elastic breaks, k becomes 0, and the equations become

$$\left.\begin{array}{l} \dfrac{dx_1}{dt} = x_2 \\[2mm] \dfrac{dx_2}{dt} = g \end{array}\right\} \qquad . \qquad . \qquad . \qquad . \quad (3)$$

Assume that the elastic breaks if it is pulled longer than X.

The events may be viewed in two ways, which are equivalent.

We may treat the change of k as a change of parameter to the 2-variable system x_1, x_2, changing their equations from (2) above to (3) (S. 21/1). The field of the 2-variable system will change from A to B in Figure 22/2/1, where the dotted line at X

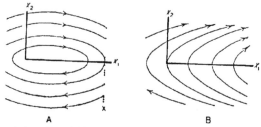

FIGURE 22/2/1 : Two fields of the system (x_1 and x_2) of S. 22/2   With unbroken elastic the system behaves as A, with broken as B. When the strand is stretched to position X it breaks.

shows that the field to its right may not be used (for at X the elastic will break).

Equivalent to this is the view which treats them as a 3-variable system : x_1, x_2, and k. This system is absolute, and has one field, shown in Figure 22/2/2.

In this form, the step-function must be brought into the canonical equations. A possible form is :

$$\frac{dk}{dt} = q\left(\frac{K}{2} + \frac{K}{2}\tanh\{q(X - x_1)\} - k\right) \qquad . \quad (4)$$

where K is the initial value of the variable k, and q is large and positive. As $q \to \infty$, the behaviour of k tends to the step-function form.

Another method is to use Dirac's δ-function, defined by $\delta(u) = 0$ if $u \neq 0$, while if $u = 0$, $\delta(u)$ tends to infinity in such a way that

$$\int_{-\infty}^{\infty} \delta(u)du = 1.$$

Then if $du/dt = \delta\{\phi(u, v, \ldots)\}$, du/dt will be usually zero ; but if the changes of $u, v, \ldots$ take ϕ through zero, then $\delta(u)$ becomes momentarily infinite and u will change by a finite jump. These

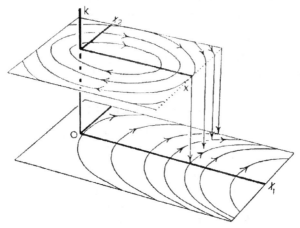

FIGURE 22/2/2 : Field of the 3-variable system.

representations are of little practical use, but they are important theoretically in showing that a step-function *can* be represented in the canonical equations.

22/3. In an absolute system, a step-function will change value if, and only if, the system arrives at certain states : the **critical**. In Figure 22/2/2, for instance, all the points in the plane $k = \mathrm{K}$ and to the right of the line $x_1 = X$ are critical states for the step-function k when it has the initial value K.

The critical states may, of course, be distributed arbitrarily. More commonly, however, the distribution is continuous. In this case there will be a **critical surface**

$$\phi(k, x_1, \ldots, x_n) = 0$$

which, given k, divides the critical from the non-critical states. In Figure 22/2/2, for instance, the surface intersects the plane $k = K$ at the line $x_1 = X$. (The plane $k = 0$ is not intersected by it, for there are no states in this system whose occurrence will result in k changing from 0.)

Commonly ϕ is a function of only a few of the variables of the

234

system. Thus, whether a Post Office-type relay opens or shuts depends only on the two variables : the current in the coil, and whether the relay is already open or shut.

Such relays and critical states occur in the homeostat. When two, three or four units are in use, the critical surfaces will form a square, cube, or tesseract respectively in the phase-space around the origin. The critical states will fill the space outside this surface. As there is some 'backlash' in the relays, the critical surfaces for opening are not identical with those for closing.

Systems with multiple fields

22/4. If, in the previous example, someone unknown to us were sometimes to break and sometimes to replace the elastic, and if we were to test the behaviour of the system x_1, x_2 over a prolonged time including many such actions, we would find that the system was often absolute with a field like A of Figure 22/2/1, and often absolute with a field like B ; and that from time to time the field changed suddenly from the one form to the other.

Such a system could be said without ambiguity to have two fields. Similarly, if parameters capable of taking r combinations of values were subject to intermittent change by some other, unobserved system, a system might be found to have r fields.

22/5. The argument can, however, be reversed : if we find that a subsystem has r fields we can deduce, subject to certain restrictions, that the other variables must include step-functions.

Theorem : If, within an absolute system $x_1, \ldots, x_n, x_p, \ldots, x_s$, the subsystem $x_1, \ldots, x_n$ is absolute within each of r fields (which persist for a finite time and interchange instantaneously) and is not independent of $x_p, \ldots, x_s$; then one or more of $x_p, \ldots, x_s$ must be step-functions.

Consider the whole system first while one field persists. Take a generic initial state $x_1^0, \ldots, x_n^0, x_p^0, \ldots, x_s^0$ and allow time t_1 to elapse ; suppose the representative point moves to $x_1', \ldots, x_n', x_p', \ldots, x_s'$, where each x' is not necessarily different from x^0. Let further time t_2 elapse, the point moving on to $x_1'', \ldots, x_n'', x_p'', \ldots, x_s''$. Now consider the line of behaviour that follows the initial state $x_1', \ldots, x_n', x_p^0, x_q^0, \ldots, x_s'$, differing from the second point only in the value of x_p : as the subsystem is absolute, an interval t_2 will bring its variables again to $x_1'', \ldots, x_n''$, i.e. these variables' behaviours are the same on the two lines   Now x_p' either is, or is not, equal to x_p^0. If unequal, then by definition (S. 14/3) $x_1, \ldots, x_n$ is independent of x_p. So the behaviour of $x_1, \ldots, x_n$ over t_2 will show either that $x_p' = x_p^0$ (i.e. that x_p did not change over t_1) or that $x_1, \ldots, x_n$ is independent of x_p. Similar tests with the other variables of the set $x_p, \ldots, x_s$ will enable them to be divided into two classes : (1) those that remained constant over t_1, and (2) those of which the subsystem $x_1, \ldots, x_n$ is independent. By hypothesis, class (2) may not include all of $x_p, \ldots, x_s$; so class (1) is not void.

When a field of $x_1, \ldots, x_n$ changes, some parameter to this system must have changed value. As $x_1, \ldots, x_n, x_p, \ldots, x_s$ is isolated, the ' parameter ' can be none other than one or more of $x_p, \ldots, x_s$. As the field has changed, the parameter cannot be in class (2). At the change of field, therefore, at least one of those in class (1) changed value. So class (1), and therefore the set $x_p, \ldots, x_s$, contains at least one step-function.

REFERENCE

ASHBY, W. Ross.   Principles of the self-organising dynamic system   *Journal of general Psychology*, 37, 125 ; 1947.

CHAPTER 23

The Ultrastable System

23/1. The definition and description already given in S. 8/6 and 7 have established the elementary properties of the ultrastable system. A restatement in mathematical form, however, has the advantage of rendering a misunderstanding less likely, and of providing a base for quantitative studies.

If a system is ultrastable, it is composed of main variables x_i and of step-functions a_i, so that the whole is absolute :

$$\frac{dx_i}{dt} = f_i(x ; a) \qquad (i = 1, \ldots, n)$$

$$\frac{da_i}{dt} = g_i(x ; a) \qquad (i = 1, 2, \ldots)$$

The functions g_i must be given some form like that of S. 22/2. The system is started with the representative point within the critical surface $\phi(x) = 0$, contact with which makes the step-functions change value. When they change, the new values are to be random samples from some distribution, assumed given.

Thus in the homeostat, the equations of the main variables are (S. 19/11) :

$$\frac{dx_i}{dt} = a_{i1}x_1 + a_{i2} x_2 + a_{i3} x_3 + a_{i4} x_4 \qquad (i = 1, 2, 3, 4)$$

The a's are step-functions, coming from a distribution of 'rectangular' form, lying evenly between -1 and $+1$. The critical surfaces of the a's are specified approximately by $|x| \pm \frac{\pi}{4} = 0$. Each individual step-function a_{jk} depends only on whether x_j crosses the critical surface.

As the a's change discontinuously, an analytic integration of the differential equations is not, so far as I am aware, possible. But the equations, the description, and the schedule of the uniselector-wirings (the random samples) define uniquely the behaviour of the x's and the a's. So the behaviour could be computed to any degree of accuracy by a numerical method. The proof given in Chapter 8, though verbal, is adequate to establish the elementary properties of the system. A rigorous statement and proof would add little of real value.

23/2. How many trials will be necessary, on the average, for a terminal field to be found ? If an ultrastable system has a probability p that a new field of the main variables will be stable, and if the fields' probabilities are independent, then the number of fields occurring (including the terminal) will be, on the average, $1/p$.

For at the first field, a proportion p will be terminal, and q ($= 1 - p$) will not. Of the latter, at the second field, the proportion p will be terminal and q not ; so the total proportion stable at the second field will be pq, and the number still unstable q^2. Similarly the proportion becoming terminal at the u-th field will be pq^{u-1}. So the average number of trials made will be

$$\frac{p + 2pq + 3pq^2 + \ldots + upq^{u-1} + \ldots}{p + pq + pq^2 + \ldots + pq^{u-1} + \ldots} = \frac{1}{p}.$$

23/3. In an ultrastable system, a field may be terminal and yet show little resemblance to the ' normal ' equilibrium which is necessary if the system is to show, after each of a variety of displacements, a return to the resting state. A field, for instance, might have a resting state at which only a single line of behaviour terminated : if the representative point were on that line the field would be terminal, but hardly any displacement would be followed by a return to the resting state.

It can, however, be shown that if a proportion of the fields evoked by the step-function changes are of this or similar type, then the terminal fields will contain them in smaller proportion. For, given a field and a closed critical surface, let k_1 be the proportion of lines of behaviour crossing the boundary which are stable. Thus in Figure 8/7/1, in I $k_1 = 0$, in II $k_1 = 0$, in III $k_1 = \frac{1}{2}$ approximately, and in IV $k_1 = 1$. To count the lines, the boundary surface could be divided into portions of equal area, small enough so that stable and unstable lines do not pass through the same area. Then if we assume that in any field the representative point is equally likely to start at any of the small areas, a field's chance of being terminal is proportional to k_1.

It follows that if the changes of step-functions evoke fields whose values of k_1 are distributed so that the probability of a field having a k_1-value between k_1 and $k_1 + dk_1$ is $\psi(k_1)dk_1$, then in the terminal fields the probablity is

$$\frac{k_1\psi(k_1)dk_1}{\int_0^1 k_1\psi(k_1)dk_1} \qquad . \qquad . \qquad . \qquad . \quad (1)$$

Figure 23/3/1 shows a possible distribution of values of k_1 in

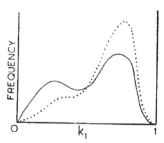

FIGURE 23/3/1 : Solid line : a distribution $\psi(k_1)$; broken line : the corresponding distribution $k_1\psi(k_1)$.

the original fields (solid line), and how k_1 would then be distributed in the terminal fields (broken line). The shift towards the higher values of k_1 is clear.

Fields with a low value of k_1, unsatisfactory for adaptation, tend therefore not to be terminal.

23/4. It was noticed in S. 13/4 that fields like A and B of Figure 13/4/1, though terminal, are defective in their persistence after small random disturbances. This idea may be given more precision.

Assume that the small random disturbances cause displacements which have some definite probability distribution, Gaussian say, so that if applied to the representative point when it is at some definite position in the field, there is a definite probability k_2 that a random displacement will not carry the point beyond the critical surface. Assume the representative point is always at the resting state or resting cycle. Then any terminal field has a unique value for k_2. If the field contains a single resting state, k_2 for that field is the probability, when the representative point

239

is at the resting state, that the application of a single random disturbance will not take the representative point beyond the critical surface. If the field has a resting cycle, k_2 is the average of the values when the representative point is on the many portions of the cycle, the value for each portion being weighted according to the time spent by the representative point in that portion. For more complex fields, k_2 could be defined, but a more detailed study is not necessary here.

Suppose that the ultrastable system, when the step-functions undergo random changes, yields terminal fields whose values of k_2 are distributed so that the proportion falling between k_2 and $k_2 + dk_2$ is $\phi(k_2)dk_2$. If to such fields, with k_2 lying between such limits, we apply one random disturbance, a proportion k_2 will not be changed ; but the proportion $1 - k_2$ will be changed, and will be replaced by new terminal fields ; their values of k_2 will be distributed again as $\phi(k_2)dk_2$, and this distribution will be added to that of the unchanged fields. In this way it is easy to show that the final distribution $\lambda(k_2)$ equals

$$A \frac{\phi(k_2)}{1 - k_2}$$

where A is a constant.

Examination of the form of the distribution $\lambda(k_2)$ shows that it is $\phi(k_2)$ heavily weighted in favour of the values of k_2 near 1. Such fields can only be those with the resting state or cycle near the centre of the region. So the result confirms the common-sense argument of S. 13/4. It will be noticed that the deduction is independent of the particular form of the distribution of disturbances.

REFERENCES

ASHBY, W Ross   The physical origin of adaptation by trial and error. *Journal of general Psychology*, **32**, 13 , 1945.
Idem.   The nervous system as physical machine : with special reference to the origin of adaptive behaviour   *Mind*, **56**, 1 ; 1947.

CHAPTER 24

Constancy and Independence

24/1. The relation of variable to variable has been treated by observing the behaviour of the whole system. But what of their effects on one another ? Thus, if a variable changes in value, can we distribute the cause of this change among the other variables ?

In general, it is not possible to divide the effect into parts, with so much caused by this variable and so much caused by that. Only when there are special simplicities is such a division possible. In general, the change of a variable results from the activity of the whole system, and cannot be subdivided quantitatively. Thus, if $dx/dt = \sin x + xe^y$, and $x = \frac{1}{2}$ and $y = 2$, then in the next 0 01 unit of time x will increase by 0 042, but this quantity cannot be divided into two parts, one due to x and one to y.

24/2. But a relationship which *can* be treated in detail is that of ' independence '. By the principle of S. 2/8 it must be defined in terms of observable behaviour.

Given an absolute system and two lines of behaviour from two initial states which differ only in their values of x_j^0 (the difference being Δx_j^0), the variable x_k is **independent** of x_j if x_k's behaviour is identical on the two lines. Analytically, x_k is independent of x_j in the conditions given if

$$F_k(x_1^0, \ldots, x_j^0, \ldots; \ t) \equiv F_k(x_1^0, \ldots, x_j^0 + \Delta x_j^0, \ldots; \ t) \quad (1)$$

as a function of t. In other words, x_k is independent of x_j if x_k's behaviour is invariant when the initial state is changed by Δx_j^0.

This narrow definition provides the basis for further development. In practical application, the identity (1) may hold over all values of Δx_j^0 (within some finite range, perhaps) ; and may also hold for all initial states of x_k (within some finite range, perhaps). In such cases the test whether x_k is independent of x_j is whether

241

$\dfrac{\partial}{\partial x_j^0}\, F_k(x_1^0,\ \ldots,\ x_n^0;\ t) \equiv 0.$ (These relations and notations are collected in S. 24/19 for convenience in reference.)

Example: In the system of S. 19/10

$$\left.\begin{aligned}
x_1 &= x_1^0 + x_2^0 t + t^2\\
x_2 &= x_2^0 + 2t
\end{aligned}\right\}$$

x_2 is independent of x_1, but x_1 is not independent of x_2.

24/3. We shall be interested chiefly in the independencies introduced when particular variables become constant : when they are part-functions, for instance. Such constancies are most naturally expressed in the canonical equations, for here are specified the properties of the parts before assembly (S. 19/19). We therefore need a method of deducing the independence from the canonical equations, preferably without an explicit integration. Such a method is developed below in S. 24/3 to 10. (The method recently developed by Riguet, however, promises to be much better.)

Given an absolute system

$$\frac{dx_i}{dt} = f_i(x_1,\ \ldots,\ x_n) \qquad (i = 1,\ \ldots,\ n) \qquad . \quad (1)$$

it is required to find whether or not x_k is independent of x_j, some region of values being assumed. The region must not include changes of values of step-functions or of activations of part-functions; for the derivatives required below may not exist, and the independencies may change.

If the functions f_i are expandable by Taylor's series around the point $x_1^0,\ \ldots,\ x_n^0$, we may write their integrals symbolically (S. 19/27) as

$$F_i(x_1^0,\ \ldots,\ x_n^0;\ t) = e^{tX}x_i^0 \qquad (i = 1,\ \ldots,\ n) \ . \quad (2)$$

where X is the operator

$$f_1(x_1^0,\ \ldots,\ x_n^0)\frac{\partial}{\partial x_1^0} + \ldots + f_n(x_1^0,\ \ldots,\ x_n^0)\frac{\partial}{\partial x_n^0}.$$

(The zero superscripts will now be dropped as unnecessary.)

Expanding the exponential, and operating on (2) with $\dfrac{\partial}{\partial x_j}$, the test whether x_k is independent of x_j becomes whether

$$\frac{\partial}{\partial x_j}X^\mu x_k = 0 \qquad (\mu = 1,\ 2,\ \ldots) \quad . \qquad . \quad (3)$$

By expanding $\frac{\partial}{\partial x_j} X$:

$$\frac{\partial}{\partial x_j} X^{\mu+1} x_k = \sum_p{}' \frac{\partial f_p}{\partial x_j} \frac{\partial}{\partial x_p} X^\mu x_k + X \frac{\partial}{\partial x_j} X^\mu x_k \qquad . \quad (4)$$

Applying the test (3), if the test for $\mu = m$ gives

$$\frac{\partial}{\partial x_j} X^m x_k = 0$$

then for $\mu = m + 1$, by using (4) we need only see whether

$$\sum_p{}' \frac{\partial f_p}{\partial x_j} \frac{\partial}{\partial x_p} X^\mu x_k = 0 \qquad . \qquad . \qquad . \quad (5)$$

24/4. We now add the hypothesis that the system is linear (S. 19/27) The restriction is unimportant as no arguments are used elsewhere which depend on linearity or on non-linearity. Further, in the region near a resting state all systems tend to the linear form (S. 20/4), and this region has our main interest.

Starting with $\mu = 1$ the tests 24/3 (5) become

$$\left.\begin{array}{c} \dfrac{\partial f_k}{\partial x_j} = 0 \\[2mm] \displaystyle\sum_p \dfrac{\partial f_k}{\partial x_p} \dfrac{\partial f_p}{\partial x_j} = 0 \\[2mm] \displaystyle\sum_p \sum_\sigma{}' \dfrac{\partial f_k}{\partial x_p} \dfrac{\partial f_p}{\partial x_\sigma} \dfrac{\partial f_\sigma}{\partial x_j} = 0 \\[2mm] \text{etc.} \end{array}\right\} \qquad . \qquad . \qquad . \quad (1)$$

These tests now use only the f's, as required. They are both necessary and sufficient. They have been shown necessary ; and by merely retracing the argument they are found to be sufficient. Only the first $n - 1$ tests of (1) above are required, for products which contain more than $n - 1$ factors must include products already given, in the first $n - 1$ tests, as zero

The tests are, however, clumsy. The simplicity and directness can be improved by using the facts that we need distinguish only between zero and non-zero quantities, and that the sums of (1) above resemble the elements of matrix products Sections 24/5–10 develop this possibility.

24/5. An **R0-matrix** has elements which can take only two values : R (non-zero) and 0 (zero). The elements therefore combine by the rules

$$R + R = R, \quad 0 + 0 = 0, \quad R + 0 = 0 + R = R,$$
$$R \times R = R, \quad 0 \times 0 = 0, \quad R \times 0 = 0 \times R = 0.$$

A sum of such elements can therefore be zero in general only if each element is zero.

24/6. In an $R0$-matrix of order $n \times n$, the zeros are **patterned** if, given any zero not in the principal diagonal, we can separate the numbers 1, 2, . . ., n into two sets α and β (neither being void) so that the minor left after suppressing columns α and rows β is composed wholly of zeros which include the given zero. For example, the $R0$-matrix

$$\begin{bmatrix} 0 & 0 & 0 & R \\ R & R & R & R \\ R & 0 & R & R \\ 0 & 0 & 0 & R \end{bmatrix}$$

has its zeros patterned. Selecting, for instance, the zero in the third row, we can make $\alpha = 1, 3, 4$ and $\beta = 2$. This leaves the minor

$$\begin{bmatrix} . & 0 & . & . \\ . & . & . & . \\ . & 0 & . & . \\ . & 0 & . & . \end{bmatrix}$$

where dots indicate eliminated elements ; the remaining elements are all zero, and they include the selected zero. The other zeros in the original matrix can all be treated similarly.

24/7. Some necessary theorems will now be stated. Their proofs are simple and need not be given here.

A matrix A is **idempotent** if $A^2 = A$.

Theorem : If an $R0$-matrix has no zeros in the principal diagonal a necessary and sufficient condition that the zeros be patterned is that the matrix be idempotent.

24/8. *Theorem :* If A is an $R0$-matrix of order $n \times n$, and I is the matrix with R's in the principal diagonal and zeros elsewhere, then the matrix

$$I + A + A^2 + \ldots + A^{n-1}$$

is idempotent.

24/9. From the f's of the canonical equations (24/8(1)) form the **differential matrix** $[f]$ by inserting, in the (hj)-th position (at the intersection of the h-th row and the j-th column) an 0 or R according as $\partial f_h/\partial x_j$ is, or is not, zero (in the region of phase-space considered). Then the square, cube, etc , of $[f]$ will contain in the (kj)-th position an element which is zero or non-zero as the second, third, etc., tests of 24/4(1) are or are not zero. If now these powers are summed, to S :

$$S = [f] + [f]^2 + \ldots + [f]^{n-1}, \qquad . \qquad . \quad (1)$$

a zero element in S at the (kj)-th position means that all the terms of the series were zero, and therefore that x_k is independent of x_j.

The same independence will make zero the element at the (kj)-th position in the matrix whose (hi)-th element is zero or non-zero as $\partial F_h/\partial x_i^0$ is or is not zero. This **integral matrix**, $[F]$, must therefore satisfy

$$[F] = S. \qquad . \qquad \qquad . \quad . \quad (2)$$

24/10. The restriction is now added that the behaviour of each variable x_i is to depend on its own starting-point. (Physical systems not conforming to this restriction are, so far as I am aware, rare and peculiar.) The principal diagonal of $[F]$ will then be found to have all its elements non-zero. In such a case, $[F]$ is not altered if we add to it the matrix I of S. 24/8, and we may sum up as follows:

If a dynamic system is specified by

$$\frac{dx_i}{dt} = f_i(x_1, \ldots, x_n) \qquad (i = 1, \ldots, n)$$

and if $[f]$ is an $R0$-matrix where each (kj)-th element is 0 or R as $\dfrac{\partial f_k}{\partial x_j}$ is or is not zero respectively (in some region within which the nullity does not change), and if $[F]$ is an $R0$-matrix where each (kj)-th element is 0 or R as x_k is or is not independent of x_j respectively in the same region, and if each x's behaviour depends on its own starting point, then

$$[F] = [f] + [f]^2 + \ldots + [f]^{n-1} \qquad . \quad (1)$$

This equation gives the independencies when the differential matrix is given; for x_k is or is not independent of x_j as the

245   R

element in the k-th row and the j-th column of the integral matrix is or is not zero respectively.

The advantage of equation (1) is that the differential matrix is often formed with ease (for only zero or non-zero values are required), and often the first multiplication shows that $[f]^2 = [f]$. When this is so, the integral matrix is at once proved to be equal to $[f]$, and all the independencies are obtained at once. A further advantage is that the theory of partitioned matrices can often be used, with considerable economy of time. The next few sections provide some examples.

24/11. In an absolute system the independencies cannot be assigned arbitrarily.

By the theorem of S. 24/8, the integral matrix, being the sum of powers, is idempotent; and therefore, by S. 24/7, has its zeros patterned. The independencies of an absolute system must always be subject to this restriction.

What is really the same line of reasoning may be shown in an alternative form. The group property requires (S. 19/10) that

$$F_k\{F_1(x^0; t), F_2(x^0; t), \ldots; t'\} \equiv F_k\{x_1^0, x_2^0, \ldots; t + t'\};$$

so if x_k is independent of x_j then x_j^0 will not appear effectively on the right-hand side, and it must therefore not appear effectively on the left. So if, say, $F_m(\ldots; t)$ contains x_j^0, then x_m^0 must not occur in F_k; so x_k must be independent of x_m as well.

24/12. If the variables of an absolute system are divisible into two groups A and B, such that all the variables of A are independent of B, but not all those of B are independent of A, then the subsystem A **dominates** the subsystem B.

Theorem : The subsystem A is itself absolute.

Write down the group equations of the A's :

$$F_A\{F_1(x^0; t), F_2(x^0; t), \ldots; t'\} \equiv F_A\{x_1^0, x_2^0, \ldots; t + t'\}$$

where the subscript A refers to all the members of A in succession. Each F_A is independent of x_B^0, so, omitting the unnecessary symbols from each side both from the F's and from the x^0's, we get

$$F_A\{F_A(x_A^0; t), \ldots; t'\} \equiv F_A\{x_A^0; t + t'\}$$

where the change of subscript means that only the members of A are now included. Inspection shows that these are the equations of a finite continuous group in the variables A. So the A's form an absolute system.

The fact of dominance may be shown in the integral matrix by finding that the deletion of columns A and rows B leaves only zeros; but the deletion of columns B and rows A leaves some non-zero elements. (If the second operation also leaves only zeros, then the system really consists of two completely independent subsystems; the whole system is 'reducible'.)

24/13. If A, B, and C are systems such that they together form one absolute system, and if A dominates B, and B dominates C, then A dominates C.

On the information given, $[F]$, in partitioned form, can be filled in but for two elements, shown as dots:

$$\begin{array}{c} \\ A \\ B \\ C \end{array}\begin{array}{ccc} A & B & C \\ \left[\begin{array}{ccc} R & 0 & . \\ R & R & 0 \\ . & R & R \end{array}\right] \end{array}$$

It must be idempotent (S. 24/11). Trying the four possible combinations of R and 0 for the two undefined elements, we find that there must be 0 at the top right corner, and R at the bottom left. A therefore dominates C.

The theorem illustrates again the importance of the concept of 'absoluteness'; for without this assumption the theorem, obvious physically, cannot be proved (for lack of the group property).

24/14. An account of the primary effects of part-functions on the independencies within an absolute system can now be given

The definition of a part-function x_p implies that over finite regions of values of $x_1, \ldots, x_n$ $f_p(x_1, \ldots, x_n)$ becomes zero. Within such a region, i.e. while not activated, the canonical equations include $dx_p/dt = 0$, which can be integrated at once to $x_p = x_p^0$; so $F_p(x^0; t) = x_p^0$, and x_p and F_p are both constant. $\partial F_p/\partial x_j$ is therefore zero for all values of j other than p. The effect of a part-function x_p being inactive is therefore to make the whole of the p-th row of the differential and integral matrices zero (except for the element in the main diagonal, which remains an R).

It will be recognised that $[f]$ and $[F]$, the differential and integral matrices, are the matrix equivalents of the diagrams of

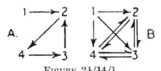

immediate and ultimate effects respectively. Thus the diagram of immediate effects A in Figure 24/14/1 yields the diagram of ultimate effects B. For the system, $[f]$ is

$$\begin{bmatrix} R & 0 & 0 & 0 \\ R & R & R & 0 \\ 0 & 0 & R & R \\ 0 & R & 0 & R \end{bmatrix}$$

assuming (S. 24/10) that the terms in the main diagonal are all R. Then

$$[f]^2 = \begin{bmatrix} R & 0 & 0 & 0 \\ R & R & R & R \\ 0 & R & R & R \\ R & R & R & R \end{bmatrix}, \quad [f]^3 = \begin{bmatrix} R & 0 & 0 & 0 \\ R & R & R & R \\ R & R & R & R \\ R & R & R & R \end{bmatrix}$$

and the sum $I + [f] + [f]^2 + [f]^3$ gives

$$\begin{bmatrix} R & 0 & 0 & 0 \\ R & R & R & R \\ R & R & R & R \\ R & R & R & R \end{bmatrix}$$

This, by S. 24/10, is the integral matrix. If it is compared directly with B of the Figure, the agreement will be found complete. Thus, it may be verified in both that x_1 dominates the system of x_2, x_3 and x_4.

The rule of S. 14/10 for the formation of the diagram of ultimate effects when a variable is an inactive part-function can now be proved. For the effect on the differential matrix of a part-function x_i being inactive is to make all the elements in the i-th row zero, except the element in the main diagonal. Exactly the same change is caused in the differential matrix if we remove those arrows whose heads are at x_i. After these two changes the correspondence continues as before. Thus, A of Figure 14/10/1 has

$$[f] = \begin{bmatrix} R & R & 0 & R \\ 0 & R & 0 & R \\ 0 & R & R & 0 \\ R & 0 & R & R \end{bmatrix} \text{ and } [F] = \begin{bmatrix} R & R & R & R \\ R & R & R & R \\ R & R & R & R \\ R & R & R & R \end{bmatrix}$$

And x_3 is not independent of x_1. But if x_2 becomes inactive,

$$[f] = \begin{bmatrix} R & R & 0 & R \\ 0 & R & 0 & 0 \\ 0 & R & R & 0 \\ R & 0 & R & R \end{bmatrix} \qquad [F] = \begin{bmatrix} R & R & R & R \\ 0 & R & 0 & 0 \\ 0 & R & R & 0 \\ R & R & R & R \end{bmatrix}$$

and x_3 is now independent of x_1

The other diagrams, B, D and E, may be verified similarly.

24/15. We can now investigate the problem of S. 14/8 : the separation of parts in a dynamic whole.

Theorem : If the variables of an absolute system are divisible into three sets, A, B, and C such that no f_A contains any of the set x_C, and no f_C contains any of x_A, i.e. so that the diagram of immediate effects is $A \underset{\leftarrow}{\overset{\rightarrow}{}} B \underset{\leftarrow}{\overset{\rightarrow}{}} C$, and if variables x_B remain constant, then A is independent of C, and vice versa.

If all variables of set B are constant, the differential matrix, in partitioned form, will be

$$\begin{array}{c} \\ A \\ B \\ C \end{array} \begin{array}{ccc} A & B & C \\ \begin{bmatrix} R & R & 0 \\ 0 & R & 0 \\ 0 & R & R \end{bmatrix}. \end{array}$$

It is idempotent, so this matrix is also the integral matrix. As the elements at the top right and bottom left corners are zero, A and C are independent of each other.

On the other hand, without further restrictions the constancy is not necessary. Thus, suppose that A and C are independent and that the differential matrix is

$$\begin{bmatrix} R & R & 0 \\ P & R & Q \\ 0 & R & R \end{bmatrix}$$

where P and Q are to be determined. For the integral matrix to have zeros in the top right and bottom left corners, it is easily found that P and Q must both be zero.   So $\partial f_B/\partial x_A$ and $\partial f_B/\partial x_C$ must be zero over the region   This can be achieved in several ways without f_B being zero, i.e. without x_B being constant.   Two examples will be given.

(1) If f_B is a constant, then x_B will increase uniformly, i.e. will not be constant, but x_A and x_C will still be independent.   Without a fourth variable, the linear change is the most which x_B can make if the system is to remain absolute.

(2) If f_B is a function of other variables not yet mentioned, y is not restricted to a constant rate of change.   Thus if there is a variable u which dominates y we could have a system

$$\left.\begin{array}{l} \dfrac{dx}{dt} = x + y \\[2mm] \dfrac{du}{dt} = 3 \\[2mm] \dfrac{dy}{dt} = \sin u \\[2mm] \dfrac{dz}{dt} = y + z \end{array}\right\}$$

which is clearly absolute.   Its solution is :

$$x = (x^0 + y^0 + \tfrac{1}{10}\sin u^0 + \tfrac{3}{10}\cos u^0)e^t - y^0 - \tfrac{1}{3}\cos u^0 \quad \cdot$$
$$- \tfrac{1}{10}\sin(u^0 + 3t) + \tfrac{1}{30}\cos(u^0 + 3t),$$

$$u = u^0 + 3t,$$

$$y = y^0 + \tfrac{1}{3}\cos u^0 - \tfrac{1}{3}\cos(u^0 + 3t),$$

$$z = (z^0 + y^0 + \tfrac{1}{10}\sin u^0 + \tfrac{3}{10}\cos u^0)e^t - y^0 - \tfrac{1}{3}\cos u^0$$
$$- \tfrac{1}{10}\sin(u^0 + 3t) + \tfrac{1}{30}\cos(u^0 + 3t).$$

Not even the rate of change of y is constant, yet x and z are independent.

Physically the conclusions are reasonable.   The various conditions which make x and z independent all have the effect of lessening or abolishing x's and z's effect on y The abolition can be done either by making y constant, or by driving y exclusively by some other variable (u).   A well-known example of the latter method is the ' jamming ' of a broadcast by the addition of some powerful fluctuating signal from another station. It may effectively render the listener independent of the broadcaster.

If to the original conditions we add the restriction that the system A is to become absolute on being made independent of C, then constancy of the variables x_B becomes necessary. For the possibilities examined in paragraphs (1) and (2) leave system A subject to parameters x_B which were assumed to be effective and which are now changing. In such conditions A cannot be absolute (S. 21/1): constancy of the variables x_B is therefore necessary.

24/16. The statement of S. 14/15, that in an absolute system an inactive variable cannot become active unless some variable directly affecting it is active, will now be proved.

Theorem : If a variable x_a is related to a set x_B so that $f_a(. . .)$ contains only x_a and x_B, and if x_a and x_B have all been constant over a finite time, and if x_a becomes active while the set x_B stays inactive, then the system cannot be absolute.

We are given that $dx_a/dt = f_a(x_a, x_B)$. As x_a remained constant (at X_a, say) while the set x_B were constant (at X_B), it follows that $f_a(X_a, X_B) = 0$. But if x_a starts to change value, dx_a/dt is no longer zero, nor is f_a, so $f_a(X_a, X_B)$ is a double-valued function of its arguments, the system is not state-determined, and it is therefore not absolute.

24/17. In the ' hour-glass ' system of S. 14/11, every variable may be shown to be dependent on every other variable. As in Figure 14/11/1, let systems A and B each act on, and be acted on, by a variable x. The differential matrix, in partitioned form, is

$$
\begin{array}{c}
 \\
A \\
x \\
B
\end{array}
\begin{array}{ccc}
A & x & B \\
\left[\begin{array}{ccc}
R & R & 0 \\
R & R & R \\
0 & R & R
\end{array}\right]
\end{array}
$$

Its square contains only R's. So none of the A's are independent of the B's, and conversely.

The proof is confirmed by the theorem of S. 19/22, which shows that, as far as system B is concerned, the values of the A's can be replaced by the derivatives of x. The behaviours of all A's variables are therefore represented in x's behaviour by x's derivatives, and B's variables are thus not independent of A's.

24/18. In S. 14/16 we wanted to compare two probabilities, each that a system would be stable, one composed of part-functions and the other of full-functions, other things being equal. The method of S. 20/12 will define the individual probabilities. The question of what we mean by ' other things ' may be treated by postulating that, regarded as two random processes, (a) the one system's full-functions and (b) the active sections of the other system's part-functions are to have the same statistical properties (when averaged over all lines of behaviour.) This postulate is stated purely in terms of the systems' observable behaviour, so that it would be easy, in a given case, to test whether the postulate was satisfied.

Now consider a system of n variables, part-functions that on the average are active over a fraction ρ of the time. The average number of variables active at one time will be $\rho n = k$, say. Suppose that, at a point Q, the average number of variables are active. For convenience, re-label the variables to list the active first. Add parameters $\alpha_1, \ldots$ to generate the distribution. At Q we have

$$
\left.
\begin{aligned}
dx_1/dt &= f_1(x_1, \ldots, x_n; \alpha_1, \ldots) \\
&\quad \cdot \cdot \cdot \cdot \cdot \cdot \cdot \\
dx_k/dt &= f_k(x_1, \ldots, x_n; \alpha_1, \ldots) \\
dx_{k+1}/dt &= 0 \\
&\quad \cdot \cdot \cdot \cdot \cdot \cdot \\
dx_n/dt &= 0
\end{aligned}
\right\}
$$

The differential matrix at this point will be formally of order $n \times n$, but the rows from $k + 1$ to n will be all zero. If now we test the probability of stability at this Q we find that in fact it depends on the probability that the α-combination has given (a) $f_1 = \ldots = f_k = 0$, and (b) that the matrix

$$
\begin{bmatrix}
\dfrac{\partial f_1}{\partial x_1} & \cdots & \dfrac{\partial f_1}{\partial x_k} \\
\cdots & \cdots & \cdots \\
\dfrac{\partial f_k}{\partial x_1} & \cdots & \dfrac{\partial f_k}{\partial x_k}
\end{bmatrix}
$$

passes Hurwitz' test. Whatever the probability may be, it is clearly equal to the probability of stability given by a system of k similar full-functions.

Conventions and symbols

24/19. The relations between the various entities defined in this chapter are here summarised for convenience of reference.

(1) (In these four statements take the upper relation in the braces in all, or the lower in all).

(a) $x_k \left\{ \begin{matrix} \text{is} \\ \text{is not} \end{matrix} \right\}$ independent of x_j

(b) $F_k(\ldots, x_j^0 + \Delta x_j^0, \ldots, t) \left\{ \begin{matrix} = \\ \neq \end{matrix} \right\} F_k(\ldots, x_j^0, \ldots t)$;

(c) $\dfrac{\partial}{\partial x_j^0} F_k(x_1^0, \ldots, x_n^0 ; t) \left\{ \begin{matrix} = \\ \neq \end{matrix} \right\} 0$;

(d) The integral matrix has $\left\{ \begin{matrix} 0 \\ R \end{matrix} \right\}$ at the (kj)-th position.

(2) The (hi)-th position is in the h-th row and i-th column :

$$\begin{bmatrix} (11) & (12) & (13) & \cdots \\ (21) & (22) & (23) & \cdot & \cdot \\ \cdot & \cdot & \cdot & \cdot & \cdot & \cdot & \cdot & \cdot & \cdot \end{bmatrix}$$

(3) The differential matrix has $\left\{ \begin{matrix} 0 \\ R \end{matrix} \right\}$ at (pq) as $\partial f_p/\partial x_q \left\{ \begin{matrix} = \\ \neq \end{matrix} \right\} 0$;

     „ integral   „   „   ··   „   „   „ $\partial F_p/\partial x_q^0$ „   „

(4) The following correspond .

     (a) In the diagram of immediate effects: $x_r \longrightarrow x_s$,

     (b) In the canonical equations : $f_s(\ldots, x_r, \quad.)$;

     (c) In the differential matrix : an R at the (sr)-th position.

(5) If sets A and B include all the variables, and if deletion from the integral matrix of :

    columns A and rows B leaves all zeros, and

    columns B and rows A leaves not all zeros,

then A dominates B.

(6) If x_p is a part-function and is inactive :

    (a) $dx_p/dt = 0$,

    (b) $x_p = x_p^0$;

    (c) $F_p(x^0 ; \ t) \equiv x_p^0$;

    (d) $\partial F_p/\partial x_q^0 = 0$ (all $q \neq p$) ;

    (e) all elements (except (pp)) of the p-th row of the differential and integral matrices are zero.

REFERENCE

RIGUET, J. Sur les rapports entre les concepts de machine de multipole et de structure algébrique. *Comptes rendus des séances de l'Académie des Sciences*, **237**, 425 ; 1953.

INDEX

INDEX

R0-matrix, 243
Robinson, E S , 194, 199
Rosenblueth, A., 71
Runaway, 52

Sea-anemone, 140, 156
Selection of fields, 91, 106
Self-correction, 54
Self-destruction, 5
Sense-organs, dispersion in, 169
Separation, 153, 160
Serum, 20
Servo-mechanism, 51
Sex hormone, 122
Shannon, C. E., 211, 215
Sherrington, C. S , 137, 138
Shivering, 58
Simple harmonic oscillator, 80
Skaggs, E B , 194, 199
Skin, 169
Skinner, B F , 190, 199
Snail, 152
Snake, 135
Sommerhoff, A , 71
Species, 8
Spectrum, 30
Speidel, C C , 127, 129
Sperry, R W , 117, 124
Spider monkey, 118
Spinal cord, transection, 159
Spinal reflexes, co-ordination between, 196
interaction between, 137
Spontaneity, 88
Stability, 47, Chapters 4 and 20
and parameter change, 78
examples, 55
is holistic, 54
nature of, 76
of homeostat, 96, 220
probability of, 56, 100, 136, 165, 221
Stalking, 132
Starling, E H., 37, 42, 64
State, 18, 203
equality of two, 19
State-determined system, 25
Statistical machinery, 145
Steady state, 43
Stentor, 103
Step-function, 80, Chapters 7 and 22
and natural selection, 123
effect of omission, 88
in Stentor, 105
in the organism, Chapter 10
nature of, 111
necessity of, 110
number necessary, 128
Stepping switch, 96
Stimuli,
addition of, 167

Stimuli, and part-functions, 166
numericising, 30, 76
repeated, 147
response to, 57
Strychnine, 130
Subjective phenomena, 10, 32
Subspaces, 87, 103
Subsystems, 171, 181
Surface, critical, 234
Surgical alterations, 117
Survival, 42, 65, 197
Swallow, 17
Switch, as step-function, 81
Switching, and part-function, 161
Symbols, collected, 253
System, 15
absolute, 24, Chapter 19
containing null-functions, 86, 228
— part-functions, 163
— step-functions, 86
hour-glass, 161, 251
independence of, 156
infinite, 203
linear, 215
regular, 23, 204
symbols for, 203
stability of, 48
with feedback, 39

Tabes dorsalis, 88
Tadpoles, 127
Taste, 169
Teleology, 9, 71
Telephone exchange, 161
Temperature, homeostasis of, 58
Temple, G , 27, 28
Temporal cortex, 170
Terminal field, 91
normality, 146
Thermostat, 43, 51, 53, 54, 67, 156
Thirst, 59
Threshold, 163, 170
Thunderstorm, 17
Time,
as variable, 15
for adaptation, 135, 141, 177, 184
Tissue culture, 126
Tokens, as reward, 186
Tongue, 7, 39
Training, 112, 187
Transducer, 121
noiseless, 211
Transformations, 168
Transient, 144
Trap, 132
Tremor, 67
Trial and error, 112, 132, 174
Trials, number of, 238
Type-problem, 11
Typewriter, 154

259

Ingram Content Group UK Ltd.
Milton Keynes UK
UKHW020931120423
420037UK00006B/239